# Regulation in the European Electricity Sector



Maciej M. Sokołowski

Routledge
Taylor & Francis Group
LONDON AND NEW YORK

First published 2016 by Routledge

2 Park Square, Milton Park, Abingdon, Oxfordshire OX14 4RN

711 Third Avenue, New York, NY 10017

*Routledge is an imprint of the Taylor & Francis Group, an informa business*

First issued in paperback 2017



*British Library Cataloguing-in-Publication Data*
A catalogue record for this book is available from the British Library

*Library of Congress Cataloging-in-Publication Data*
Sokolowski, Maciej M., author.
Regulation in the European electricity sector / Maciej M. Sokolowski.
pages cm. – (Routledge studies in energy law and regulation)
1. Electric utilities–Law and legislation–European Union countries.
2. Electric utilities–Law and legislation–Europe. I. Title.
KJE6852.S65 2016
343.2409'29–dc23 2015036072

ISBN: 978-1-138-96341-2 (hbk)
ISBN: 978-0-8153-5831-2 (pbk)

Typeset in Goudy
by Wearset Ltd, Boldon, Tyne and Wear

*To my wife Kinga*

# Contents

# Preface

Electricity is one of the main factors influencing the forward development of every country. This situation results in the state having a particular interest in the provision, maintenance and development of electrical systems. The state's interest is reflected by the existence of legal instruments and institutions dedicated to the sector.

Since the very beginning of European integration, electricity has been within the legal sphere of the European Union (EU). Much of this is found within the binding European acts making up the framework of the Energy Package. The established legal institutions have a significant impact on the shape of the energy market in Europe (*inter alia*, Third Party Access, unbundling, independent market regulator, "3 × 20% goals"). Nevertheless, the European energy market still seems to be in the process of development, as demonstrated by the current lively discussion about the state of the Energy Union.

These considerations make it necessary to reflect on some of the primary issues related to the public legal impact on the European energy sector. What legal measures are used by the EU to determine the shape of the sector? Is the regulatory model of the European internal energy market complete? Will its reform be in further EU scope of action? These are just some of the questions that my book raises and attempts to answer.

In this context, the book delves into European energy law. It is aimed at giving the reader a deep insight into the nature of the state's presence in the power sector, examining its legal form, and suggesting the place for public law regulation in the EU's energy market. Herein, such main themes emerge:

i ways that the state impacts on the energy market;
ii definitions of public law regulation;
iii EU legal measures to determine the shape of the energy sector;
iv impact of EU legislative packages on the Member State's public regulation;
v institutionalisation of public law regulation;
vi dimension of public law regulation of the Member States;
vii future of public law regulation.

To analyse them, several different perspectives are taken into consideration (methodologies). The book is based on European law, Member States' national legislation, and certain examples of law relevant to the energy sector (particularly within the US). With regard to law influencing the energy sector, the European Union's three legal acts are of particularly great importance. These are directives on the electricity market, established as key elements of Liberalisation Packages adopted by the EU at the turn of the century. Remarks on them are supplemented with comments on numerous strategic European documents, which directly or indirectly influenced the law-making process (e.g. COM documents), as well as other policy and working papers developed by the EU or international organisations like the Organisation of Economic Co-operation and Development (OECD). Moreover, important considerations are grounded by findings derived from the literature on energy law, state impact on the economy, and public law regulation.

Seen in this light, I really do hope that presented to the reader is a book that provides a rationale for the requirements stipulated by the relevant law on public regulation. I wanted to show not only the substance of the law, but also illustrate the considerations that have influenced the reasoning of the EU regarding liberalisation of the electricity sector. Therefore, the book presents analysis of European and national laws, as well as considering their interpretation.

I trust that the interdisciplinary methodology applied in the book offers a brief explanation of the background operation of the electricity sector, as well as of liberalisation within the area. My aim was to help all those interested with addressing the different theories of public law regulation, its types, and mechanisms as well as to trace the evolution of the EU's approach towards the issue of public law regulation within the electricity sector. I sincerely hope my readers will consider that I managed to achieve this goal.

Maciej M. Sokołowski

# Acknowledgements

To begin, I am deeply grateful to Professor Christa Tobler and Doctor Torbjörn Odolow for their help and support during my research stays in Switzerland (University of Basel) and Sweden (University of Gothenburg), where I explored the regulatory issues related to the European energy sector and EU law.

Furthermore, I would like to express my deep appreciation and gratitude to my supervisor, Professor Marek Wierzbowski, for his thought-provoking feedback and for supervising my work with patience and understanding. His experience in energy law, insight, and academic rigour was invaluable and is deeply appreciated.

I also owe many thanks to Professor Anna Walaszek-Pyzioł and Professor Marcin Dyl for the time they spent reviewing my dissertation and for providing their recommendations. Moreover, I wish to express my deepest and most sincere gratitude once more to Professor Anna Walaszek-Pyzioł for her energy, helpful guidance, and inestimable support throughout my scientific career.

Apart from this, the reviewers of this book deserve special thanks for their thoughtful comments and useful remarks. I also thank colleagues from Montreal, Zack Parker and Stephen Hill, who provided proofreading of my text, which I really do appreciate. Additionally, this book would not have been completed without the kindness of librarians from the University of Bern, University of Basel, University of Gothenburg, and McGill University who offered me their expertise and skills during the long hours spent there. Furthermore, I am grateful to Doctor Dawei (David) Sun, Vishal Ranjan, and Christian Lauchenauer, whom I am honoured to call friends, and with whom I have shared great moments in Basel during my time off from writing.

Herein, I also thank my dad, Professor Marek Sokołowski, who encouraged me into scientific work and taught me its basics, and for all his practical advice and experience which he shared with me. I truly cannot thank him enough.

Last but not least, I am extremely grateful to my dear wife Kinga. She gave me the encouragement and inspiration to carry out my actions and plans. Without her I would not have written this book.

Maciej M. Sokołowski

# Abbreviations

| | |
|---|---|
| ACER | Agency for the Cooperation of Energy Regulators |
| ACM | *Autoriteit Consument & Markt* |
| AEEG | *Autorità per l'Energia Elettrica e il Gas* |
| CEER | Council of European Energy Regulators |
| CNE | *Comisión Nacional de Energía* |
| CR | Committee of Regions |
| CRE | *Commission de Régulation de l'Énergie* |
| DERA | Danish Energy Regulatory Agency |
| DSO | Distribution System Operator |
| EC | European Commission |
| ECSC | European Coal and Steel Community |
| EdF | *Électricité de France* |
| Ei | *Energimarknadsinspektionen* |
| ENEL | *Ente Nazionale per l'Energia Elettrica* |
| ENTSO | European Network of Energy Transmission System Operators |
| EP | European Parliament |
| ERGEG | European Regulators' Group for Electricity and Gas |
| ESC | Economic and Social Committee |
| EU | European Union |
| EU ETS | European Union Emission Trading System |
| Euratom | European Atomic Energy Community |
| GHG | greenhouse gases |
| GWh | gigawatt-hour |
| IEA | International Energy Agency |
| IPPs | Independent Power Producers |
| ISO | Independent System Operator |
| ITO | Independent Transmission Operator |
| J L | *Journal of Laws* |
| MW | megawatt |
| OECD | Organisation of Economic Cooperation and Development |
| OFGEM | Office of Gas and Electricity Markets |
| OJ | *Official Journal* |
| PPAs | Power Purchase Agreements |

| | |
|---|---|
| SEP | *Samenwerkende elektriciteitsproductiebedrijven* |
| TEC | Treaty Establishing the European Economic Community |
| TEN-E | Trans-European Energy Networks |
| TFEU | Treaty on the Functioning of the European Union |
| TPA | third party access |
| TSO | Transmission System Operator |
| TWh | terawatt-hour |
| UK | United Kingdom |
| UNFCCC | United Nations Framework Convention on Climate Change |

# 1 Introduction

In the reality of the twenty-first century, electricity has become one of the key (strategic) factors determining the level of economic development of every country. Access to an uninterrupted supply of electricity at an acceptable price stabilises socio-economic relations, both at national and global levels.

Seen in this light, Peter D. Cameron, an acclaimed author of papers on competition in regulated sectors, describes the key drivers encouraging the state to enter, remain, or develop a position within the energy sector. Among these factors there is a nature of energy services (services provided by energy companies seen as essential to society, what is followed by state control over electricity prices), the strategic importance of the energy sector for the whole economy, or capital intensity and a high degree of technical complexity of investment in the energy sector (Cameron 2007, pp. 6–7). This situation results in the particular interest of the state towards the energy sector. The interest is reflected by the existence of available legal instruments dedicated to the sector.

Energy, including electricity, since the very beginning of European integration has been in the sphere of the legal impact of the European Union (EU). It is evidenced by the fact that two of the three European Communities were strongly associated with energy matters (with its legal basis in the treaties). These were the European Coal and Steel Community (ECSC) and the European Atomic Energy Community (Euratom). In addition, already in the 1960s, the first action in the field of EU energy policy had already been undertaken. It was done by adopting an inter-state legal agreement on energy policy (Protocol of Agreement 1964), and by issuing guidelines for an energy policy of the Community (European Commission 1968). The following years brought new strategic documents calling for action in relation to the EU's energy policy (e.g. European Commission 1973, 1985, 1974a, 1974b, 1978, Council Resolution 1974).

The year 1986, was an important turning point in the timeline of European legislative actions with regard to the energy sector. In this year, a vital document for European integration called "the Single European Act" was issued.[1] Despite the lack of explicit references to the energy market, the Act intensified integration in the area of energy, since the decisions necessary for the accomplishment of the common internal market had to be made before 1 January

1993. Two years after the adoption of the Single European Act, in 1988, the Commission explicitly presented the main objectives for the establishment of the internal energy market (European Commission 1988).

Binding European legal acts supported the mentioned actions of a political-strategic orientation, which have been adopted since the early 1990s. Together, they can be enclosed in a framework of the three *Energy Packages* (or *Liberalisation Packages*), supplemented by the acts preceding them, as well as of the *Climate and Energy Package*. Within these packages, as their part, legal acts (regulations, directives, and decisions) on the energy sector were adopted. They established legal institutions of significant importance on the shape of the energy market in Europe. These included, *inter alia*, third party access, unbundling, the Transmission System Operator, and the independent market regulator, which derived from the Liberalisation Packages. Furthermore, the provisions of the Climate and Energy Package introduced "3 × 20% goals" to support renewable energy, reduce greenhouse gas emissions, and improve energy efficiency.

Nevertheless, the energy market still seems to be in the process of development. Not all of the Member States have timely and properly implemented provisions of the Packages, or have not complied with them causing formal infringement proceedings.[2] For example, in February 2014, the European Commission (EC)[3] referred Ireland to the Court of Justice of the EU for failing fully to transpose the EU rules on the internal energy market (European Commission 2014b). Until the end of January 2014 a few Member States had opened infringement procedures in the field of the implementation of the Packages' Directives on electricity,[4] on gas,[5] or on renewable energy sources.[6] Furthermore, even after passing the Third as well as the Climate and Energy Package, the European Union has adopted new legal acts[7] and proposed flag ideas[8] covering issues from the area of energy and climate, or the internal energy market.

## Main research assumptions

The aforementioned conditions were the basis for conducting a legal analysis of the issue of the impact of the European legislation – included in the framework of the *legislative packages* – on the scope of public law regulation of the electricity sector. As can be seen, the book's reference point is limited to electricity. This is because the width and depth of all energy matters make it impossible to cover this vast subject in several hundred pages (or even more) without losing the quality of conducted research. Further, other energy sectors are characterised by different material (e.g. technical, financial, economic) and formal (legal) determinants. The remarks here refer especially to the fuel sector. Gas, due to the dual nature of European legislation on energy liberalisation (where one legal act concerns electricity and another gas), has more similarities to electricity. So wherever appropriate, I refer also to the gas sector.

Bearing in mind these considerations, I noticed the need to reflect on and analyse some of the primary issues related to the European energy sector. I address them in the framework of the following questions:

i What is the nature of the state's presence in the electricity sector? Which legal form has it, and how does it change? Where is the place for public law regulation? How it is positioned with respect to other aspects of a state's impact on the energy market?

ii How can public law regulation be defined? What are its essential elements? What is its range? How can this concept be classified?

iii What legal measures are used by the EU to determine the shape of the energy sector? What is the role of the legislative packages? How can the idea of legislative package be defined?

iv How do the EU's legislative packages influence Member States' public regulation? What is their impact on national regulatory authorities? What are their aims and direction?

v What is the role of the Agency for the Cooperation of Energy Regulators for energy regulation in Europe? What is its legal status? Can it be qualified as an energy regulator?

vi Is the regulatory model of the European internal energy market complete? Will it be in the EU's further interest? Would this result in adoption of new legal acts determining the dimension of public law regulation of Member States? If so, will it take the form of a legislative package, i.e. the *Fourth Energy Package*?

## Structure of this book

Seen in this light, I gathered and recalled issues concerning the impact of European energy legislation (*Energy Packages*) on the scope of *public law regulation* of the *electricity sector* in the EU in 11 chapters of this book, gathering them in four main parts.

Omitting the first chapter which does not need broader comments as it is the book's Introduction, I go straight to presenting the substantive part of this work. In Chapter 2, I provide general remarks on electricity and energy cooperation in Europe. Such issues as electricity demand, specific electricity features, future energy market scenarios as well as the significance of electricity for the European economy and society are examined there. As the market is a key notion for the concept of the internal energy market, different ways of defining market are explained there. This chapter also covers remarks on the legal character of electricity as well as providing findings on the place of energy issues within the EU and its Treaties, with the Treaty on the Functioning of the European Union.

Chapter 3 addresses the description of the electricity market and its players as well as different market models that enable electricity trade. It is supplemented with legal definitions of market players within the electricity sector. Moreover, Chapter 3 describes how states influenced the electricity sector and how it was shaped in Europe. Herein, the first steps towards liberalisation of the energy market are demonstrated. It includes presenting the EU's complex approach to the energy sector, which takes the form of legislative packages –

i.e. the Energy Packages (the *Liberalisation Packages*) and the Climate and Energy Package. As a result of these considerations I propose the definition of legislative packages.

Energy Packages are aimed at realising reforms in the energy sector. Their essence is to liberalise the energy market, including electricity. Thereby in Chapter 4 the most important principles of liberalism are provided. These cover the notions of the night-watchman, *laissez-faire*, as well as limits of liberalism and the possible space for public action. Moreover, the application of liberal ideas into legal systems from a historical perspective is considered there. In addition, this chapter addresses an example of deregulation conducted in the 1990s in the electricity sector in California. Finally, in comparison to these remarks, an approach that can be contrasted with the market-based approach is presented. This concerns delving into the state-based system that involves a much more intensive level of the state's influence on the economy.

Further, in Chapter 5, the idea of public law regulation is discussed. I outline definitions of public law regulation. The analysis includes different regulatory approaches, regimes, and ways of understanding the narrow and broad sense of regulation. Using available literature regarding regulation I broadly introduce this concept in an attempt to examine its every nature, including the legal dimension. Due to the fact that the institution is a crucial element, I review various models of the administrative bodies. This is complemented with an analysis of the tools of regulation with which the regulatory authorities are equipped to realise the public interest and implement public policy goals. Lastly, in reference to the institution of energy market regulators in the European Union, I propose the concept of the day-watchman state, as a balanced way of performing the public functions with respect to market.

However, this assumption of market regulators needs public law regulation to be enhanced. The EU's legal practice shaping the energy sector and public regulation, takes the form of legislative packages. This legal measure of achieving the EU's policy agenda covers a broad range of public law regulation. With their use so important for conducting energy sector reform institutions like third party access, unbundling, as well as national regulators were introduced to the system of European law. For the electricity sector, due to the breakdown by sector of electricity and gas adopted within Energy Packages, Electricity Directives are of particular importance. With their use the concrete rules of public law nature were adopted.

Continuing this theme, in Chapters 6, 7, and 8 the issue of European Energy Packages' influence (the First, the Second, and the Third) on the scope of public law regulation is examined in detail. In each chapter the legislative process is highlighted. It includes specific European documents, which influence the law-making process as well as statements of the European institutions engaged in it, i.e. the Commission, the Council, the Parliament, the Committee of Regions, and the Economic and Social Committee. Moreover, particular attention is given to the provisions imposing obligations for Member States.

A constant element of the conducted analysis is characteristics of the national regulatory authorities. It takes into account their competencies, powers, and obligations. This part of the work demonstrates a practical application of the previous findings.

Chapter 9 complements the preceding remarks. Under the provisions of the Third Energy Package public law regulation is raised to the European level. This was done by the establishment of the Agency for the Cooperation of Energy Regulators (ACER). Thereby, in this chapter, I analyse the Agency's role in relation to national regulatory authorities. This includes a juxtaposition of functions performed by the Agency. I compare it with the function performed by classic regulators trying to show how close (or how far) the ACER is from them. Furthermore, a deeper examination of regulatory authorities makes it necessary to apply general remarks to the Member States' situation, and the way that the institutionalisation of public law regulation is shaped under national law, influenced by the European legislation. Accordingly, I conduct a review of certain European Union countries, outlining their electricity markets and position of the national regulatory authorities.

Finally, Chapter 10 examines the European approach to regulation. It covers the issue of the EU's regulatory goals steering public law regulation. Apart from promoting competition, European regulation is extended by two other directions: energy security with security of supplies, as well as the environment with the climate agenda. In this chapter I trace these two policy goals: competition and environment. I analyse the latter in a broader view, tracing down provisions of European legislation on reduction of emissions, renewable energy sources, and climate. A special place is devoted here to the Climate Energy Package, which is analysed in reference to the legislation on the internal energy market, particularly the Third Electricity Directive.

The overall impact of the EU's Energy Packages on the scope of public law regulation of the electricity sector is depicted in Chapter 11 which is a summary of the book. At this point, I recapitulate the discussed issues and the book's most important findings. Wherever necessary, I provide additional explanations and clarifications. In particular, this outlines the prospects for the future of public law regulation.

## Methodology applied

This work is elaborated on the basis of European Union law, the Member States' national legislations, and certain examples of law relevant to the energy sector (particularly the US). With regard to law influencing the energy sector, which is the reference point of this book, the EU's three legal acts are of particularly great importance. These are three directives on the electricity market, adopted as key elements of Liberalisation Packages adopted by the EU at the turn of the century: the First Electricity Directive of 1996 (Directive 96/92/EC), the Second Electricity Directive of 2003 (Directive 2003/54/EC), and the Third Electricity Directive of 2009 (Directive 2009/72/EC). Due to their primary role in the development of the common internal energy market in the European Union they are presented in more detail. In addition, in the book's scope of analysis are numerous strategic European documents, which directly or indirectly influenced the law-making process (e.g. COM documents), as well as other policy and working papers developed by the EU or international organisations like the OECD. Moreover, important considerations are grounded by the findings derived from the literature on energy law, state impact on the economy, and public law regulation.

The research methodology used in the book is a dogmatic approach. It serves as an instrument for analysing legislation in the field of electricity, and providing a rationale for the requirements stipulated by the relevant law on public regulation. Not only is this methodology applied to compare the substance of law, but also to illustrate the considerations that have influenced the reasoning of the European Union regarding liberalisation of the electricity sector. Furthermore, it helps in addressing the different theories of public law regulation, its types, and tools.

Second, a very important element of the conducted research includes the comparative method, necessary for proper analysis of European and national laws, as well as their interpretation. Third, in some examined areas it is necessary to engage the historical method (especially in the field of legislation processes in the EU). It allows the tracing of the evolution of the EU's approach towards the issue of public law regulation within the electricity sector.

Last, in this work, empirical and interdisciplinary methodologies are used. The empirical approach adduces the data regarding the electricity market, *inter alia*, electricity consumption, market opening, market concentration, etc. Interdisciplinary methodology offers a brief explanation of the background operation of the electricity sector to show its characteristics and growing importance, as well as of liberalisation that is necessary for the elucidation of the aims of the EU's legislation on the energy sector. Although, what must be emphasised herein, this methodology is ancillary to the previous one. Thereby it is limited so as not to distort the predominantly legal nature of this work.

Regardless of the apparent breadth and depth of the scope of the conducted analysis, the book does not close studies on public regulation, including regulation in the energy sector. The presented work covers only a part of them. However, it may constitute a contribution to further discussion and legal examination of electricity – the strategic sector for the state, its economy, society, as well as its influence from European public law regulations.

## Notes

1 OJ L 169, 29 June 1987.
2 In November 2013, the EC referred Austria to the Court of Justice of the European Union for failing to transpose provisions of the Climate and Energy Package on renewable energy sources (see European Commission 2013b), or in June 2013 the Commission decided to refer Poland to the Court for failing to comply with the EU internal energy market rules on gas (see European Commission 2013a).

3 The abbreviation "EC" may also refer to European Community in historical references; in this historical context it appears in the book only in terms of legal acts (e.g. Directive 2003/54/EC). The name "European Commission" is also used where necessary instead of the former name "Commission of the European Communities".
4 Estonia, Finland, Ireland, Lithuania, Romania, and Slovenia.
5 Estonia, Finland, Lithuania, Poland, Romania, and Slovenia.
6 Austria, Belgium, Cyprus, the Czech Republic, Spain, Finland, Ireland, Italy, the Netherlands, and Poland. See European Commission 2014a.
7 For example, Regulation (EU) No. 347/2013, Directive 2012/27/EU.
8 For example, an idea of an Energy Union (see European Commission 2015).

## References

Cameron, P.D. 2007, *Competition in energy markets: law and regulation in the European Union*, 2nd edn, Oxford University Press, Oxford.

Council Resolution of 17 September 1974 concerning a new energy policy strategy for the Community, OJ C 153, 9 July 1975.

Directive 2003/54/EC of the European Parliament and of the Council of 26 June 2003 concerning common rules for the internal market in electricity and repealing Directive 96/92/EC, OJ L 176, 15 July 2003.

Directive 2009/72/EC of the European Parliament and of the Council of 13 July 2009 concerning common rules for the internal market in electricity and repealing Directive 2003/54/EC, OJ L 211, 14 August 2009.

Directive 2012/27/EU of the European Parliament and of the Council of 25 October 2012 on energy efficiency, amending Directives 2009/125/EC and 2010/30/EU and repealing Directives 2004/8/EC and 2006/32/EC, OJ L 315, 14 November 2012.

Directive 96/92/EC of the European Parliament and of the Council of 19 December 1996 concerning common rules for the internal market in electricity, OJ L 27, 30 January 1997.

European Commission 1968, *Commission Memorandum to the Council of 18 December 1968: first guidelines for a Community Energy Policy*, COM (68) 1040, Supplement to EC Bulletin No. 12/1968.

European Commission 1973, *Communication from the Commission to the Council presented on 27 April 1973: guidelines and priority actions under the Community energy policy*, Brussels, 19 April 1973, SEC (73) 1481 final.

European Commission 1974a, *Communication and proposals from the Commission to the Council: towards a new energy policy strategy for the European Community*, Brussels, 26 June 1974, COM (74) 550 final/2.

European Commission 1974b, *Communication from the Commission to the Council: Community Energy Policy. Objectives for 1985*, Brussels, 27 November 1974, COM (74) 1960 final.

European Commission 1978, *Communication from the Commission to the Council: energy objectives for 1990 and programmes of the Member States*, Brussels, 16 November 1978, COM (78) 613 final.

European Commission 1985, *Communication from the Commission to the Council: new community energy objectives*, Brussels, 28 May 1985, COM (85) 245 final.

European Commission 1988, *Commission Working Document: the Internal Energy Market*, Brussels, 2 May 1988, COM (88) 238 final.

European Commission 2013a, *Internal gas market: the Commission takes Poland to Court over regulated gas prices for business consumers*, Brussels, 20 June 2013, IP/13/580. Available from: http://europa.eu/rapid/press-release_IP-13-580_en.htm [16 June 2015].

European Commission 2013b, *Renewable energy: Commission refers Austria to Court for failing to transpose EU rules*, Brussels, 20 November 2013, IP/13/1113. Available from: http://europa.eu/rapid/press-release_IP-13-1113_en.htm [12 June 2015].

European Commission 2014a, *Table of infringement procedures open for non-communication of national transposition measures: situation 23.01.2014*. Available from: http://ec.europa.eu/energy/infringements/doc/infringements_energy.pdf [15 June 2015].

European Commission 2014b, *Internal Energy Market: Commission refers Ireland to Court for failing to transpose EU rules*, Brussels, 20 February 2014, IP/14/155. Available from: http://europa.eu/rapid/press-release_IP-14-155_en.htm [16 June 2015].

European Commission 2015, *Communication from the Commission to the European Parliament, the Council, the European Economic and Social Committee, the Committee of the Regions and the European Investment Bank a framework strategy for a resilient Energy Union with a forward-looking climate change policy*, Brussels, 25 February 2015, COM (2015) 80 final.

Protocol of Agreement on energy matters concluded the governments of the Member States of the European Communities on 21 April 1964, Official gazette of the European Communities No. 69, 30 April 1964.

Regulation (EU) No 347/2013 of the European Parliament and of the Council of 17 April 2013 on guidelines for trans-European energy infrastructure and repealing Decision No 1364/2006/EC and amending Regulations (EC) No 713/2009, (EC) No 714/2009 and (EC) No 715/2009, OJ L 115, 25 April 2013.

# PART I

# Energy

The road to use it, the road to regulate it

# 2 Importance of electricity

> There are many reasons why electricity has become the preferred form of energy and why it is, in many ways absolutely essential for the normal functioning of a modern civilization. Electricity's use results in … benefits unsurpassed by any fuel, as it offers superior final conversion efficiencies, unmatched productivity, and unequalled flexibility, with uses [in different sectors].
>
> (Smil 2010, p. 39)

It can be "simply transmitted, safely consumed with no emissions, and, owing to the technological developments, it can be generated in a multitude of ways" (European Association of the Electricity Transmission 2008). Electricity can be precisely controlled in the phase of its delivery (regardless of its volume), it supplies devices in every possible scale, is noiseless, and easy to use (turning on the switch) (Smil 2010, p. 39).

## Electricity features and demand for energy

Specific electricity features are: lack of storage potential, high costs of outages, fluctuation, transformation, and technical specifications (Cameron 2007, pp. 22–23). Storing electricity, in a large volume and at a low cost is currently impossible.[1] The supply (with power generation) has to cover the load. The demand for electricity varies, *inter alia*, throughout the day and night; what causes the problem of a "peak demand". The load has to be supplied. To do so, the power capacity always has to equal or exceed the load. Otherwise, accidental interruption in supply may occur ("brownouts" or "blackouts"). Electricity requires also to be transformed into final forms: light, heat, cooling- or motion-power. Cameron (2007, pp. 22–23) concludes "[i]t means that some of the input energies to electricity such as natural gas are also its competitors in final energy markets". Finally, there are considerable differences among power stations (renewable, nuclear, oil, natural gas, and coal power plants), which arise from their nature, both technical and financial (different technologies installed, different fuel used). These specifications result in the power units' various flexibilities, and therefore different reactions to changes in demand (Cameron 2007, pp. 22–23).

The flexibility determines the distinction between load power plants: base, intermediate, and peak. Coal and nuclear power sources are generally considered base load plants, and oil- and gas-fired units are typically intermediate load plants. For the needs of peak load (due to the quick start) turbines fired by natural gas are used (Blok 2007, p. 92).[2] This is because electricity demand is heterogeneous in nature. Besides the mentioned daily variations, different weekly and seasonal volumes can be distinguished. Electricity demand has significant regional differences as well. Obviously, it also varies between countries. Due to the significance of the several trends emerging in the electricity sector, this issue requires further attention.

In terms of electricity demand, one general trend can be highlighted: more and more, electricity plays an important role in the modern world, struggling for supremacy over other types of energy. Thus, electricity is a growing market. Its share in the global energy markets confirms this tendency. In 1973, consumption of electricity accounted for 11 per cent of the total world energy demand. In 2007, it had grown to almost 18 per cent (Burger, Bernhard, & Schindlmayr 2007).

Global electricity generation from 1971, rose at an average annual rate of 3.7 per cent, reaching greater than 2.2 per cent growth in 2010 (in total primary energy supply). This was an effect of the growing use of electrical appliances and electrical heating (in developed countries), as well as the introduction of electrification programmes (in developing countries) (OECD 2013, p. 112). As a result, in 2010, world electricity generation exceeded 21 000 TWh (OECD 2013, p. 113). In 2012 it reached 22 668 TWh (IEA 2014, p. 24). Furthermore, according to the International Energy Agency (IEA), electricity demand between 1990 and 2009 increased in the OECD countries by almost one-third (e.g. in Europe). In non-OECD countries growth was approximately one-half (IEA 2011, p. 176). In terms of power plant types, in that period the biggest growth was noted in renewable energy sources, which ranged from threefold to eightfold growth. However, both in 1990 and 2009, the majority of electricity was generated by conventional, fossil fuel-fired sources (IEA 2011, p. 178).

Growth in the demand for electricity did not stop in the first decade of the twenty-first century. In the World Business Council for Sustainable Development's opinion (2005, p. 4) demand is determined, *inter alia*, by such trends as "improvements in electrical applications, including automation", "increasing numbers of electrical appliances", "information technology and the Internet", and "continuous urbanization". These are also the basis for the preponderance of electricity, whose usage – in comparison to other kinds of energy – grows much faster.

This assumption is repeated and confirmed in numerous reports on the shape of the future energy market. For example, in the report "Power Choices: Pathways to Carbon-Neutral Electricity in Europe by 2050" (EURELECTRIC 2010, p. 4) a shift to electricity in the final demand (the Power Choices scenario) is foreseen. It states:

> [t]he scenario indicates very strong reduction in the end use of gas and oil – down from 52% of final energy demand under baseline to only 34% … [with] a consequent increase in the proportion of electricity … – up from 20% to 45.5%.

Similarly, the increase of electricity's role and its importance in "every aspect of our lives", is highlighted in the report by the Edison Foundation's Institute for Electric Efficiency (2012, p. 1). Furthermore, in the IEA's main scenario: "the New Policies Scenario" (IEA 2012), the global demand for electricity is predicted to continue rapid growth by 2035 (over 70 per cent increase).

Finally, in discussions about the role of electricity, two important factors of the energy sector emerge. First, not taking into account energy efficiency, "increasing economic activity leads to an increase in energy consumption and production". Second, "the energy sector is an important source of economic activity itself" (Blok 2007, 101). On the other hand, economic and social progress determines the development of the energy sector.

In the classic sense, energy development should simultaneously follow the first two factors mentioned in the previous paragraph, being their catalyst and allowing increased production and life activity. Consequently, economic growth and social development are correlated with an increased consumption of what determines an increase in energy production.

These issues highlight the importance of the sector for the economy, society, and the state. The industry's significance correlates with state control over the energy sector. This relationship developed in an interesting period in the post-war years in Europe.

## Energy issues under European primary rules

A firm legal impact on the energy industry, as well as the electricity sector, started in Europe just after 1945. When the Second World War was over "hard" branches of European industry (i.e. coal, coke, and steel) were extremely important for speeding up the post-war economy. Accordingly, each of them has something in common with electricity: electricity is needed in the production process (steel) or may be used to generate it (coal).

The rapid post-war development of these branches could have resulted in over-production. International cooperation with coordination of investment plans could, however, prevent it (Jovanovic 2005, p. 8). A very first step towards the realisation of these assumptions was made in 1945 when a French planning officer, Jean Monnet, proposed a plan for the modernisation of the French economy. It was based on the idea that France would control German coal production and the steel industry so that it would not compete with France (Fimister 2008, p. 178).

### *A very first European energy integration*

To plan the output and allocation of Ruhr coal resources, France proposed the establishment of an international body. This was to be the International Ruhr Authority (Milward 2002, p. 43). Finally agreed in 1948, it had only general supervisory power to allocate Ruhr's coal (Chick 2007, p. 36). After objections from the Allies, particularly the US not wanting to weaken the economy of

West Germany, Monnet's original outline evolved towards a more international arrangement which would involve the control of the coal and steel industries in France and Benelux as well (see Raitio 2003, p. 16; Wunderlich 2007, p. 59; Milward 2002).

In May 1950, the arrangement was strengthened by political action by the French foreign minister, Robert Schuman (Jovanovic 2005, p. 8), who announced that the French government proposed "to place all Franco-German coal and steel production under a common High Authority, in an organization open to the participation of other countries of Europe" (Willis 1965, p. 80). This unusual concept of transferring national sovereignty to a supranational authority responsible for managing an important part of France's and West Germany's economies found a positive response in Germany. It was Chancellor Konrad Adenauer who perceived it as a chance to improve Germany's subordinate post-war position and, as a result of this international cooperation, an opportunity to regain equality with other states (Jovanovic 2005, p. 8). The neighbouring states quickly recognised the potential of this bilateral cooperation. Belgium, the Netherlands, Luxemburg, and Italy accepted the integration plan for the coal and steel branches. As a result, in April 1951, six European partners signed the Treaty of Paris,[3] which established the ECSC (Dinan 2004, p. 55).

On the basis of Article 2, the Treaty had to enable economic expansion, growth of employment, and a rising standard of living. This was to be done through the common market for coal and steel, with the equal positioning of its players (equal market entry, equal access to the sources of production). To do so, the Treaty of Paris established a new, separate institution – the High Authority. Pursuant to the Treaty's provision, the High Authority received a set of tasks and competences in the field of public law regulation. For example, under Article 46 the High Authority was in force periodically to "draw up programmes indicating foreseeable developments in production, consumption, exports and imports" or "lay down general objectives for modernisation, long-term planning of manufacture and expansion of productive capacity". More direct rights of the High Authority concerned procurement of the funds it required to conduct its task. On the basis of Article 49, the High Authority could impose levies on the production of coal and steel, and contract loans. Moreover, this Community's institution could grant loans (or guarantee other loans) to support investment programmes. However, the most powerful regulation that might be used by the High Authority was a power deriving from Article 64. According to that, when some infringements of the Treaty of Paris occurred, the High Authority could impose undertakings fines.

Naturally, the ECSC did not erase all barriers of European trade. Desmond Dinan (2004, p. 55) highlights that, apart from tariffs and quantitative restrictions, which were eliminated in the coal and steel sectors, non-tariff barriers proved to be more problematic to identify and remove. Due to these reasons the market continued to be defragmented, still uncompetitive (or not so competitive), not improving in productivity, as well as targeted by cartels.

However, apart from some drawbacks, the establishment of the ECSC was an important political and institutional step towards European integration. It was also a new element of the regulatory agenda, which under law (international agreement of a public law regulatory character) enabled a realisation of European policy in terms of strategic resources and industries of a key-value for the electricity sector. According to François Duchêne (cited in Dinan 2004, p. 57), the "narrow, technocratic view of relations between the High Authority and the industries and governments [developed into] a political system, which is substantially that of the Europe today". Moreover, aimed at coal – the leading energy fuel at that time – regulation of the ECSC had a great impact on the European energy sector. Thereby, the Treaty Establishing the European Coal and Steel Community can be considered as the first legal source of a key character for European interests in energy.

Further legal basis for energy issues and public law regulation was provided by the Treaties of Rome: the Treaty Establishing the European Atomic Energy Community and the Treaty Establishing the European Economic Community (TEC).[4] Within them, two of three European Communities were concerned with energy exclusively. However, each Treaty had something in common with energy matters. Thus, from the very beginning, energy issues in the European Communities were divided among the ECSC for coal, the Euratom for nuclear power, and the European Economic Community[5] which dealt with oil, gas, and electricity (see Hitiris 2003, p. 312). However, the TEC did not place energy in the field of explicit Community competence. It addressed issues of economic integration, but energy was not expressly mentioned (Cameron 2007, p. 13). Furthermore, no specific Title on Energy was introduced by the European Union, Amsterdam and Nice Treaties (Mathijsen 2004, p. 419).

### *The new European chapter of 2009*

The situation changed in December 2009, with the entry into force of the Treaty of Lisbon (2007), when the EU established the basis for shaping the energy sector. It is Article 194 of the Treaty on the Functioning of the European Union (TFEU)[6] which constitutes Title XXI "Energy". It provided a firm basis for the EU's activity within the energy sector, making it responsible for (a) ensuring the functioning of the energy market, (b) security of the energy supply in the Union, as well as (c) promoting energy efficiency and energy savings and the development of new and renewable forms of energy, and (d) the interconnection of energy networks.

Before 2009, energy matters were not so directly addressed as they are in the TFEU. Some scholars assess this previous absence of concrete provisions on energy as a mistake (see Cameron 2007, p. 42). However, the possibility of shaping the energy sector with the use of a legal instrument existed also under provisions of the TEC. To do this, the European Community institutions could make use of Article 175 TEC (environmental protection), Article 95 TEC (internal market), Articles 155 and 156 TEC (trans-European networks), and Article 100 TEC (difficulties in supply) (Piris 2010, p. 318).[7]

The EU's activity under Article 194 TFEU derives from the establishment and functioning of the internal market as well as the need to preserve and improve the environment. To achieve the listed objectives, the European Parliament and the Council, acting in accordance with the ordinary legislative procedure, may establish necessary measures. However, as stated in Article 194 (2), the EU does not have an unlimited field of action. The mentioned measures (with one derogation)[8] shall not affect a Member State's right to determine the conditions for exploiting its energy resources, its choice between different energy sources, and the general structure of its energy supply.[9]

In the literature concerning Article 194 TFEU, two main approaches appear. The first finds the increasing influence of the European Union on the energy sector. However, it assumes some limitations – as stated in Article 194. The second is based on the fact that the European Union has already used the legal basis provided by the TEC to impact the energy sector. That is why the status quo of this impact is more or less maintained.

Stephen C. Sieberson's opinion (2008, p. 232) may be considered as an example of the first approach. In his early assessment of the new title on energy he wrote:

> [t]he Lisbon Treaty's unprecedented approach may spur greater EU activity in this field, and if so, the level of Member State action may be correspondingly diminished. Furthermore, the classification of energy as a shared competence may prevent national action where it had previously permitted. However, the Lisbon Treaty will leave in the Member States control the critical choice and structure of their energy sources, and it will require that fiscal measures relating to energy be unanimously approved on the Council. The Lisbon Treaty may shift the energy divided line toward Brussels, but it also offers important safeguards for national sovereignty in this field.

On the other hand, commenting on Article 194, Jean-Claude Piris (2010, p. 319) argues that it is difficult to affirm the opinion that the EU increased its competence in the area of energy. Taking into account the possibilities the EC already had to act on the basis of Articles 95, 155, or 156, as well as 175 and 308 of the TEC, the new title within TFEU has rather made these competences explicit and codified in a single Article. Hancher and Salerno (2012, p. 381) perceive this matter in a similar way. In their view the TEC

> already allowed the Community to realize far-reaching structural changes in the ownership of key infrastructure and to consolidate a considerable shift of regulatory power in the Commission in order to realize and subsequently supervise the mechanics of the internal energy market.

Apart from a firm legal basis for having an impact on the electricity sector, the EU, and earlier the EC, provided strategic documents in the field of energy policy. The first steps in this respect were taken in 1964 when the ECSC adopted a protocol on energy (Protocol of Agreement 1964) and, in 1968, with publishing the First Guidelines for a Community Energy Policy. This trend continued and, as a result, every year the European energy policy is becoming more complex and harmonised.

## The harmonisation of European law and policy on energy

Recognising the significance of electricity for the European economy and society, the EU has a policy of harmonisation aimed at the establishment of a fully integrated internal energy market. EU harmonisation is a way to create a common standard across its internal market. It is a method to achieve uniformity in the laws of Member States (Turnbull 2010, pp. 135–154). It is built on the common agreement of all interested parties. Harmonisation seeks to coordinate legal systems. It eliminates major differences. It establishes minimum requirements or standards (Turnbull 2010, pp. 135–154). It makes Member States adjust their national law to these rules (Pennings 2003, p. 289).

Eva J. Lohse (2011, p. 313) defines harmonisation of EU law with the use of three elements. These are "a process", "a result" (intended), and "a function". First, harmonisation starts with a concept at the European level. It is a standard which national law has to follow (Lohse 2011, p. 313). In this context, it is also an attempt to make the defragmented domestic law of the Member States more coherent (see Havu 2012, pp. 26–27). Second, harmonisation has an intended result. It creates a uniform law which is needed for goals to be achieved. Finally, it serves as a function to pursue the tasks of the EU. This can be the establishment of the European internal market (Lohse 2011, p. 313).

The internal market (its creation and development) is a common denominator of many actions in the field of harmonisation in the EU (see Ohly 2009, pp. 621–622, Kur & Dreier 2013, p. 245, Reich 2008, pp. 41–42). One of these is the internal energy market. Not referring to the past activity in this area (which is done in the following chapters) at this point, let us address the far-reaching Conclusions of the European Council of February 2011. They provide the very recent important steps for harmonisation bringing in the main policy goals in the field of energy, as well as electricity. As the Council announced (pp. 1–2):

> [s]afe, secure, sustainable and affordable energy contributing to European competitiveness remains a priority for Europe. Action at the EU level can and must bring added value to that objective. Over the years, a lot of work has been carried out on the main strands of an EU energy policy, including the setting of ambitious energy and climate change objectives and the adoption of comprehensive legislation supporting these objectives…
>
> The EU needs a fully functioning, interconnected and integrated internal energy market…
>
> The internal market should be completed by 2014 so as to allow gas and electricity to flow freely. This requires in particular that in cooperation with

> ACER national regulators and transmission systems operators step up their work on market coupling and guidelines and on network codes applicable across European networks.

The priorities of the EU – energy security (pro-security), sustainability (pro-environmental), and affordability (pro-consumer) – within the energy market are correlated with the competitiveness of the European economy, which cannot be achieved without a solid energy sector. These objectives due to their complexity are not yet established in the European agenda. Their realisation requires comprehensive action, carried out by different actors, on the European and national levels.

A common feature for the priorities is that they are anchored in the *internal energy market*. Depending on the context, it may be a goal or a measure for achieving primary European energy objectives. Thus, the internal energy market can be considered in a dualistic relation (*a mirror reflection*). The strategic documents of the European Union seem to confirm this implication:

> Europe's energy markets have been opened up to enable citizens to benefit from more reliable, competitive prices as well as more sustainable energy. This potential will not be fully realised unless robust efforts are made to create a more integrated, interconnected and competitive market.
>
> (European Commission 2010, p. 9)

or

> [t]he European Union needs an internal energy market that is competitive, integrated and fluid, providing a solid backbone for electricity and gas flowing where it is needed. To tackle Europe's energy and climate challenges and to ensure affordable and secure energy supplies to households and businesses, the EU must ensure that the internal European energy market is able to operate efficiently and flexibly.
>
> (European Commission 2012b, p. 2)

Therefore, achieving the internal energy market contributes to the realisation of the objectives sought by the EU, e.g. promotion of the sustainable energy, or establishing reliable prices for energy services. Furthermore, improving competition in the energy markets, which is a prerequisite of the internal energy market, can enhance the incentives for the investments required and reducing their cost to what is necessary (which meets the criteria of energy security or reliability of prices).

Seen in this light, one may ask, in scenarios for the future of the internal energy market, in which direction does this take the EU, and what importance does it attach to electricity? Answers to these crucial questions may be found in the strategic documents of the EU. Despite their non-binding character (the Commissions' communications), they drive the public discussion and political agenda of the Union, link each legislative initiative, and provide a future outlook for the European energy sector, giving the strategic response in the context of its shape. Moreover, they show the importance that the EU attaches to the energy sector:

> [e]nergy is the life blood of our society. The well-being of our people, industry and economy depends on safe, secure, sustainable and affordable energy.... The energy challenge is ... one of the greatest tests which Europe has to face.... Yet the decisions to set us on the right path are needed urgently as failing to achieve a well-functioning European energy market will only increase the costs for consumers and put Europe's competitiveness at risk.
>
> (European Commission 2010, p. 2)

Quoted from the EC's Communication "Energy 2020", this text underlines one key message: the energy sector is extremely vital for the European Union, its economy, and its citizens; although, it requires improvements which are a result of Europe's energy situation (*inter alia*, dependence and lack of diversification of energy routes and sources).[10] As of May 2013 the European Council noticed in the Conclusions (p. 3):

> [t]he EU's energy policy must ensure security of supply for households and companies at affordable and competitive prices and costs, in a safe and sustainable manner. This is particularly important for Europe's competitiveness in the light of increasing energy demand from major economies and high energy prices and costs.

This also concerns the electricity sector where energy security is linked with developing the interconnectors, rebuilding European infrastructure (generation and network), and optimising the energy mix with the use of new sources like renewables. However, as in the other energy sectors (fuel and gas), electricity in other Member State countries is rather different.[11] Naturally, this general remark covers competition in energy markets.[12]

Thereby, the dynamic growth of electricity use does not only have a technical background (i.e. technologies of electricity transmission and distribution, the installed capacity, the growing demand for energy, etc.). It has its economic dimension, which simply comes from the fact that electricity can be traded. The security of market transactions requires law that establishes market rules and ensures compliance with them.

These features complement the technical conditions in such a way that electricity is sold for commercial purposes. That makes it necessary to set a specific trading platform for this commodity – already mentioned several times – the energy market.[13] The importance of the *market* for the concept of the *internal energy market* (as the first is a key element of the latter) makes it reasonable to delve into definitions of market and other terms related to market.

## Market, internal energy market, and electricity market

The idea of *market* is a very core concept of economy and law. Mark Blaug (1985, p. 6), in his *Economic Theory in Retrospect*, even defines the whole history of economic thought through the prism of market. In his words, it is "nothing but the history of our efforts to understand the working of economy based on market transactions". Due to its importance for the functioning of the economy, in the context of strict correlation of law and economy, also from the legal point of view, market is a term of great importance. As defined in *Black's Law Dictionary*, market is "a place of commercial activity in which goods or service are bought and sold".[14] It can also be described as a "geographic area or demographic segment considered as a place of demand for particular goods or services, especially prospective purchase of goods, wherever they are".[15] The geographic aspect of a market definition plays a crucial role in antitrust law, where "geographic market" is defined "as a part of relevant market that identifies the region in which a firm might compete".[16]

### *Relevant market as a point of reference*

The market definition, in particular "relevant market", is an analytical tool of great significance for competition law. It enables authorities to tackle competition problems. Originally, this was a response to strengthening of market power (OECD 2012, pp. 91–92). Currently, in general the definition is intended "to calculate market shares, identify competitors, measure concentration and make inferences about market power" (OECD 2012, p. 81).

For introducing the market definition into law two approaches can be distinguished: hard or soft law instruments. Kenneth Abbott and Duncan Snidal propose a useful explanation of what should be considered as hard law. In their definition it is grounded on "legally binding obligations that are precise (or can be made precise through adjudication or the issuance of detailed regulations) and that delegate authority for interpreting and implementing the law" (cited in Shaffer & Pollack 2010, pp. 706–799). With respect to soft law, in principle it does not have a binding character, but may have practical effects (see Snyder 1993, pp. 19–65). However this must be decided from case to case (Mörth 2004, p. 5). Additionally, Abbott and Snidal propose three determinants which weaken legal arrangements: obligation, precision, delegation. If formally binding legal provisions are under the impact of any of them, they should be qualified as soft law (cited in Shaffer & Pollack 2010, p. 715).[17]

With regard to practice, in many national legal systems soft law is used as a tool for setting guidance or notices on market issues (e.g. relevant product, geographic market). Authorities issue guidelines or notices to establish a reference point (the "analytical framework") for introducing an idea of a relevant market. This is aimed at the enforcement of competition law (OECD 2012, pp. 81–82). The European Commission's 1997 "Notice on the definition of the relevant market" is in line with this concept. According to it:

> [m]arket definition is a tool to identify and define the boundaries of competition between firms. It serves to establish the framework within which competition policy is applied by the Commission. The main purpose of market definition is to identify in a systematic way the competitive constraints that the undertakings involved [i.e. in the case of a concentration, the parties to the concentration] face. The objective of defining a market in both its product and geographic dimension is to identify those actual competitors of the undertakings involved that are capable of constraining those undertakings' behaviour and of preventing them from behaving independently of effective competitive pressure.

In soft law, as highlighted in the OECD's report (2012, p. 82) the market definition may be provided in categorised guidelines (on specific groups of cases), like the European Commission's guidelines (e.g. Commission Notice Guidelines 2004) or the "US Horizontal Merger Guidelines" (US Department of Justice 2010). For example, these "US Horizontal Guidelines" summarise "the principal analytical techniques, practices, and the enforcement policy of the Department of Justice and the Federal Trade Commission ... with respect to mergers and acquisitions involving actual or potential competitors ('horizontal mergers') under the federal antitrust laws".[18]

The market can be also defined through hard law. As a result, market definition takes the form of a "statutory prerequisite" (OECD 2012, p. 82). Such approaches exist in many national legal systems, both in Europe and in the world. For example, in Poland, under the provisions of the Act on Competition and Consumer Protection (*Ustawa z dnia 16 lutego 2007 r. o ochronie konkurencji i konsumentów*) in Article 4 (9) a "relevant market" (*rynek właściwy*) is defined.[19] This issue is similarly regulated in other national competition legislation. OECD (2012, p. 82) lists here Slovakia, Hungary, India, or Mexico.

### *Defining energy market*

The presented considerations apply to the market in general, although the subject of this book concerns only a part of it – the electricity market. In finding its definition, one may recall the concept of "Organized Electricity Market" established in the US Code of Federal Regulations, which means:

> an auction-based day ahead and real time wholesale market where a single entity receives offers to sell and bids to buy electric energy and/or ancillary services from multiple sellers and buyers and determines which sales and purchases are completed and at what prices, based on formal rules contained in Commission-approved tariffs, and where the prices are used by a transmission organization for establishing transmission usage charges.
>
> (18 CFR 42.1)

No matter how much the US energy law is helpful in understanding the issues of how law steers the energy sector (how it is shaped, with established conditions for operation within it, etc.), the subject of this book is correlated with European energy law, and the European electricity sector. Therefore, US law and theory can be only an auxiliary research instrument, used when comparisons are necessary.

In the European Union the electricity market is part of the internal energy market. It is clearly confirmed by the EU's strategic documents as well as by the Electricity Directives. The European Union perceives it through internal markets goals, rules, and institutions which it established for its needs; naturally, these find an application in the electricity sector. These indicated circumstances are proved by the Commission. "The architecture for the internal energy market is clear. It is laid out in the Third energy package and in complementary legislation. The building blocks are there", the EC figuratively addresses (European Commission 2012b, p. 7).[20] Noteworthy remarks were made by the Commission in the "before-liberalisation era". In 1988 the Commission discussed the issue of the internal energy market in the following context:

> [t]he commonly used expression "energy market" could give one the impression that energy is a comparatively homogeneous sector. However, if one looks at this sector in greater detail it is quite evident that this market is extremely diverse in terms both of products and of end-uses ... [and] is still comparatively partitioned in the Community and there are therefore many barriers to the free movement of energy products.
>
> (European Commission 1988, pp. 4–5)

Underlining the diversity of the energy market the Commission placed it in the context of the free movement of energy products,[21] linking it with the European internal market based on the Single European Act,[22] and of the Treaties, which provide the following definition of an internal market: "an area without internal frontiers in which the free movement of goods, persons, services and capital is ensured in accordance with the provisions of the Treaties".[23] The electricity market is an element of it.

Although, in defining an electricity market, it is necessary to answer the question: "what is the real trading product?" (Burger, Bernhard, & Schindlmayr 2007, p. 27). From a legal point of view it is a tradable "good". The rationale for it is provided by the European Court of Justice judgements. For example, in its judgement in *Costa v ENEL* the Court accepted that electricity may fall within the scope of European Union competition law (Cameron 2007, p. 42). In *Gemeente Almelo and others v Energiebedrijf IJsselmij* the European Court of Justice noticed that both "in Community law, and ... in the national laws of the Member States, it is accepted that electricity constitutes a good". Further, in the European legal system, electricity is regarded as a good under the common tariff nomenclature.

The European Court of Justice's judgements confirm the applicability of European law to electricity trade, especially the principle of the free movement of goods. However, this principle is not easy to execute within the electricity market in the European Union due, *inter alia*, to a number of electricity's specific features, including technical and economic reasons. Because of these facts, linked with the role that energy plays for the European economy, as well as for European society, as already mentioned, energy issues are subject to EU legislation, at the highest level in the hierarchy of European law – Treaties, with TFEU at the forefront.

Having outlined the features of electricity, its importance in global relations, as well as the approach of the European Union towards it, where it is a component of the internal energy market, let us move forward. Because of the latter I find it necessary to discuss briefly the practical dimension of the *electricity market* and its players. Undoubtedly, electricity does not function in a vacuum, but needs a specific utilitarian application. This establishes the conditions for electricity trade.

Furthermore, besides Treaties, which gave a very concrete basis for the operation of the EU's electricity sector, the crucial steps for the electricity market were undertaken with the use of secondary law. In the European Union's legal system this activity took the shape of the Energy Packages.

## Notes

1 However, the new technologies for electricity storage are being developed (e.g. batteries, flywheels). In addition, hydro sources give some storage possibilities (hydroelectric pumped storage). Although this requires specific geographical conditions and involves pumping water to reservoirs when the energy demand is low, and pumping it out for generation needs when the demand increases (Energy Regulatory Commission 2012, p. 2).

2 Blok (2007, p. 92) rightly explains:

> [b]ase load power plants have high capital costs and low variable operational costs (mainly fuel costs) and are hence suitable if they run for many hours a year (i.e., if they have a high load factor). For peak load power plants, the opposite is true. Intermediate load plants are in between.

3 The Treaty Establishing the European Coal and Steel Community was signed on 18 April 1951 by France, West Germany, Italy, Belgium, Luxembourg, and the Netherlands. The Treaty entered into force on 23 July 1952, with a validity period limited to 50 years. The Treaty expired on 23 July 2002.

4 Both Treaties were signed on 25 March 1957 and they entered into force on 1 January 1958.

5 After the Treaty of Maastricht (Treaty on European Union, OJ C 191, 29 July 1992) the EEC became the European Community. Thus, herein the abbreviation TEC is used.

6 Consolidated version 2012, OJ C 326, 26 October 2012.

7 Besides Article 95 Paul Craig (2010, p. 321) adds here a conjunction of Article 47 and 55 as a basis for measures enacted on energy.

8 As an exception, pursuant to Article 194(3) the Council, acting in accordance with a special legislative procedure, shall unanimously and after consulting the European Parliament, establish the measures referred to therein when they are primarily of a fiscal nature.

9 Although, as underlined in the judgement of the General Court in Case T-370/11 *Republic of Poland v European Commission* [2013],

> it is true that, under the second subparagraph of Article 194 (2) TFEU, measures established in accordance with the procedure laid down in the first subparagraph of that paragraph and necessary to achieve the policy objectives of the European Union in the area of energy, referred to in paragraph 1 of that article, cannot affect the right of a Member State to determine the conditions for exploiting its energy resources, its choice between different energy sources and the general structure of its energy supply. However, there is no reason to suppose that the second subparagraph of Article 194 (2) TFEU establishes a general prohibition to assign that right that is applicable in European Union policy in the area of the environment (see, to that effect, Case C 490/10 *Parliament v Council* [2012] ECR I-0000, paragraph 77). On the one hand, Article 194 TFEU is a general provision which relates solely to the energy sector and, consequently, delineates a sectoral competence.... On the other hand, it should be noted that the second subparagraph of Article 194 (2) TFEU expressly refers to point (c) of the first subparagraph of Article 192 (2) TFEU. Indeed, the second subparagraph Article 194 (2) TFEU provides that the prohibition on affecting the right of a Member State to determine the conditions for exploiting its energy resources, its choice between different energy sources and the general structure of its energy supply applies without prejudice to point (c) of the first subparagraph of Article 192 (2) TFEU. While it is true that that latter provision is only procedural in nature, it none the less provides specific rules relating to the environment policy of the European Union.

Seen in this light, where the decisions are qualified as actions taken by the European Union within the framework of its environment policy Article 194 (2) TFEU is not applicable as in Case T-370/11. Compare an opposite opinion regarding qualification of circumstances of this judgement. See Nowacki 2012, pp. 26–35.

10 Since 1995, the European Union's total import dependency has grown from 43.2 per cent in 1995 to 53.8 per cent in 2011, and accordingly from 21.4 to 41.4 per cent in solid fuels, in petroleum from 74.3 to 84.9 per cent, and in gas from 43.5 to 67.0 per cent. The EU depends on a few leading suppliers for its oil (mostly Russia 35 per cent, Norway 12 per cent, Saudi Arabia 8 per cent) and gas supplies (Russia 30 per cent, Norway 28 per cent, Algeria 13 per cent, Qatar 11 per cent). See European Commission 2013, pp. 22–24.

11 For example, at the end of 2011 the installed electricity capacity (MW) in Germany was at the level of 171 681 out of 919 275 for EU-27. For comparison in France it was 131 353, and in Poland 34 554, Denmark 13 580, Bulgaria 10 236, or just 3 691 in Lithuania and 571 on Malta (European Commission 2013, p. 77).

12 As it was proved in the report "Energy markets in the European Union in 2011" by 2011, the 18 Member States had more than 20 electricity suppliers in retail, while there were three or more main electricity suppliers in 20 Member States. Concentration in electricity continued to be high in most Member States, while the total number of power generation companies present in the market reached a three- to four-digit figure in a few Member States. The market share of the largest producers, where one generator reached more than 50 per cent, existed in 11 Member States, and where the generator reached the level of 80 per cent in six Member States. Further, major differences persisted between prices in different EU Member States (European Commission 2012a, pp. 8–9).

13 Before moving forward, one issue requires clarification. Herein, I propose to analyse the market. However, in the book, or in this chapter, I also use the term "sector". This derives from a broader context which follows this term, mostly the industrial background of this word. Thus, it allows finding a more public perspective, which is

not strictly linked with private market transactions. Thereby, I propose to see the market through a prism of sector. However, in terms of practice, a close meaning of the above-mentioned terms allows for using them as synonyms where possible.

14 *Black's Law Dictionary*, 8th edn, s.v. "market", similarly in *Oxford Dictionary of Law*, 5th edn, s.v. "market is a facility for the sale and purchase of goods".

15 *Black's Law Dictionary*, s.v. "market".

16 *Black's Law Dictionary*, s.v. "geographic market".

17 Shaffer and Pollack (2010, p. 715) provide a practical description of each dimension. For example,

> if an agreement is formally binding but its content is vague so that the agreement leaves almost complete discretion to the parties as to its implementation, then the agreement is soft along a second dimension. Finally, if an agreement does not delegate any authority to a third party to monitor its implementation or to interpret and enforce it, then the agreement again can be soft (along a third dimension).

18 Section 7 of the Clayton Antitrust Act of 1914, 15 U.S.C. §18, Sections 1 and 2 of the Sherman Antitrust Act of 1890, 15 U.S.C. §§1, 2, and Section 5 of the Federal Trade Commission Act of 1914, 15 U.S.C. §45, US Department of Justice and the Federal Trade Commission 2010, p. 1.

19 As stated there, the relevant market means the market for goods, which, due to their purpose, price, and features, including quality, are considered by their buyers as substitutes, and are offered in the area in which, due to their nature and characteristics, the existence of barriers to market, consumers' preferences, significant differences in prices, and transport costs, there are similar conditions of competition.

20 Within "complementary legislation" the EC recognises particularly Regulation (EU) No 994/2010, Regulation (EU) No 1227/2011, and Regulation (EU) No 347/2013.

21 "An increase in trading between Member States is one of the results which might be expected from the internal energy market" (European Commission 1988, p. 6).

22 "The single market is a means of cementing the economic integration of the Community" (European Commission 1988, p. 5). See also European Commission 1988, pp. 2–5.

23 Introduced in Single European Act, now Article 26 TFEU, ex Article 14 TEC.

## References


Abbott, K.W. & Snidal, D. 2000, "Hard and soft law in international governance", *International Organization*, 54, pp. 421–456.

Blaug, M. 1985. *Economic theory in retrospect*, 4th edn, Cambridge University Press, Cambridge.

Blok, K. 2007, *Introduction to energy analysis*, Techne Press, Amsterdam.

Burger, M., Bernhard, G., & Schindlmayr, G. 2007, *Managing energy risk: an integrated view on power and other energy markets*. John Wiley & Sons Ltd, Chichester.

Cameron, P.D. 2007, *Competition in energy markets: law and regulation in the European Union*, 2nd edn, Oxford University Press, Oxford.

Case 6/64 *Costa v ENEL* [1964] ECR 1141.

Case C-393/92 *Gemeente Almelo and others v Energiebedrijf IJsselmij* [1994] ECR I-1477.

Case C-490/10 *Parliament v Council* [2012] ECR I-0000.

Case T-370/11 *Republic of Poland v European Commission* [2013], not yet published.

Chick, M. 2007, *Electricity and energy policy in Britain, France and the United States since 1945*, Edward Elgar, Cheltenham.

Code of Federal Regulations, 18 CFR 42.1.

Commission Notice Guidelines on the application of Article 81 of the EC Treaty to technology transfer agreements, OJ C 101, 27 April 2004.

Commission Notice on the definition of the relevant market for the purposes of community competition law, OJ C 372, 9 December 1997.

Council of the European Union 2011, *Council Conclusions of 4 February 2011*, Brussels, 8 March 2011, EUCO 2/1/11, REV 1.

Council of the European Union 2013, *Council Conclusions of 22 May 2013*, Brussels, 23 May 2013, EUCO 75/1/13, REV 1.

Craig, P. 2010, *The Lisbon Treaty: law, politics, and treaty reform*, Oxford University Press, Oxford.

Dinan, D. 2004, *Europe recast: a history of European Union*, Lynne Rienner, Boulder, CO.

Duchêne, F. 1994, *Jean Monnet: the first statesman of interdependence*, Norton, New York.

Energy Regulatory Commission 2012, *Energy primer: a handbook of energy market basics*. Available from: www.ferc.gov/market-oversight/guide/energy-primer.pdf. [19 June 2015].

European Association of the Electricity Transmission and Distribution Equipment and Services Industry 2008, *Position paper for energy policy T&D Europe WG1 – V3*. Available from: www.tdeurope.eu/data/file/Position%20Paper%20for%20Energy%20Policy%20T&D%20Europe%20WG1-V3.pdf [22 June 2015].

European Commission 1968, *Commission Memorandum to the Council of 18 December 1968: first guidelines for a Community Energy Policy*, COM (68) 1040, Supplement to EC Bulletin No. 12/1968.

European Commission 1988, *Commission Working Document: the Internal Energy Market*, Brussels, 2 May 1988, COM (88) 238 final.

European Commission 2010, *Communication from the Commission to the European Parliament, the Council, the European Economic and Social Committee and the Committee of the Regions: Energy 2020: a strategy for competitive, sustainable and secure energy*, Brussels, 10 November 2010, COM (2010) 639 final.

European Commission 2012a, *Commission Staff Working Document: energy markets in the European Union in 2011*, Brussels, 15 November 2012, SWD (2012) 368 final.

European Commission 2012b, *Communication from the Commission to the European Parliament, the Council, the European Economic and Social Committee and the Committee of the Regions: making the Internal Energy Market work*, Brussels, 15 November 2012, COM (2012) 663 final.

European Commission 2013, *EU energy in figures: pocketbook 2013*. Available from: https://ec.europa.eu/energy/sites/ener/files/documents/2013_pocketbook.pdf [22 June 2015].

Fimister, A.P. 2008, *Robert Schuman: neo scholastic humanism and the reunification of Europe*, P.I.E. Peter Lang, Brussels.

Hancher, L. & Salerno, F.M. 2012, "Energy policy after Lisbon", in *EU law after Lisbon*, eds A. Biondi, P. Eeckhout, & S. Ripley, Oxford University Press, Oxford, pp. 367–402.

Havu, K. 2012 "Quasi-cogerence by harmonisation of EU competition law-related damages actions?" in *Coherence and fragmentation in European private law*, eds P. Letto-Vanamo & J. Smits, Sellier European Law Publishers, Munich, pp. 25–42.

Hitiris, T. 2003, *European Union economics*, 5th edn, Prentice Hall/Financial Times, Harlow.

IEA 2011, *World energy outlook 2011*, International Energy Agency, Paris. Available from: www.iea.org/publications/freepublications/publication/WEO2011_WEB.pdf [16 June 2015].

IEA 2012, *World energy outlook 2012 factsheet: how will global energy markets evolve to 2035?* Available from: www.worldenergyoutlook.org/media/weowebsite/2012/factsheets.pdf [17 June 2015].

IEA 2014, *Key world energy statistics*. Available from: www.iea.org/publications/freepublications/publication/keyworld2014.pdf [12 June 2015].

Institute for Electric Efficiency, Edison Foundation 2012, *IEE 2012 annual report*. Available from: www.edisonfoundation.net/iee/Documents/IEE_2012_AnnualReport.pdf [22 January 2015].

Jovanovic, M.N. 2005, *The economics of European integration: limits and prospects*, Edward Elgar, Cheltenham.

Kur, A. & Dreier, T. 2013, *European intellectual property law: text, cases and materials*, Edward Elgar, Cheltenham.

Lohse, E.J. 2011, 'The meaning of harmonisation in the context of European Union Law: a process in need of definition', in *Theory and practice of harmonisation*, eds M. Andenas & C. Baasch Andersen, Edward Elgar, Cheltenham, pp. 282–313.

Mathijsen, P.S.R.F. 2004, *A guide to European Union law*, 8th edn, Sweet & Maxwell, London.

Milward, A.S. 2002, *The rise and fall of a national strategy, 1945–1963*, vol. 1 of *The United Kingdom and the European Community*, Frank Cass Publishers, London.

Mörth, U. 2004, "Introduction", in *Soft law in governance and regulation: an interdisciplinary analysis*, ed. U. Mörth, Edward Elgar, Cheltenham, pp. 1–10.

Nowacki, M. 2012, "Swoboda państwa w zakresie kształtowania krajowej struktury zaopatrzenia w energię w świetle prawa Unii Europejskie" [Freedom of state in the field of shaping national energy supply structures in the light of European Union Law], in *Wybrane węzłowe zagadnienia współczesnego prawa energetycznego* [Selected nodal contemporary issues of modern energy law], ed. A. Walaszek-Pyzioł, AT Wydawnictwo, Cracow, pp. 17–35.

OECD 2012, *Market definition 2012*. Available from: www.oecd.org/daf/competition/Marketdefinition2012.pdf [17 June 2015].

OECD 2013, *OECD factbook 2013: economic, environmental and social statistics*, OECD Publishing, Paris. Available from: http://dx.doi.org/10.1787/factbook-2013-43-en [16 June 2015].

Ohly, A. 2009, "Economic rights", in *Research handbook on the future of EU copyright*, ed. E. Derclaye, Edward Elgar, Cheltenham, pp. 612–641.

Pennings, F. 2003, *Introduction to European social security law*, 4th edn, Intersentia, Antwerp.

Piris, J.-C. 2010, *The Lisbon Treaty: a legal and political analysis*, Cambridge University Press, Cambridge.

Protocol of Agreement on energy matters concluded the governments of the Member States of the European Communities on 21 April 1964, Official gazette of the European Communities No. 69, 30 April 1964.

Raitio, J. 2003, *The principle of legal certainty in EC law*, Kluwer Academic Publishers, Dordrecht.

Regulation (EU) No 347/2013 of the European Parliament and of the Council of 17 April 2013 on guidelines for trans-European energy infrastructure and repealing Decision No 1364/2006/EC and amending Regulations (EC) No 713/2009, (EC) No 714/2009 and (EC) No 715/2009, OJ L 115, 25 April 2013.

Regulation (EU) No 994/2010 of the European Parliament and of the Council of 20 October 2010 concerning measures to safeguard security of gas supply and repealing Council Directive 2004/67/EC, OJ L 295, 12 November 2010.

Regulation (EU) No 1227/2011 of the European Parliament and of the Council of 25 October 2011 on wholesale energy market integrity and transparency (REMIT), OJ L 326, 8 December 2011.

Reich, N. 2008, "Crisis or future of European consumer law", in *The yearbook of consumer law 2009*, eds D. Parry, A. Nordhausen, G. Howells, & C. Twigg-Flesner, Ashgate Publishing, Farnham, pp. 3–67.

Shaffer, G. & Pollack, M.A. 2010, "Hard vs. soft law: alternatives, complements and antagonists in international governance", *Minnesota Law Review*, 94, pp. 706–799. Available from: www.minnesotalawreview.org/wp-content/uploads/2011/08/Shaffer-Pollack_MLR.pdf [18 June 2015].

Sieberson, S.C. 2008, *Dividing lines between the European Union and its Member States: the impact of the Treaty of Lisbon*, T.M.C. Asser Press, The Hague.

Smil, V. 2010, *Energy transitions: history, requirements, prospects*. ABC-CLIO, Santa Barbara, CA.

Snyder, F. 1993, "The effectiveness of European community law: institutions, processes, tools and techniques", *Modern Law Review*, 56, pp. 19–65. Available from: www.francis-snyder.com/tl_files/contents/articles/The_Effectiveness_of_European_Community_Law.pdf [18 June 2015].

Treaty of Lisbon Amending the Treaty on European Union and the Treaty Establishing the European Community, signed at Lisbon, 13 December 2007, OJ C 306, 17 December 2007.

Treaty on the Functioning of the European Union, consolidated version 2012, OJ C 326, 26 October 2012.

Turnbull, J. 2010, "Harmonisation of the law and legal cultures in the EU: a linguistic approach", in *Researching language and the law: textual features and translation issues*, eds D.S. Giannoni & C. Frade, Peter Lang, Bern, pp. 135–154.

Union of the Electricity Industry EURELECTRIC 2010, *Power choices: pathways to carbon-neutral electricity in Europe by 2050. Full report*, Brussels. Available from: www.eurelectric.org/PowerChoices2050/ [18 June 2015].

US Department of Justice and the Federal Trade Commission 2010, *Horizontal merger guidelines 2010*. Available from: www.ftc.gov/os/2010/08/100819hmg.pdf [17 June 2015].

*Ustawa z dnia 16 lutego 2007 r. o ochronie konkurencji i konsumentów* [Act of 16 February 2007 on competition and consumer protection], *Dz.U. Nr 50, poz. 331, ze zm.* [J.L. No. 50, item 331, with amendments].

Willis, F.R. 1965, *France, Germany, and the new Europe, 1945–1967*. Stanford University Press, Stanford, CA.

World Business Council for Sustainable Development 2005, *Pathways to 2050: energy & climate change*. Available from: www.leonardo-energy.org/sites/leonardo-energy/files/root/Documents/2009/pathways.pdf [18 June 2015].

Wunderlich, J.-U. 2007, *Regionalism globalisation and international order: Europe and Southeast Asia*, Ashgate Publishing, Aldershot.

# 3 Models of the electricity sector and the "package approach"

As already discussed, the features and significance of electricity imply a need to create a suitable trading platform, which will meet electricity characteristics. For example, a distinguishing feature of electricity in comparison to the other commodities is the fact that electricity is not storable. As a result, supply is to exactly match demand every time.

Moreover, the supplier has no possibility of forecasting precisely the demand of customers. That is why an entity that balances supply and demand is needed (Burger, Bernhard, & Schindlmayr 2007, pp. 27–28). This impossibility of forecasting demand simply differs electricity from other goods. In establishing the market for electricity these factors must be taken into account.

## Market models for the electricity sector

To address, *inter alia*, these issues, as well as to enable electricity trade, different market models adjusted to the characteristics of electricity have been established. They can be classified by various criteria (subjective, e.g. market players; objective, e.g. fuel mix; quantitative, e.g. volume of electricity produced; qualitative, e.g. energy security measures, etc.). One of them is the level of market opening (qualitative).[1]

Using this criterion herein some of the models are briefly presented, i.e. Single Buyer Model, Wholesale Competition Model, and Retail Competition Model in centralised or decentralised variant (de Vries 2007, p. 10).

### *Simple market structure*

The first of the listed models, the Single Buyer Model, was a popular market structure in the 1990s, when governments in several countries (in particular developing) established it aiming at relieving capacity shortages while maintaining "scarce public resources" (Lovei 2000, p. 1). In this model competition exists only in electricity production.[2] A significant part of the market is a monopoly (de Vries 2007, p. 10), which proves that it is a transition model (from monopoly to competition).

In the model of national power utility, very often a former monopolist, may be divided into generation, distribution, and transmission companies (Lovei 2000, p. 1), is the state-owned single buyer, who purchases, and has exclusive rights to, electricity from Independent Power Producers (IPPs) (Lovei 2000, p. 1) – and all electricity within the public grid must be sold to it (de Vries 2007, p. 10). Usually, the utility holds a position of a strategically important Transmission System Operator (Lovei 2000, p. 1). Parenthetically, Harris (2006, p. 163) distinguishes another extreme option of the Single Buyer Model. In this market formula the Single Buyer is a short-term intermediary coordinator for generators, transmitters, and suppliers.

Often the power purchasing authority operates its own generation units; although a single buyer "may also be prohibited from owning and operating generation facilities himself" in order to improve competition (de Vries 2007, p. 10). The single buyer determines capacity requirements. By setting appropriate conditions in the call for tender for new capacity, he can influence the market player's choice of technology (Petrov 2010, p. 2).[3] As a result, with the use of long-term Power Purchase Agreements (PPAs) the national power utility can ensure construction of necessary power plants when and where it needs them (Lovei 2000, p. 1).

These PPAs are the basis for electricity trade in this model (Yang & Sharma 2012, p. 4).[4] They include provisions on "take-or-pay quotas" or "fixed capacity charges" in order to minimalise the market risk borne by the investor (Lovei 2000, p. 1). On the other hand, all risks (as well as ownership responsibilities) are assigned to the PPA provider.[5] PPAs have a broad spectrum of types (Harris 2006, p. 163). In practice PPAs' scope contain, *inter alia*, provisions on the length, specifics of electricity trade, curtailment agreements, transmission, credit, insurance and environmental issues, credits, disputes, etc. (Windustry 2007).

Laurens de Vries (2007) provides further characteristics of the Single Buyer Model. As its important advantage he qualifies the model's simplicity. "The minimum requirement, starting from a monopoly situation, is to allow private investment in generating capacity and to give the monopolist the task of coordinating the purchase of electricity". This market structure, due to private capital engagement, enables it to achieve cost savings in generation, which is one of the most capital-intensive sub-sectors of electricity (de Vries 2007, p. 10). On the other hand, the model's main weakness is the fact that the power purchasing authority "may have the same tendency to over invest as a monopoly, limiting the benefits of competition". By this inefficiency the Single Buyer Model remains a position close to a monopoly. However, its efficiency can be improved by generation where competition appears, and – what should be noted – by regulation (de Vries 2007, p. 11).

### *Extended market models*

To tackle drawbacks of the Single Buyer Model, the market structure of the Wholesale Competition Model can be introduced. This requires the withdrawal of the power purchasing authority from the market. Thereby, distribution companies (or large consumers) can buy electricity directly from producers (de Vries 2007, p. 11). According to de Vries (2007, p. 11), two conditions are required to ensure competition. First, several distributors must be on the market. Second, an established Transmission System Operator (TSO) must be separated (unbundled) from other activities in the electricity market (and entities which carry it out).[6] In terms of the model's efficiency, in industrial countries wholesale competition has mainly worked without obstacles. As stated in the World Bank's policy report (Kessides, Bogetic, & Maurer 2007, p. 81), this was "because of excess capacity, moderate demand growth, and the availability of natural gas (which enabled the entry of gas-fired plants at modest scale and relatively low cost)". On the contrary, in many developing countries it has faced problems, i.e. "capacity shortages, enormous excess demand, and periodic blackouts" (Kessides 2004, p. 9).

In terms of the Competition Model's advantages, they can be found in generation where the market is "two-sided", in contrast to the "one-sided" Single Buyer Model. "Being competitors of each other in the purchase of electricity, utilities are likely to put more pressure on generating companies for being efficient than a power purchasing authority" (de Vries 2007, p. 11). With respect to the model's disadvantages within a retail market a monopoly is maintained. This means that regulation is required (as well as the unbundling of the TSO).[7]

The mentioned monopoly in a part of the market does not appear in the Retail Competition Model. There, all consumers have a guaranteed choice of electricity seller. "Thus there are two markets: a wholesale market ... and a retail market, in which the retail companies compete with each other for small end consumers" (de Vries 2007, p. 11). This market requires stricter unbundling (retail from distribution). As a result, instead of integrated utilities dealing with retail and distribution, retail companies are established. They purchase electricity in the wholesale market and resell it to consumers. In some variations of the model, they can purchase some services associated with distribution network services (de Vries 2007, p. 12). The model's main advantage refers to its name: simply, it is competition in retail. That affects retail companies forcing them to act in more cost-effective and consumer-friendly ways (de Vries 2007, p. 12).

Competitive wholesale markets can be organised in a centralised (integrated) or decentralised (disintegrated) way. De Vries (2007, p. 12) denotes the role of a system operator in managing the electricity pool, as the basic difference between the two models – in an integrated model the system operator is responsible for the pool's operation, while in the decentralised one the operator "has nothing to do with the matching of supply and demand in the market".

In the integrated model, electricity is traded with the use of the mentioned marketplace called a "pool". The pool can be either of a mandatory or a voluntary character (Onaiwu 2010, p. 2). In a mandatory pool, generated electricity must be sold in the pool. In the voluntary pool, "generators can participate in the pool, or the buyer and seller can request dispatch to meet a bilateral contract between them" (Harris 2006, p. 163). The pool is a tool of facilitating competition between generators. On the buyers' side it enables the calculation of the price paid for electricity (Onaiwu 2010, p. 2). The offered price can be grounded on "predetermined variable costs" (in Cost Based Pools) or the generators have the possibility of offering whatever price they deem appropriate (in Price Based Pools) (Barroso *et al.* 2005, p. 2).

In the pool model, electricity is purchased on "short-term" grounds. Typically, it is constructed on three pillars: "a day-ahead market", "several adjustment markets" (except US markets), and "balancing markets" (or "real-time markets") (Conejo, Carrión, & Morales 2010, p. 2). However, it can also be based on different combinations of several markets (day-ahead, intra-day, and five minutes-ahead) (Barroso *et al.* 2005, p. 2). Generally, the main part of daily transactions is conducted on the day-ahead and adjustment market. Both markets are very similar. The difference lies in the distance of power delivery: adjustment markets are much closer to it ("may cover a shorter trading horizon"). Finally, the balancing markets enable the coverage of: dispatched power (for the short term), load deviations, and transmission constraints (Conejo, Carrión, & Morales 2010, p. 2). In addition, electricity trading is supplemented by the "futures market". This is a trading platform based on a medium- or long-term horizon. It enables purchasing and selling "derivatives" or "derivative products" (Conejo, Carrión, & Morales 2010, pp. 2–3).

Furthermore, due to the security of the system's operation the "reserve" and "regulation" markets are established. The former, guarantees the coverage of interruptions in system operation (generation, as well as grid) by providing "spinning" or "non-spinning" standby power. It also concerns covering changes in demand (high volume fluctuations), as well as intermittent generation from non-dispatchable sources (e.g. wind, solar) (Conejo, Carrión, & Morales 2010, p. 3). The latter – the regulation market – "provides up and down real-time load-following capability to enforce continuously the balance between production and consumption (and to keep fixed the system frequency)" (Conejo, Carrión, & Morales 2010, p. 2).

Analysed in this section, circumstances highlight the role that energy market actors play on the market. Different energy market models determine (as well as require) different structures of entities engaged in specific activities within the electricity sector – its market players. The structure of entities complements the structure of the energy market. It therefore needs to be introduced in a few comments.

## Market players of the electricity sector

The structure of entities operating in the energy market is naturally different. It varies within mentioned models, taking a more or less complex shape. The models may be described as finding their functional (operational) dimension, which derives from the theory of business and economy, as well as by applying a legal approach. Furthermore, as the legal approach has a more formal nature, it is narrower in scope, whereas the functional (operational) dimension may cover more entities, even not so directly involved in the operation of the electricity market.

### *The functional dimension of market entities*

Agents operating in the electricity market are briefly presented by Antonio J. Conejo, Miguel Carrión, and Juan M. Morales. According to these authors among the entities (market players) operating in the electricity market two main categories can be set: "non-institutional" and "institutional". In the first category there are "consumers", "retailers", "producers", as well as "non-dispatchable producers" (2010, pp. 4–6). They describe them as follows (pp. 4–5):

i consumers: "[t]hey are the end users of the electricity. They may purchase energy in the pool or in the futures market, or may sign bilateral contracts with producers or be supplied by retailers."
ii retailers: "[t]hey provide electricity to those consumers that do not participate directly in the electricity markets. Retailers do not generally own production units and they purchase the electricity to be supplied to their clients through bilateral contracts, in the futures market, and in the pool."
iii producers: "[t]hey are the entities owning the production units that are in charge of the electricity generation. A producer may sell electric energy either to the electricity markets (pool and futures market) or directly to the consumers and the retailers through bilateral contracts."
iv non-dispatchable producers: "[t]hey are producers with non-dispatchable sources, such as wind or solar-thermal power plants. All market agents must cope with the intermittency and time-dependent nature of non-dispatchable sources."

Within this classification further specification (as well as a more detailed description) can be made. Using the criterion of ownership among producers one may distinguish: investor-owned (private), publicly owned, cooperative, and nationalised entities. Further, these entities may be engaged in all or only some aspects of the energy industry (operational criterion), or be regulated by local or national authorities (regulation criterion) (Rademaekers, Slingenberg, & Morsy 2008, p. 15).

Institutional market entities (market players) include: the Market Operator, the Independent System Operator, and the Regulator. Their role in the energy market can be summarised in the following way (Conejo, Carrión, & Morales 2010, p. 6):

i Market Operator: "[an] entity responsible for the economic management of the marketplace as a whole. In addition, the market operator administers the market rules and determines the prices and quantities of energy traded in the market."
ii Independent System Operator: "[an] entity in charge of the technical management of the electric energy system pertaining to the electricity market. The independent system operator should provide equal access to the grid to all consumers, retailers and producers, and strive to facilitate the commerce

among buying and selling agents. The independent system operator manages generally the reserve and the regulation markets, and assists the market operator to clear the balancing market."

iii Market Regulator: "government-independent entity whose function is to oversee the market and to ensure its competitive and adequate functioning. Additionally, the regulator promotes and enforces orders and regulations."

Often, it is possible (and right) to expand the list with entities not necessarily directly involved in the generation, distribution, or transmission, as well as regulation of electricity. These are, *inter alia*, banks and financial institutions (hedge funds, investment banks, and speculative traders) whose presence on the energy market derives from volatility in the market (Rademaekers, Slingenberg, & Morsy 2008, p. 15). Besides them, the use of the broad approach to the electricity market's actors enables qualification herein of other entities (e.g. consumer advisers (see Ei 2012, p. 2), electricity brokers).

## The legal dimension of market entities

The structure of market players in the electricity market is not a matter of a business model derived from economic theories alone. It is shaped in a formal way under the provisions of law. In the European Union, market players are covered by European law, i.e. the *Electricity Directives*. Not delving into the details of their importance for the EU's electricity sector at this point – as this is covered in the following chapters of this book – to underline the legal dimension of the European electricity market, I list the definitions of entities operating within it.

First, Directive 96/92/EC (the First Electricity Directive) provided the legal basis for crucial categories of entities operating in the energy market (Article 2). Among them were entities responsible for electricity generation – "producers" (natural or legal person), with a special category of producers generating electricity for their own use ("autoproducers"), and producers who do not "carry out electricity transmission or distribution functions in the territory covered by the system where [they are] established" ("independent producers"). These were supplemented by electricity consumers, *inter alia*, "wholesale"[8] or "final customers".[9] Directive 96/92/EC also set a broad group of "system users" which were any natural or legal persons "supplying to, or being supplied by, a transmission or distribution system", where "transmission" was defined as "the transport of electricity on the high-voltage interconnected system with a view to its delivery to final customers or to distributors", and accordingly distribution as "the transport of electricity on medium-voltage and low-voltage distribution systems with a view to its delivery to customers". In addition, with reference to the presented Single Buyer Model, the Directive formed its core definition of a "single buyer". This meant "any legal person who, within the system where he is established, is responsible for the unified management of the transmission system and/or for centralized electricity purchasing and selling".

Mentioned categories were broadened or amended by Directive 2003/54/EC (the Second Electricity Directive). This legal act introduced new definitions of consumers ("household"[10] and "non-household customers",[11] as well as "eligible consumers").[12] Moreover, the Directive established a legal meaning for "transmission" and "distribution system operator". Respectively, these were the

> natural or legal person responsible for operating, ensuring the maintenance of and, if necessary, developing the transmission system [or a distribution] in a given area and, where ever applicable, its interconnections with other systems, and for ensuring the long-term ability of the system to meet reasonable demands for the transmission [or distribution] of electricity.

In addition, Directive 2003/54/EC slightly altered the meaning of some definitions. For example, in new wording the previous definition of "final customer" became plural ("customers"), and "purchase" was used instead of ("buy") as the expression of their activity on the electricity market.

Finally, actors of the energy market are naturally established under the provisions of the latest Directive 2009/72/EC (the Third Electricity Directive). In the area of definitions, Directive 2009/72/EC is based mainly on the prior Directive of 2003. Its slight difference in comparison to the former legislation is in the use of the singular with regard to definitions of market entities.[13] Other minor changes involved the modification of the wording of provisions.[14] Further, Directive 2009/72/EC also introduced new definitions in the field of the structure of analysed players. Among them, in Article 2 (35), a definition of "electricity undertaking" can be found.[15] It is:

> any natural or legal person carrying out at least one of the following functions: generation, transmission, distribution, supply, or purchase of electricity, which is responsible for the commercial, technical or maintenance tasks related to those functions, but does not include final customers.

The Directives laid the foundations for the establishment of the very first idea of the common energy market. Further, they have driven its development, and made it possible to launch policy debate about the *internal energy market* in the European Union. Nevertheless, no matter how great the impact of the Directives on the energy market in the EU has been, they are *secondary law* of the European Union. They can be amended or overruled. However, they are firmly rooted in the *primary law* of the Union – i.e. the Treaties (see Hofmann, Rowe, & Türk 2011, pp. 67–116). This is especially clear in the current legal situation in which the role of energy, in accordance with the provisions of the Treaties in force, was strengthened (see Talus 2013, pp. 289–290). Seen in this light, the next part of this chapter is devoted to the legal analysis of electricity with particular attention to the European approach in this respect.

## "Package approach"

From the 1990s the EU has been shaping its electricity sector with the use of legal acts gathered in the form of *packages*. This term appears in many different connotations and contexts relating to the energy sector. For example, in December 2013, Joaquín Almunia, Vice President of the European Commission responsible for Competition Policy in his speech on state aid and an integrated EU energy market complained about completing the Single Market for energy. "Reform efforts – including the third Energy Package ... are taking longer than expected to have an impact on the ground", said Commissioner Almunia (European Commission 2013c). Regarding energy, *package* appeared and appears in the statements of many other European politicians.[16] This proves the popularity of the term, permanently embedded in the European energy agenda (e.g. Council of the European Union 2008). In this respect, four European legislative actions in the energy sector field can be identified with the word *package*. These are: three *Energy Packages* (*Liberalisation Packages*), and the *Climate and Energy Package*.

However, *package* is not a word reserved only for energy issues. It occurs in relation to legislation introduced in other sectors. That is why apart from Energy Packages the European Union has established (or is working on) the "Long-Term Guarantee Package" (LTG Package) for the insurance regulatory regime (European Commission 2013b), the "Connected Continent Package" for the telecoms sector (European Commission 2015b), the package for Cohesion Policy 2014–2020 (Lithuanian Presidency of the Council of the European Union 2013a), the "External Relations Package" (European Commission 2013d), the "Payments Package" which gives legal foundation for the creation of an EU-wide single market for payments (European Commission 2015c), "Asylum Package" (United Nations High Commissioner for Refugees 2013), "Schengen Governance Package" (Council of the European Union 2013), as well as packages for the aviation sector, i.e. "Single European Sky" (European Commission 2015a) or railways (European Commission 2013a). Naturally, this is not a closed list. Multiplicity of such EU initiatives emphasises the importance that is attached to packages gathering together specific European legislation. In this sense, taking into account the already mentioned Energy Packages, it is necessary to define what are *packages* (often called *legislative packages*) adopted by the EU.

### *The package in different contexts*

Referring to the dictionary definitions, the English word *package* which originated in mid-sixteenth century (as a noun denoting the action or mode of packing goods)[17] means "[a] bundle of things packed or tied up together", "[a] set or interdependent or related abstract entities", "[a] group of related objects viewed or organized as a unit",[18] or "a complete unit consisting of a number of component parts".[19] In legal dictionaries the word "package" occurs in a combination with "mortgage" as "package mortgage" which is "[r]eal property mortgage which also finances the purchase of home appliances",[20] or with insurance where "package policy" is defined as "an insurance policy providing protection against multiple perils and losses of both insured and third parties",[21] although separate definitions can be found. For example, according to John Bouvier's dictionary, "package" is "[a] bundle put for transportation or commercial handling".[22] Finally, in many legal dictionaries other definitions, not corresponding to this book's subject, appear.[23]

Packages also have a binding legal context. This is provided by the EU's legislation, where "package" occurs in numerous references. For instance, tracing only the latest examples of legislative activity of the EU, in a legal sense the *package* is used in reference to carriage of goods and passengers by rail and road (Decision No 1/2013 of the Community/Switzerland Inland Transport Committee), the European Structural and Investment Funds (Regulation (EU) No 1303/201), markets in agricultural products (Regulation (EU) No 1308/2013), the European Globalisation Adjustment Fund (Regulation (EU) No 1309/2013), association of the overseas countries and territories with the European Union (Council Decision 2013/755/EU), interoperability of spatial data sets and services (Commission Regulation (EU) No 1253/2013), the European Border Surveillance System (Regulation (EU) No 1052/2013), the tariff and statistical nomenclature (Commission Implementing Regulation (EU) No 1001/2013), the protection of geographical indications (Commission Implementing Regulation (EU) No 716/2013), and many others fields.

Moreover, some of the European legal acts refer to packages even more directly. Packages occur not only in legal texts, but also in titles and in legal definitions created on their basis. These concern, *inter alia*, "package codes" (see Council Decision of 17 October 2013), as well as definitions of specific packages established on the basis of provisions on energy labelling: "package of water heater and solar device",[24] and "package of space heater, temperature control and solar device", and "package of combination heater, temperature control and solar device".[25]

## *The legislative package and its elements*

Of course, not all of these examples relate to packages in the sense which corresponds to this book. The subject of the work covers only *legislative packages*, shortened to *packages* where appropriate (as in its title). At this point a question should be raised as to what legislative packages are issued by the European Union? In giving an answer, already made arrangements on packages are very useful, in particular cited dictionary definitions; although they have to be supplemented by remarks on *the legislative character* of these packages. For this purpose, once again, dictionary definitions constitute a firm basis for further considerations.

According to *Black's Law Dictionary*, the adjective "legislative" means something of a character "relating to lawmaking or to the power to enact laws".[26] The *Oxford Dictionary of English* defines it likewise, as "having the power to make laws".[27] Similarly, "legislative power" is "[t]he authority ... to make laws, and to alter and repeal them".[28] In other definitions it is "[t]hat legislates, that has the function of legislation, that has the power to legislate",[29] "having the function of making laws",[30] "relating to laws and the process or function of making new laws".[31] Its core consists of the verb "to legislate" which connotes "[m]ake or enact laws, make provision by laws".[32] It corresponds to "legislation" – "the action of making or giving a positive law in written form, according to some type of formal procedure".[33]

By combining these definitions I propose the following reasoning of *legislative package*, which I define as *a set of interdependent or related legal acts viewed or organised as a unit*. In the case of the European Union this is legislation (*legal acts*) issued by the empowered EU institutions. It includes regulations, directives, and decisions (see Craig & de Búrca 2011, pp. 104–107). As a rule, the legislation considers correlated fields (*interdependence or related*), i.e. sectors of industry (railroads, aviation, banking, telecoms, energy, etc.), or specific issues (payments, asylum, border policy, climate, etc.). And finally, these legal acts are usually published in the same *Official Journal* (*organised as a unit*).[34] If not (but it is rather an exception), in public discussion as well as by European institutions, they are perceived as one interrelated block of legal acts (*viewed as a unit*).[35]

Finally, besides the presented theoretical definition of packages it must be noted that in European law one may find a practical dimension of packages' definition. Furthermore, this example refers to the area of this book: energy law and the electricity sector. It concerns Decision No 1386/2013/EU of the European Parliament and of the Council of 20 November 2013 on the General Union Environment Action Programme to 2020 "Living Well, within the Limits of Our Planet". As stated in Recital 8, the Decision finds it necessary to build the Seventh Environment Action Programme on policy initiatives in the Europe 2020 strategy (European Commission 2010), including the "Union Climate and Energy Package".[36] In an evident way, this proves the transition of the "package" concept, from a language of political debate to legal language used for the needs of European legislation. Moreover, using the above-mentioned Decision on the General Union Environment Action Programme it is possible to define the *Climate and Energy Package*. These are acts to which a reference linked to the package is made in the Decision's footnote 7:

> Regulation (EC) No 443/2009 of the European Parliament and of the Council of 23 April 2009 setting emission performance standards for new passenger cars as part of the community's integrated approach to reduce $CO_2$ emissions from light-duty vehicles, Directive 2009/28/EC of the European Parliament and of the Council of 23 April 2009 on the promotion of the use of energy from renewable sources and amending and subsequently repealing Directives 2001/77/EC and 2003/30/EC, Directive 2009/29/EC of the European Parliament and of the Council of 23 April 2009 amending Directive 2003/87/EC so as to improve and extend the greenhouse gas emission allowance trading scheme of the Community, Directive 2009/30/EC of

the European Parliament and of the Council of 23 April 2009 amending Directive 98/70/EC as regards the specification of petrol, diesel and gas-oil and introducing a mechanism to monitor and reduce greenhouse gas emissions and amending council directive 1999/32/EC as regards the specification of fuel used by inland waterway vessels and repealing Directive 93/12/EEC, Directive 2009/31/EC of the European Parliament and of the Council of 23 April 2009 of the geological storage of carbon dioxide and amending council Directive 85/337/EEC, European Parliament and Council Directives 2000/60/EC, 2001/80/EC, 2004/35/EC, 2006/12/EC, 2008/1/EC and Regulation (EC) No 1013/2006, Decision No 406/2009/EC of the European Parliament and of the Council of 23 April 2009 on the effort of member states to reduce their greenhouse gas emissions to meet the Community's greenhouse gas emission reduction commitments up to 2020.[37]

The foregoing list defines in a formal way the legal acts which constitute the EU Climate and Energy Package. In this enumerative way already presented, the *theoretical definition of packages* finds its practical application. Furthermore, it is strengthened by the European law that is in force.

Used by EU legal instruments, the packages, dedicated to the energy sector including their part relating to electricity, were passed for specific purposes. These were, establishing and enhancing the internal energy market (Energy Packages) as well as making it more sustainable (Climate and Energy Package). As the Energy Packages were an initiating step for the EU's energy market, let us focus on them in the next part of the book. Their common feature is that of being an element of European public law[38] and they were used for the needs of broad market reform of the European energy sector based on a paradigm of market liberalisation.

## European public law for the needs of liberalisation of the electricity sector

The history of the development of electricity shows that throughout the twentieth century, states and their governments controlled electricity markets in most countries. In many countries electricity companies on all levels were owned by government or were subjected to government (Blok 2007, p. 93). In various forms (municipal, provincial, national) governments have participated (as a regulator or as an owner) in the electricity sector (Hausman, Hertner, & Wilkins 2008, p. 23). An important cut-off date for public impact on the energy sector is 1945. Post-war Western Europe was dominated by the view that the state should control the main industries with the energy sector at the forefront. Peter D. Cameron (2007, p. 12) justifies this reasoning as a necessary measure for "the reconstruction of Western Europe and the creation of the new post-War society". Due to these circumstances core industries were nationalised, and their assets were overtaken by state agencies or state enterprises and subjected to strict government control in their operation. In many countries a concentration of capital occurred. In 1946, the French *Électricité de France* (EdF) was set up. In 1957, in the UK, the Central Electricity Generation Board was created. In 1962, Italy nationalised the electricity sector and established the *Ente Nazionale per l'Energia Elettrica* (ENEL) (Cameron 2007, p. 12).

Cameron (2007, pp. 6–7) considers this movement as "a normal practise" of government in every industrialised country. He describes five principal factors that encourage a state to do so:

> i [electricity industries] are elements of natural monopoly in transmission and distribution which stimulate vertical integration of the activities of a single company. Those companies have traditionally been obliged by the government to provide and supply electricity ... and have in return been granted exclusive rights to supply over a specific area or a territory...;
>
> ii [t]he services provided by these companies have traditionally been seen as essential for communities, and obligation to supply has often been imposed by governments on the companies – electricity prices normally being controlled by government and based on costs;
>
> iii [t]he electricity ... [sector is] strategic for overall economy and for the military capability of the nation-state;
>
> iv [the electricity sector is] capital-intensive ... with a high degree of technical complexity, which creates entry barriers and necessitates technical co-ordination.... This has led to a structure of regulation that places stronger emphasis on reliability of transmission and delivery. This has been evident in electricity sector, because electricity cannot be stored; rapid changes in demand can occur throughout any given day, and each request must be linked with supply;
>
> v [t]here is a measure of integration between the various energy subsectors, so the regulatory status of one influences others. Electricity is a secondary form of energy that derives from various primary natural sources such as gas, oil, coal, water, uranium. [For comparison] [g]as is commonly found in conjunction with oil. But both electricity and gas can be substituted for each other and so compete for end-use in consumer markets.
>
> (Cameron 2007, pp. 6–7)

These can be summed up with the following consideration: the state has an influence on the energy sector because of the specific nature of electricity, as well as related with its need (dependence) for electricity usage. This is correlated with an impact on society (which stands behind government – an emanation of the state) as well as on the economy (which implicitly sets up social peace and the strength of the state).

A practical example of these circumstances was the electricity sector in Western Europe before the 1990s. At this time, the sector was run by national and state-owned monopolies. In the areas of purchase, import and export, or infrastructure they were granted either *de jure* or de facto exclusive power (Jones 2010, p. 1). Cameron (2007, p. 8) links this with a "traditional paradigm" that required central control over a synchronised network, in which it was assumed that they were strategic assets for a national economy, which made it necessary to provide them exclusive rights in the field of electricity production, transmission, and distribution. Further characteristics of this system included: operation of vertically integrated entities, remuneration based on historical costs, a high degree of planning, the objectification of consumers, and, as a result, closure to competition (Cameron 2007, p. 8).

At the turn of the 1980s and 1990s the European Commission took the steps to overcome these monopolies and their exclusive powers. First, this was applied in the telecommunication sector and, afterwards, in the energy industry (Jones 2010, p. 2). However, as Christopher Jones (2010, p. 2) rightly indicates, "[a]t this time... there was no realistic chance of getting the agreement of.... Member States to agree to liberalise the energy and other markets at the Community level". That is why the Commission decided to use competition law and, starting from the telecommunication sector, eliminate the harm to competition and free movement of goods monopolies (Jones 2010, p. 2).

In this context, with the use of Article 86 (2) TEC,[39] the Commission launched antitrust proceedings against telecom sector entities. In the beginning of the 1990s, separate proceedings reached the energy sector (electricity and gas). On the basis of infringements of Article 31 TEC (free movement of goods) the Commission took action against eight Member States (Jones 2010, p. 2).

This European movement steered Member States' actions at the national level. It would not be possible without the necessity of implementation of European legislation, which appeared as binding legal acts in the mid-1990s. As a result, European countries began to change rules for the electricity sector. An idea was to eliminate the monopoly rights and to enable different suppliers to compete for customers, as well as to rebuild the electricity sector on the market basis (Cameron 2007, pp. 7–10). Therefore, in the 1990s the earlier actions of the European Commission were strengthened by binding legislation that needed implementation. This had already been done with the already mentioned packages of the 1990s. They started the movement which had its second and third phase: the subsequent packages of 2003 and 2009. Together they are called *Liberalisation Packages*. Parenthetically, besides this common name, the phrase *Energy Packages* is treated as their synonym. Both are widely accepted names of this legislation. This designation can be found in the public debate and official European materials (see European Commission 2012b; *Lithuania Tribune* 2013; EurActiv 2008), as well as in the literature on the electricity sector (see Jones 2010; Swora 2011; Eikeland, 2008). Depending on needs, different types of legal acts were adopted within them. These were regulations, directives, as well as decisions. They did not emerge independently – as part of broader legislative action, they were passed. Thereby, the EU proposed a complex approach, as a result of which the European Union established a set of rules, which took the form of legislative packages dedicated to the energy sector.

The packages are an instrument that has been used by the European Union to introduce broad reform of the energy sector, with electricity as its part. The essence of the reform, with packages its name, is to liberalise the energy market. Herein one may ask what does that mean, what is liberalisation, what is its nature, is there any place for the law and for the state? Is there any place for public law regulation within this concept? These are just some of the many questions that accompany the notion of liberalisation which motivated the European Union's action in the electricity sector. To delve into them, it is necessary to present certain principles of liberalism and their legal dimension.

Further, the notion of *public law regulation* should be discussed. Liberalisation does not preclude an active role of the state, or an involvement of the public factor provided by the European Union as an organisation of states. Rules on unbundling, third party access, as well as an independent regulator clearly shows the state's impact on the electricity sector. Moreover, it seems that Liberalisation Packages are based and steered by *public law regulation*. To prove this, an area occupied by public law regulation should be delimited.

In this regard, in the following chapters, starting with remarks on liberalisation, I trace the public approach by providing definitions of regulation, as well as different regulatory models presented in the literature on this issue. They correlate with institutionalisation of regulation and regulatory tools. Together, these observations allow an exploration of the essence of public law regulation used by the European Union to influence the Member States and their electricity sectors.

## Notes

1 Not always do they form a rigid division, i.e. the example can be found in different division criteria. It depends on what is being analysed, e.g. level of market opening can be expressed as a percentage (quantitative), or as described in the model (qualitative).

2 However, this can be limited to new capacity, "while the continued operation of plants with respect to output would be exempt from competition and would rather run under [P]ower [P]urchase [A]greements" (Petrov 2010, p. 2).

3 However, "the power purchasing authority has the ability to plan the entire system, including generating capacity, and coordinate between investment in generation and network capacity". Seen in that light the utility "can contract for plants with specific characteristics and in specific locations". That is why it should own generating capacity (de Vries 2007, p. 10).

4 Nowadays, PPAs are used to support renewable energy production, mainly solar and wind. In his study, Park (2009, pp. 93–98) addresses this issue concisely.

5 "A PPA provider will own, operate, maintain, and clean the system for optimal performance. The PPA provider will also have sophisticated real-time monitoring services to verify the system is working properly" (Park 2009, pp. 93–94).

6 Additionally, de Vries (2007) lists some results of insufficiently unbundled TSO. In such a situation a TSO

> can use his position to hamper access to the network by other generating companies, he can use network revenues to cross-subsidize his electricity generation activities, and through his knowledge of electricity flows he can obtain sensitive information about competing generating companies.

7 De Vries (2007) underlines that the unbundled TSO in this model can have some difficulties in coordination investment in generation and network capacity.

8 Pursuant to Article 2 (8)

> "wholesale customers" shall mean any natural or legal persons, if the Member States recognize their existence, who purchase or sell electricity and who do not carry out transmission, generation or distribution functions inside or outside the system where they are established.

9 As stated in Article 2 (7) "'final customer' shall mean a customer buying electricity for his own use".

10 "[C]ustomers purchasing electricity for their own household consumption, excluding commercial or professional activities."

11 "[N]atural or legal persons purchasing electricity which is not for their own household use and shall include producers and wholesale customers."

12 According to Article 2 (12) these were "customers who are free to purchase electricity from the supplier of their choice within the meaning of Article 21 of this Directive".

13 For example, these concern "customer", "wholesale customer", "final customer", "household customer", "non-household customer", and "eligible customer".

14 For example, the meaning of "customer" has been delimited with the use of "or" (in place of "and" – and defined as "a wholesale or final customer of electricity").

15 Although this expression appeared in an earlier Directive (as a part of other definitions, or just as a point of reference) it was not defined. Thus, the new Directive has a clarifying value.

16 For example, Günther Oettinger (European Energy Review 2014), Jaroslav Neverovič, former Minister of Energy of Lithuania (Lithuanian Presidency of the Council of the European Union 2013b), or Jerzy Buzek, former President of European Parliament (Buzek 2013).

17 *Oxford Dictionary of English*, 3rd edn, s.v. "package". As noted in *Oxford Dictionary of English* it comes from the verb "pack" and "age", compare with Anglo-Latin *paccagium*.

18 The *New Shorter Oxford English Dictionary on Historical Principles*, 3rd revd edn, vol. 2, s.v. "package".

19 *Collins English Dictionary*, 5th edn, s.v. "package".

20 *Modern Dictionary for the Legal Profession*, 4th edn, s.v. "package mortgage".

21 *Black's Law Dictionary*, s.v. "package policy".

22 *John Bouvier's Law Dictionary*, 15th edn, vol. 2, s.v. "package".

23 For example, s.v. "original package doctrine" in *Barron's Law Dictionary*, 6th edn, or other definitions of "package" in *Bouvier's Law Dictionary*, vol. 2.

24 Article 2 (13) "'package of water heater and solar device' means a package offered to the end-user containing one or more water heaters and one or more solar devices" (Commission Delegated Regulation (EU) No 812/2013).

25 Article 2 (19) "'package of space heater, temperature control and solar device' means a package offered to the end-user containing one or more space heaters combined with one or more temperature controls and/or one or more solar devices", as well as Article 2 (20) "'package of combination heater, temperature control and solar device' means a package offered to the end-user containing one or more combination heaters combined with one or more temperature controls, and/or one or more solar devices" (Commission Delegated Regulation (EU) No 811/2013).

26 *Black's Law Dictionary*, s.v. "legislative".

27 *Oxford Dictionary of English*, s.v. "legislative".

28 *Bouvier's Law Dictionary*, vol. 2, s.v. "legislative power".

29 *New Shorter Oxford English Dictionary*, vol. 1, s.v. "legislative".

30 *MacQuarie Dictionary*, 4th edn, s.v. "legislative".

31 *Dictionary of Politics and Government*, 3rd edn, s.v. "legislative".
32 *New Shorter Oxford English Dictionary*.
33 A *Dictionary of Modern Legal Usage*, 2nd edn, s.v. "legislation" and s.v. "legislative". See also *Garner's Dictionary of Legal Usage*, 3rd edn, s.v. "legislation" and s.v. "legislative".
34 For example, Capital Requirements Package, Zoonoses Package, Single Supervisory Mechanism (SSM) Package, Financial Regulation and Supervision Package, or the Third Railway Package.
35 For example, the Second Single European Sky Package was published in different issues of the *Official Journal*, OJ L 300, 14 November 2009 and OJ L 309, 24 November 2009, just as the Defence Package, OJ L 146, 10 June 2009 and OJ L 216, 20 August 2009. First, generally the time between subsequent issues does not exceed a few months. Second, they are repeatedly called "packages" (European Commission 2012a). See also Fiott 2013, p. 2.
36 Capitalisation mine.
37 OJ L 140, 5 June 2009.
38 In defining public law I use, distinguished by John Bell, *the French-influenced system*, where public law

> is the governing administrative activity in the broadest sense and is not necessarily limited to public bodies. This activity is done in the public interest as opposed to the private interest, and it leads to a distinction between public and private law (though there are degrees of intensity in this distinction) which affects both substantive law and procedure.
>
> (Bell 1998, p. 149)

39

> Undertakings entrusted with the operation of services of general economic interest or having the character of a revenue-producing monopoly shall be subject to the rules contained in this Treaty, in particular to the rules on competition, insofar as the application of such rules does not obstruct the performance, in law or in fact, of the particular tasks assigned to them. The development of trade must not be affected to such an extent as would be contrary to the interests of the Community.

## References

Barroso, L.A., Mercados de Energia, P.S.R., Cavalcanti, T.H., Giesbertz, P., & Purchala, K. 2005, "Classification of electricity market models worldwide", *CIGRE/IEEE PES International Symposium*, New Orleans, LA, 5–7 October 2005. Available from: http://ieeexplore.ieee.org/stamp/stamp.jsp?tp=&arnumber=1532720 [1 March 2015].

Bell, J. 1998, "Mechanisms for cross-fertilisation of administrative law in Europe", in *New directions in European public law*, eds J. Beatson & T. Tridimas, Hart Publishing, Oxford, pp. 147–167.

Blok, K. 2007, *Introduction to energy analysis*, Techne Press, Amsterdam.

Burger, M., Bernhard, G., & Schindlmayr, G. 2007, *Managing energy risk: an integrated view on power and other energy markets*. Hoboken, Chichester.

Buzek, J. 2013, *Keynote speech by Jerzy Buzek, MEP "Energy solidarity in Europe – moving towards a European Energy Community (EEC)"*, Vilnius, 20 September 2013. Available from: http://buzek.pl/en/node/7612 [21 June 2015].

Cameron, P.D. 2007, *Competition in energy markets: law and regulation in the European Union*, 2nd edn, Oxford University Press, Oxford.

Capital Requirements Package, OJ L 176, 27 June 2013.

Commission Delegated Regulation (EU) No 811/2013 of 18 February 2013 supplementing Directive 2010/30/EU of the European Parliament and of the Council with regard to the energy labelling of space heaters, combination heaters, packages of space heater, temperature control and solar device and packages of combination heater, temperature control and solar device, OJ L 239, 6 September 2013.

Commission Delegated Regulation (EU) No 812/2013 of 18 February 2013 supplementing Directive 2010/30/EU of the European Parliament and of the Council with regard to the energy labelling of water heaters, hot water storage tanks and packages of water heater and solar device, OJ L 239, 6 September 2013.

Commission Implementing Regulation (EU) No 716/2013 of 25 July 2013 laying down rules for the application of Regulation (EC) No 110/2008 of the European Parliament and of the Council on the definition, description, presentation, labelling and the protection of geographical indications of spirit drinks, OJ L 201, 26 July 2013.

Commission Implementing Regulation (EU) No 1001/2013 of 4 October 2013 amending Annex I to Council Regulation (EEC) No 2658/87 on the tariff and statistical nomenclature and on the common customs tariff, OJ L 290, 31 October 2013.

Commission Regulation (EU) No 1253/2013 of 21 October 2013 amending Regulation (EU) No 1089/2010 implementing Directive 2007/2/EC as regards interoperability of spatial data sets and services, OJ L 331, 10 December 2013.

Conejo, A.J., Carrión, M., & Morales, J.M. 2010, *Decision making under uncertainty in electricity markets*, Springer, New York.

Council Decision of 17 October 2013 on the Position to be adopted, on behalf of the European Union, in the EU–EFTA Joint Committee on common transit concerning the adoption of a decision amending the Convention of 20 May 1987 on a common transit procedure, as regards the modification of HS Codes and Package Codes, OJ L 282, 24 October 2013.

Council Decision 2013/755/EU of 25 November 2013 on the association of the overseas countries and territories with the European Union ("Overseas Association Decision"), OJ L 344, 19 December 2013.

Council of the European Union 2008, *2875th Council Meeting Transport, Telecommunications and Energy*, Luxembourg, 6 June 2008, PRES/08/162. Available from: http://europa.eu/rapid/press-release_PRES-08-162_en.htm?locale=en [9 June 2015].

Council of the European Union 2013, *Council and the European Parliament Reach a Provisional Agreement on the Schengen Governance Legislative Package*, Brussels, 30 May 2013, PRESSE 221. Available from: www.consilium.europa.eu/uedocs/cms_data/docs/pressdata/en/jha/137348.pdf [12 June 2015].

Craig, P. & de Búrca, G. 2011, *EU law: text, cases, and materials*, 5th edn, Oxford University Press, Oxford.

de Vries, L. 2007 "Design choices for electricity markets: a systematic analysis", *20th World Energy Congress*, Rome, 11–15 November 2007. Available from: www.worldenergy.org/documents/p000905.doc [17 June 2015].

Decision No 1/2013 of the Community/Switzerland Inland Transport Committee of 6 December 2013 amending Annex 1 to the Agreement between the European Community and the Swiss Confederation on the carriage of goods and passengers by rail and road, OJ L 352, 24 December 2013.

Decision No 1386/2013/EU of the European Parliament and of the Council of 20 November 2013 on a General Union Environment Action Programme to 2020 "Living well, within the limits of our planet", OJ L 354, 28 December 2013.

Ei 2012, *Descriptions of the actors on the electricity and natural gas markets*. Available from: www.ei.se/Documents/Publikationer/rapporter_och_pm/Rapporter%202012/EI%20PM2012_07.pdf [19 June 2015].

Eikeland, P.O. 2008, "EU internal energy market policy: new dynamics in the Brussels policy game?" *CANES Working Paper*. Available from: www.fni.no/doc&pdf/FNI-R1408.pdf [23 June 2015].

EurActiv 2008, *Discussing the impact assessment of the "third energy liberalisation package"*. Available from: www.euractiv.com/energy/discussing-impact-assessment-third-energy-liberalisation-package/article-174498 [21 June 2015].

European Commission 2010, *Communication from the Commission EUROPE 2020: a strategy for smart, sustainable and inclusive growth*, Brussels, 3 March 2010, COM (2010) 2020 final.

European Commission 2012a, *Air: Single European Sky II*. Available from: http://ec.europa.eu/transport/modes/air/single_european_sky/ses_2_en.htm [23 June 2015].

European Commission 2012b, *Energy and environment: overview*. Available from: http://ec.europa.eu/competition/sectors/energy/overview_en.html [22 June 2015].

European Commission 2013a, *Rail: railway packages*. Available from: http://ec.europa.eu/transport/modes/rail/packages/index_en.htm [11 June 2015].

European Commission 2013b, *Solvency II prudential framework for the insurance sector: report on the long-term guarantee assessment by the European Insurance and Occupational Pensions Authority*. Available from: http://ec.europa.eu/internal_market/insurance/docs/solvency/20130614-report-eiopa-technical-findings_en.pdf [10 June 2015].

European Commission 2013c, *State aid modernisation for an integrated EU energy market*. Available from: http://europa.eu/rapid/press-release_SPEECH-13-1005_en.htm [17 June 2015].

European Commission 2013d, *The multiannual financial framework: the external action financing instruments*, Brussels, 11 December 2013, MEMO/13/1134. Available from: http://europa.eu/rapid/press-release_MEMO-13-1134_en.htm [16 June 2015].

European Commission 2015a, *Air: single European sky*. Available from: http://ec.europa.eu/transport/modes/air/index_en.htm [22 June 2015].

European Commission 2015b, *Connected continent legislative package*. Available from: http://ec.europa.eu/digital-agenda/en/connected-continent-legislative-package [23 June 2015].

European Commission 2015c, *Directive on payment services (PSD)*. Available from: http://ec.europa.eu/internal_market/payments/framework/index_en.htm [22 June 2015].

European Energy Review 2014, *Günther Oettinger on the completion of the EU internal energy market "getting to 2014"*. Available from: www.europeanenergyreview.eu/site/pagina.php?id=3249 [12 June 2015].

Financial Regulation and Supervision Package, OJ L 331, 15 December 2010.

Fiott, D. 2013, "More competitive, more efficient? The 2013 European Commission Defence Communication", *Security Policy Brief*, no. 49, pp. 1–7. Available from: www.egmontinstitute.be/wp-content/uploads/ [22 June 2015].

Harris, C. 2006, *Electricity markets: pricing, structures and economics*, John Wiley & Sons, Chichester.

Hausman, W.J., Hertner, P., & Wilkins, M. 2008, *Global electrification: multinational enterprise and international finance in the history of light and power, 1878–2007*, Cambridge University Press, Cambridge.

Hofmann, H.C.H., Rowe, G.C., & Türk, A.H. 2011, *Administrative law and policy of the European Union*, Oxford University Press, Oxford.

Jones, C. 2010, "Introduction", in *The internal energy market: the Third Liberalisation Package*, ed. C. Jones, vol. 1 of *EU energy law*, 3rd edn, Claeys & Casteels, Leuven, pp. 1–14.

Kessides, I.N. 2004, *Reforming infrastructure: privatization, regulation, and competition*, World Bank/Oxford University Press, Washington, DC. Available from: www-wds.worldbank.org/external/default/WDSContentServer/IW3P/IB/2004/06/16/000012009_20040616143838/additional/310436360_20050007115940.pdf [19 June 2015].
Kessides, I.N., Bogetic, Z., & Maurer, L. 2007, "Current and forthcoming issues in the South African electricity sector", *World Bank Policy Research Working Paper 4197*, April 2007. Available from: https://openknowledge.worldbank.org/bitstream/handle/10986/7026/wps4197.txt?sequence=2 [1 November 2015]
*Lithuania Tribune* 2013, "Minister of Economy says Lithuania could delay EU's Third Energy Package". Available from: www.lithuaniatribune.com/33154/minister-of-economy-says-lithuania-could-delay-eus-third-energy-package-201333154/ [21 June 2015].
Lithuanian Presidency of the Council of the European Union 2013a, *EU Council signs the legislative package for cohesion policy 2014–2020*. Available from: www.eu2013.lt/en/news/pressreleases/eu-council-signs-the-legislative-package-for-cohesion-policy-20142020 [21 June 2015].
Lithuanian Presidency of the Council of the European Union 2013b, *Speech by Jaroslav Neverovič, Minister of Energy, at the Joint Committee Meeting on the EU Internal Energy Market for the 21st Century*. Available from: www.eu2013.lt/en/news/statements/speech-by-jaroslav-neverovic-minister-of-energy-at-the-joint-committee-meeting-on-the-eu-internal-energy-market-for-the-21st-century- [21 June 2015].
Lovei, L. 2000, "The single-buyer model: a dangerous path toward competitive electricity markets", *Public Policy for the Private Sector*, 225, pp. 1–4. Available from: www.erranet.org/index.php?name=OE-eLibrary&file=download&id=1294&keret=N&showheader=N [16 June 2015].
Onaiwu, E. 2010, "How does bilateral pooling differ from electricity pooling?" *Centre for Energy, Petroleum and Mineral Law Annual Review*, 13, pp. 1–12. Available from: www.dundee.ac.uk/cepmlp/gateway/files.php?file=cepmlp_car13_67_116710412.pdf [17 June 2015].
Park, R. 2009, "The power purchase agreement (PC for solar)", in *Energy project financing: resources and strategies for success*, eds A. Thumann & E.A. Woodroof, Fairmont Press, Lilbrurn, ch. 5.
Petrov, K. 2010, "Electricity markets and principle". Available from: www.leonardo-energy.org/sites/leonardo-energy/files/root/pdf/2010/Electricity%20Markets%20Paper.pdf [16 June 2015].
Rademaekers, K., Slingenberg, A., & Morsy, S. 2008, *Review and analysis of EU wholesale energy markets: historical and current data analysis of EU wholesale electricity, gas and CO2 markets*, ECORYS Nederland BV, Rotterdam. Available from: http://ec.europa.eu/energy/gas_electricity/studies/doc/2008_eu_wholesale_energy_market_historical.pdf [17 June 2015].
Regulation (EU) No 1052/2013 of the European Parliament and of the Council of 22 October 2013 establishing the European Border Surveillance System (Eurosur), OJ L 295, 6 November 2013.
Regulation (EU) No 1303/2013 of the European Parliament and of the Council of 17 December 2013 laying down common provisions on the European Regional Development Fund, the European Social Fund, the Cohesion Fund, the European Agricultural Fund for Rural Development and the European Maritime and Fisheries Fund and laying down general provisions on the European Regional Development Fund, the European Social Fund, the Cohesion Fund and the European Maritime and Fisheries Fund and repealing Council Regulation (EC) No 1083/2006, OJ L 347, 20 December 2013.

Regulation (EU) No 1308/2013 of the European Parliament and of the Council of 17 December 2013 establishing a Common organisation of the markets in agricultural products and repealing Council Regulations (EEC) No 922/72, (EEC) No 234/79, (EC) No 1037/2001 and (EC) No 1234/2007, OJ L 347, 20 December 2013.

Regulation (EU) No 1309/2013 of the European Parliament and of the Council of 17 December 2013 on the European Globalisation Adjustment Fund (2014–2020) and repealing Regulation (EC) No 1927/2006, OJ L 347, 20 December 2013.

Single Supervisory Mechanism (SSM) Package, OJ L 287, 29 October 2013.

Swora, M. 2011, "Smart grids after the third liberalization package: current developments and future challenges for regulatory policy in the electricity sector", *Yearbook of Antitrust and Regulatory Studies*, V, pp. 9–22.

Talus, K. 2013, *EU energy law and policy: a critical account.* Oxford University Press, Oxford.

Third Railway Package, OJ L 315, 3 December 2007.

United Nations High Commissioner for Refugees 2013, *Moving further toward a common European asylum system: UNHCR's statement on the EU Asylum Legislative Package June 2013*. Available from: www.unhcr.org/51b7348c9.html [16 June 2015].

Windustry 2007, *Chapter 13: power purchase agreement.* Available from: www.windustry.org/community-wind/toolbox/chapter-13-power-purchase-agreement [17 June 2015].

Yang, M. & Sharma, D. 2012, "The impacts of electricity industry reforms on electricity prices" presentation, *3rd IAEE Asian Conference: growing energy demand, energy security and the environment in Asia – challenges under enormous uncertainty*, Kyoto, 20–22 February 2012. Available from: http://eneken.ieej.or.jp/3rd_IAEE_Asia/pdf/paper/123p.pdf [20 June 2015].

Zoonoses Package, OJ L 325, 12 December 2003.

# PART II

# Energy markets

## Between liberalisation and intervention

# 4 The market or the state?

The state is considered a representation of the public sphere, while the market is a synonym for private property. The same distinction applies to the electricity sector (see Hogan 1999; Rudkevich, Lazebnik, & Sorokin 2010; Metais 2013; Bjørnebye 2010; Veith 2010; pp. 45–55; Serati, Manera, & Plotegher 2008; KPMG 2013). Generally, this division seems to be very simple. Although various issues that may arise during the analysis of the relations between the state and market make it much more complicated. Among them, using Sikor, Barlösius, and Scheumann's reasoning (2008, p. 4), such questions may emerge: what actions should the state undertake? What kinds of social interaction should take place in the market? Under what conditions and how should the state intervene in the market? What are appropriate roles for the state and market? Where should the boundary between state and market be drawn?

Ambiguous answers can raise other discussions, which in turn can encompass multiple questions. However, the limited framework of this book does not allow room to cover all aspects in a comprehensive way. On the other hand the analysis of public law regulation requires the theoretical background, presented from different perspectives, with the use of various scientific fields. Therefore, in view of these circumstances, for the needs of this work I select important concepts, ideas, and theories that might better elucidate the theory of public law regulation occurring in the energy sector.

## A total subordination vs a complete release

"Markets do not exist independently of mankind. Markets are a function of the strategic actions of business … law, and moral rules.… Each is a function of the forces acting on and through it, and each influence those same forces." Among these forces Warren J. Samuels (2011, p. 185) finds law. This enables the provision of the notion of a broader perspective of the market. Behind the law stands the state, with its bodies involved in the process of law-making, like the parliament or the government.

Using the mentioned relation, one can see the state as a force "acting on and through" the market. Market also means economy, and the electricity sector, which is a significant part. Both of these assumptions enable reference to the issue of the state's presence in the electricity sector (this presence in every industrialised country is normal practice). The state's role comes from the observation that the market is inefficient. This can be simplified to the conclusion: "[t]he allocation of resources in a market economy is imperfect, and the government might be able to improve it" (Leach 2004, p. 390).

In a natural way, depending on the adopted socio-economic system, the degree of public involvement in the electricity sector varies. On the axis of this impact, two extreme points may be distinguished: "a total subordination" and "a complete release" (Sokołowski 2013, p. 309). The first of these themes can be described as a situation in which the state not only passes legislation, but executes it in an exclusive way, as well as manages the electricity sector with the use of subordinate bodies such as state enterprises. This structure is characterised by a strong and centralised hierarchy with the state's strict interaction within the electricity sector, either via direct influence (command) or by the existence (and maintenance) of many monopolistic structures. In the second theme, there is a high degree of competition in the electricity market, resulting from the existence of a number of companies offering their services to large volumes of consumers. In this model there are no entry barriers and operating on the electricity market is free. This structure is dominated by private property (Sokołowski 2013, p. 310).

Both approaches have their key elements. It is either "market" or "state" that steers the electricity sector. This draws a public/private dichotomy, a distinction between state administration and market economy, where the state is responsible for the general interests of society and private matters are left to the self-regulating market, in which private individuals conduct multilateral voluntary transactions (Sikor, Barlösius, & Scheumann's reasoning 2008, p. 4). Anthony I. Ogus draws the legal nature of these two systems. In the market system, individuals pursue their own welfare goals. They are left free, subject only to certain basic restraints. According to Ogus (1994, p. 1) "[t]he legal system underpins these arrangements but predominantly through instruments of private law; regulation … has no significant role". In systems in which the state has a stronger position and "corrects deficiencies in the market system in meeting collective or public interests goals" it uses regulation (Ogus 1994, pp. 1–2).

Due to their extreme nature they are very different, almost opposite. However, their differences enable the presentation of their background to public law regulation. In this sense, it fills a space between them. This space is occupied by a mixed economy, with regulation. To analyse *public law regulation* I propose the concept of *a day-watchman state* which I established on the basis of texts of political, legal, and economic classic thinkers.[1]

The idea of the day-watchman state is strongly correlated with the concept of *a night-watchman state* originating from (or anchored in) liberal philosophy. Due to this fact, in this book, the market-based approach is described first. This notion is an important driver for the EU Liberalisation Packages for electricity. What should be emphasised is the fact that in common perception liberalism is very often only linked with the economy, and economic analysis. However in this book I present its broader *legal dimension*. This is based on liberal thinkers' views of such important legal matters as the state, the government, and the law. Only, in this context, I refer to the public influence (or its lack) on the market, economy, as well as the electricity sector.

## Basic principles of liberalisation

Liberalisation may be examined from different perspectives. In this book I propose to look at it through the prism of the night-watchman state, a concept which in public debate is identified with liberalism and liberalisation. This notion of the night-watchman state, so strongly identified with liberalism in its classic formula, was not, however, presented until the nineteenth century. Paradoxically, the first time it was mentioned in a public debate was not by a supporter of liberalism, but by its opponent. It was German socialist Ferdinand Lasalle who used this catchy phrase of the "night-watchman" to criticise liberal thinking and liberal construction of the state with such words:[2]

> the middle class [bourgeoisie] conceives the moral object of the State. This object consists simply and solely in securing the personal freedom of the individual and his property. This is the night-watchman theory, gentlemen, for this conception [one] can regard the State only under the form of a night-watchman whose duties are confined to preventing burglary and theft.
>
> (Brandes 1911, pp. 125–126)

Commenting on Lasalle's notion, Ludwig von Mises (1985, p. 37) considered that he

> tried to make the conception of a government limited exclusively to [the function that the liberal doctrine assigns to the state: the protection of property, liberty, and peace] ... appear ridiculous by calling the state constituted on the basis of liberal principles the "night-watchman state".[3]

Ludwig von Mises wrote about Lasalle's trial. History has shown that this was a successful attempt. The prevalence of these words in the context of liberal philosophy proves that Ferdinand Lasalle managed to build a firm link between the night-watchman state and liberalism. Thus, nowadays it is assumed that the idea of the night-watchman is a concept (and a symbol) of the state and the government limited to some functions. Among them Robert Nozick (2006, p. 26) lists protection of all its citizens (against violence, theft, and fraud), and enforcement (of contracts). In portraying an illustration of a night-watchman state, Immanuel Wallerstein (1999, pp. 23–24) uses a figure of an ordinary watchman who "sits in relative darkness,... occasionally twirling his baton or revolver when not asleep, and waiting. His function is to ward off intruders who intend to pilfer property. He does this primarily just by being there."

### *Laissez-faire and the invisible hand of the market*

The night-watchman state interacts with a notion of *laissez-faire*. With respect to the practical application of *laissez-faire*, it is often suggested that it was introduced in Great Britain between the end of the Napoleonic wars and about 1850. Christopher Hill (2002, p. 297) points out an even earlier time perspective (the second half of the seventeenth, and the first part of the eighteenth century), when "most European populations groaned under vastly expansive bureaucracies, [while] far the heaviest English government expenditure was on the armed forces which fought off trade rivals". As Hill (2002, p. 297) claims "[i]t was a *laissez-faire* state, whose chief internal function was to hinder hindrances to the sway of the 'natural rulers,' just as in the economy there was internal free trade and external protection". One may agree with it or not,[4] however it is a fact that it was in Britain where people, considered to be the founding fathers of classic liberalism, began their public activity bearing in mind "the conviction that liberty was conducive to the well-being of humankind" (Hudelson 1999, p. 59). Herein, it is impossible to omit John Stuart Mill. Steven Pressman (2014, p. 61) notes that Mill's *On Liberty* of 1859 "was a ringing endorsement of *laissez-faire* ... [which for Mill was] desirable because it enhanced individual growth and development". In his work Mill presented the limits of a government's action, as well as highlighting the restrictions of individual freedom. As Pressman (2014, p. 61) finds, "Mill argued that the state and society had a right to restrict individual freedom only to keep individuals from harming another individual". Furthermore, in Richard Hudelson's opinion (1999, p. 59) Mill's thoughts have also a broader dimension. Seen in this light, Mill "provided powerful arguments for the view that political and social institutions granting the maximal amount of liberty to individual citizens were likewise conducive to the greatest happiness possible for society as a whole".

Nevertheless, not denying John Stuart Mill's contribution to the theory of state and law, he was a successor of another great thinker of liberal philosophy – Adam Smith, who was an unquestionable leading figure of the eighteenth century liberal movement. Smith's liberal philosophy, expressed in his attitude to state, society, and economy, derives from his written works, including his *magnum opus*, published in 1776, *An Inquiry into the Nature and Causes of the Wealth of Nations* (Labio 2006, p. 151). Paul Turpin (2011, p. 8) claims that it "was a decisive milestone in promulgating the concept of the self-regulating market" based on an idea "that markets would provide for the material subsistence of society as long as they were left open to competition instead of being controlled by the state". This involves Smith's deep belief in individualism that could positively affect society. Jan Horst Keppler (2010, p. 136) underlines that "[l]iberalism and the pursuit of economic self-interest remain [Smith's] answers to the question of what is the best manner for enabling social life to produce lasting benefits for the community as a whole". This may be reflected in Adam Smith's well-known metaphor of the "invisible hand":

> every individual ... intends only his own gain, and he is in this, as in many other cases, led by an invisible hand to promote an end which was no part of his intention. Nor is it always the worse for the society that it was no part of it. By pursuing his own interest he frequently promotes that of the society more effectually than when he really intends to promote it. I have never known much good done by those who affected to trade for the public good. It is an affectation, indeed, not very common among merchants, and very few words need be employed in dissuading them from it.
>
> (Smith 1904, www.econlib.org/library/Smith/smWN13.html)

Craig Smith (2006, p. 1) qualifies the quoted Scottish thinker's words about the "invisible hand" as "perhaps the most famous phrase to have emerged from the political philosophy of Adam Smith". Nobel laureate in economics James Tobin (1983, p. 4) considered the "invisible hand" as "one of the Great Ideas of intellectual history". Indeed, to this day Adam Smith's idea stimulates minds and steers a discussion on their "pure and real nature". In many views it is linked with a notion of a free and open market (de George 2004, p. 46). Christina Petsoulas (2001, p. 34) notices that Smith's metaphor presents an "order that results as the unintended consequence of many independent individual actions". Others highlight the "process" nature of the theory rather than its "end-state" (Aydinonat 2008, p. 3). Some, like Kaushik Basu (2011, p. 16), read Smith's words as a key element of the free market system which in Smith's view "is like an invisible hand that can unobtrusively coordinate the behaviour of a multitude of individuals, interested only in maximizing their selfish utility, so as to bring about efficiency and a socially optimal outcome". In this context, "[t]he core theorem of the invisible hand theory is that the common good of efficiency and wealth creation is realized in a market society as a side effect of the pursuit of self-interest" (Koslowski 2004, p. 14). As an effect, in a free market state "the self-interested actions of many individual people have the unintended result of promoting the common good" (Bishop 2000, p. 10). Thus individual interests promote interests of the society (van Suntum 2005, p. 5). Certain authors find a social-ethical side of Smith's concept. According to Jerry Evensky (1998, p. 7) "if individuals are to enjoy the fruits of a classical liberal society the invisible hand must not only coordinate individuals' choices, it must shape the individuals into constructive social beings – ethical beings". John Douglas Bishop reminds us about two popular moral corollaries originating from Smith's vision of the invisible hand. First, "since free markets promote the common good ... [they] are morally justified". Second, "since self-interested actions promote the common good ... self-interest is morally acceptable, perhaps even morally obligatory" (Bishop 2000, p. 10). However, in referring to Adam Smith's work and view, an ongoing dispute about the contexts of him using the phrase "invisible hand" cannot be omitted.[5]

## *Space for public action in liberal theory*

Regardless of which interpretation of Smith's idea of the invisible hand is more closely related to the original assumptions, this notion had an influence on the *laissez-faire* philosophy and other liberal concepts that appeared after Adam Smith.[6] In this approach

> the market should be allowed to function without intervention of the state because self-interest in a free society would lead to the most rapid progress and growth a nation was capable of achieving. This meant the individual should be left free to pursue and advance his own ideas.
>
> (MacDonald, Hughes, & Crum 2000, p. 30)

Some authors claim even that Smith's views are "a systemic rationale that provided the foundation of laissez-faire ideology" (MacDonald, Hughes, & Crum 2000, p. 30) and they explain the doctrine of *laissez-faire*.[7] Seen in this light, Adam Smith "accepts the need for a gradual movement toward *laissez-faire* through the elimination of tariffs and subsidies" (Foley 2006, p. 38).

However this reasoning is also ambiguous. Adam Smith is believed to be "the main promoter of laissez-faire" (Tanzi 2011, p. 49), or to be "the champion of *laissez faire*" (Buchan 2006, p. 2). Gavin Kennedy (2012) denies that Adam Smith used the words "*laissez-faire*" in any work he published, both in his lifetime and posthumously.[8] Jacob Viner tried to explain this issue in his well-written, still current essay from 1927. As he summarised his reflections on Adam Smith and *laissez-faire*:

> Adam Smith was not a doctrinaire advocate of *laissez faire*. He saw a wide and elastic range of activity for government, and he was prepared to extend it even farther if government, by improving its standards of competence, honesty, and public spirit, showed itself entitled to wider responsibilities. He attributed great capacity to serve the general welfare to individual initiative applied in competitive ways to promote individual ends. He devoted more effort to the presentation of his case for individual freedom than to exploring the possibilities of service through government.... But ... Smith saw that self-interest and competition were sometimes treacherous to the public interest they were supposed to serve, and he was prepared to have government exercise some measure of control over them where the need could be shown and the competence of government for the task demonstrated.
>
> (Viner 1927, pp. 231–232, italics added)

In Viner's view, driven by natural law philosophy, Adam Smith noted the need for the simultaneous existence of state and government. Although, his belief in individualism resulted in his approach to favour individual liberty rather than governmental control. Jacob Viner describes it as follows:

> [Smith] had little trust in the competence or good faith of government. He knew who controlled it, and whose purposes they tried to serve, though against the local magistrate his indictment was probably unduly harsh. He saw, nevertheless, that it was necessary, in the absence of a better instrument, to rely upon government for the performance of many tasks which individuals as such would not do, or could not do, or could do only badly. He did not believe that *laissez faire* was always good, or always bad. It depended on circumstances; and as best he could, Adam Smith took into account all of the circumstances he could find.
>
> (Viner 1927, p. 232, italics added)

Also, Swedish Nobel Prize winner Gunnar Myrdal (1953, p. 114) agreed that Adam Smith (and David Ricardo as well) "admitted certain exceptions to *laissez-faire*, usually on grounds of what they called practical considerations". This does not influence Myrdal's general interpretation of Smith's attitude to *laissez-faire*, who considered some works on this topic as a revisionism:

> [n]ow there have been repeated attempts to show that neither Adam Smith nor Ricardo believed in laissez-faire, a term which has in the course of time acquired a bad flavour. These attempts are usually made by neo-classical authors who try to defend the classics on all fronts. Such attempts are well-meant but misconceived and dangerous. We are not yet sufficiently free from dogmatism to be able to dispense with an honest and thorough criticism of the masters.
>
> (Myrdal 1953, p. 114)

Nevertheless, not trying to decide which approach is appropriate, Smith's thoughts have been used by proponents of *laissez-faire*, and even Viner's explanation does not change this fact. Many of these came from France and were the opponents of the growing role of the French government during the Industrial Revolution (Tanzi 2011, p. 52). In particular, this concerns the role of Jean-Baptiste Say in "dissemination" of Smith's ideas (or "laissezfairesation" of Smith's theory). In 1897, influential Italian author of a public finance textbook, Augusto Graziani, accused him of vulgarising Smith's doctrine (Tanzi 2011, p. 52). As Vito Tanzi (2011, p. 52) compares, "Say wanted the state to be out of the way, whereas Smith wanted to give the state a limited, well-defined, useful and productive role". Besides Say, Kennedy distinguishes Frédéric Bastiat's involvement. These two French economists "were prominent in cries for *laissez-faire*, using Adam Smith's name as cover for its popularity among politicians and merchant campaigners against the 'Corn Laws'[9] and the newly passed but limited Factory Acts" (Kennedy 2012).

In conclusion it should be emphasised that Smith's belief in individualism resulting in better society building together the common good, linked with free, open market, had its borders and limits. It is not a libertarian concept where state abandons the economy and does not use its legal instrument to influence it. In contrast, liberalisation does not imply complete withdrawal from public involvement in the economy and its sectors. It can cover a broad, elastic range of governmental activity. As Viner clearly indicated, Smith perceived traps of self-interest and competition. Thus, his attitude to liberalism did not exclude public instruments of control. However, individual liberty prevails over governmental control. A watchman may be its symbol. An answer, if it is a night-watchman, depends on the scope of public impact – as individuals have to rely upon the state without which many of their tasks would not or could not be realised, or could be only badly performed. Before examining the matter of this influence and presenting it within the European electricity sector, let us focus on the legal basis for liberalisation and how this doctrine of individual liberty was put into practice.

## The legal dimension of liberalisation

Liberalism is not just a theory. Through the centuries before its application in sectors of the economy like aviation, telecommunication, or energy it had been used in numerous contexts. Many of them had a legal background. With respect to practical examples of liberalism, *laissez-faire*, and the night-watchman state formula, John Braithwaite (2008, p. 15) emphasises that the nineteenth century state was mostly a *laissez-faire* state. Willam G. Clarence-Smith (1999, p. 121) recalls colonies and the golden rule of colonialism which induced establishment of a minimalist night-watchman administration ("the enterprise should not cost anything to the metropolitan tax payer"). For example, Thomas Balogh (1962, p. 14) considers India under the British Civil Service a night-watchman state. Judith Maxwell distinguishes the *laissez-faire* concept in Canada at the time of the Confederation (1860s): "The state served as a glorified night-watchman. It provided defence, it meted out justice, it regulated foreign trade, and it helped private agents to build railways and canals.... The state was limited mainly to economic and judicial affairs" (Grady, Howse, & Maxwell, 1995, p. 3). Further, Carin Lee Holroyd (2002, p. 40) writes about *laissez-faire* in providing assistance (the most basic) by Canada, New Zealand, and Australia to entities wanting to expand foreign investments for much of the twentieth century.

The *laissez-faire* system did not function in isolation from the legal system. On the contrary, it was implemented and executed by means of specific legislation. Due to the hierarchy of legal acts, in each democratic state of law (even in the early eighteenth and nineteenth century's formula) a constitution is an act of principal importance. With respect to *laissez-faire*'s legal basis, Jan Art (2004, p. 113) evokes the Belgian constitution of 1830 which he considers the most liberal in continental Europe on its adoption. Under its provision "[t]he Belgian state was 'a night watchman state,' only operating when local and private initiatives failed".

A noteworthy context of application of the night-watchman concept has emerged in US judicial history. In the beginning of the twentieth century, in the well-known case, *Lochner v New York*, the US Supreme Court used the

Fourteenth Amendment to the United States Constitution's due process clause to invalidate a state labour law that set maximum working hours for employees (bakery workers) (Ryan 2011, p. 81). *Lochner* was not the only case that referred to this topic. It initiated a line of cases which, on the basis of the Fourteenth Amendment, were to protect freedom of contract and were against state law interference, thereby limiting Congress's commerce authority aiming at achieving similar objectives (Ryan 2011, p. 81). Some authors justify this "judicial era" by "contract liberty ideals", followed by suggesting that "the cases also contain important themes of judicial concern for governmental neutrality, other fundamental rights, and even means-end reasonableness" (Ryan 2011, pp. 81–82). Erin Ryan (2011, p. 82) writes that the *Lochner* period is often referred to as "a period of rampart antiregulatory activism", in which the Supreme Court verified in much more detail governmental interference in the economy. Jed Handelsman Shugerman (2010, p. 1125) suggests that the *Lochner* era was preceded by "the doctrine of vested property rights" which was raised under the 1846 convention, "with newly elected judges relying on substantive due process to limit the Married Women's Property Act of 1848 and the Anti-Liquor Act of 1855". With the use of Edward S. Corwin's research (1917, pp. 281–313), Shugerman (2010) assesses that New York's constitutional convention of 1846 helped establish the foundation for post-Civil War *laissez-faire* constitutionalism.[10]

However, the mentioned examples show how difficult it is to find a homogeneous public governance regime that can be described as a *laissez-faire* state. Exploration of this issue therefore requires making a reference to *laissez-faire*'s philosophical background and its roots. This needs a broader presentation of an already invoked and partially described classic philosophy thought.

Trying to summarise this part of the book while linking it with the previous section, I would like to refer to Warren J. Samuels and some of his views on liberalism and *laissez-faire*. He distinguishes three contexts for using *laissez-faire*. First, is the minimisation of legal change; second, a particular vision of an economy; and third, a legal change to bring about that particular vision.[11] As Samuels writes focusing on the first of them:

> [t]he concept of *laissez-faire* is simultaneously unambiguous and ambiguous.... Both sentimentally and substantively, it stands for ... system based upon institutions of private property, free enterprise, competition, markets, meaningful private choice, and a presumption against government activism [where] markets govern resource allocation.
>
> (Beckert & Zafirovski 2011)

Seen in this light, the difference for a state-based, public approach derives from prevailing governmental action, where government acts as a representative of the state. Keeping in mind remarks on liberalisation stemming from Smith's thoughts and a place for state in this concept, what is interesting is the similarity in both approaches. In practice, similarity may be found in sectors where liberalisation has been conducted, i.e. aviation, railroad, telecommunication, or energy, etc. Besides liberalisation, public influence is still very strong there. This makes it necessary to find an answer for the dilemma which may be posed in the following question: to what extent do the two concepts – liberal, market-based on the one hand, and public, state-based approach on the other – lie completely outside each other, or is there any convergence between them, and, if so, might the point of contact be found?

Nevertheless, before moving on to this issue, let us discuss a process of liberalisation of the electricity sector which was conducted in a very unfortunate way. It is the case of the California energy crisis of 2000–2001.

## Application of liberal models in the electricity sector: the California energy crisis

Liberalisation is a concept that affects, more or less intensively, all areas of the economy. It also finds its application in the energy sector and, as will be presented in the following chapters of this book, is an integral part of European policy on the energy market. At this point, I would like to recall an example of a deregulation that was implemented in the US. This is a case of fallen liberalisation of the electricity sector in California.

The California model of liberalisation had been presented as a perfect solution, thereby many countries adopted it in local formats (e.g. Spain) (Cortina 2002, p. 4). In 1996, with the passing of the California Assembly Bill 1890, a radical restructuring of the state's electricity sector began (Weare 2003, p. 1). James L. Sweeney describes the background for that movement as follows:

> California had very good reasons for restructuring its energy supply system. First, many experts believed that the vertically integrated system in place was not operating as efficiently as it could. Second, the system had very high costs. Third, the system did not seem to provide enough incentives for investments in new generating plants.
>
> (n.d., p. 2)

The started deregulation of the California power sector covered providing a retail rate cap, introducing compulsory use of the spot market, and assuring the free choice of supplier (Cortina 2002, p. 4). These actions were complemented with an unbundling of energy companies to separate generation, transmission, distribution, and sales of electricity (Sweeney n.d., p. 2). To steer the new markets, the law of 1996 established the Power Exchange and the California Independent System Operator. Nevertheless, the markets were not an integrated system, but two separate organisations vulnerable to market inefficiencies and full of opportunities for manipulation, with fixed retail price controls, causing an isolation of the consumer from the producer of electricity (Sweeney n.d., p. 2).

However, in the early years after April 1998, when the competitive wholesale power markets were inaugurated, the new system functioned relatively well (Weare 2003, p. 1). Although, between 1998 and 2000, the market structure in

California met the actions of privately owned suppliers and retailers to maximise their profits, accordingly from selling wholesale power or selling electricity to final consumers (Wolak 2005, p. 147).

Beginning in late May 2000, electricity markets in California entered a hard time. Cumulative problems which consisted of skyrocketing prices, the collapse of the California Power Exchange, bankruptcy of the state's largest utility, as well as the first blackouts since the Second World War began to choke the economy (Knittel & Metaxoglou 2008, p. 2). Christopher Weare describes the shortcomings in the supplies of electricity in the following way:

> On June 14, 2000, rolling blackouts in San Francisco caused by a Bay Area heat wave signaled the beginning of rough times. In 2000, electricity was turned off to customers with special interruptible contracts on 13 other days. During 2001, "load shedding" occurred on 31 days. On nine of these days customers experienced involuntary rolling blackouts for a total of 42 hours of outages. During these nine outages, California experienced an average shortfall of 600 MW of electricity, enough energy to power over 450,000 households. On the worst day, January 18, the equivalent of almost one million households lost electricity.
>
> (2003, p. 2)

In terms of prices, they rose significantly from approximately $30 per megawatt-hour in April to more than $100 by June, and, in November 2000, prices had increased to between $250 and $450 (Sweeney n.d., p. 6). David Watts and Rafael Ariztía (n.d., p. 3) list the factors that raised wholesale prices. Among them they find

> significant demand growth (12.7 per cent in June 2000) due to an extremely hot summer, unexpected increase in natural gas prices (more than 10× between 1999 and 2000), increase in NOx emission permit prices and considerable reduction in energy [imports] due to the low level of the reservoirs in the Northeast of the country.

Moreover, an important cause of the crisis was also a lack of new generation capacity that resulted from "environmental restrictions, long and complicated site approval procedures, and inadequate regulatory legislation that failed to stimulate investment" (Cortina 2002, p. 5). Increasing demand was not followed by growth of generation capacity ("capacity remained stagnant"). Among other factors that ignited the crisis was the generation ownership which was too concentrated (Bushnell 2004, p. 1052).

Additionally, at that time California was also hit by unfavourable weather conditions: the winters of both 2000 and 2001 were relatively dry, and, consequently, the amount of hydro-generation available was inadequate. Furthermore, a very hot summer of 2000 drove up electricity demand throughout the western states (Weare 2003, p. 21).

Regulation is a vital aspect of the case. A lack of it as well as wrong actions and decisions taken by the authorities contributed largely to the crisis. With this respect, reducing the role of the California Energy Commission in the field of energy planning was a mistake. As Weare (2003, p. 25) reports "[b]efore deregulation, the California Energy Commission produced comprehensive biannual evaluations of the state of the California electricity sector, but its role in resource planning was significantly diminished with the advent of deregulation".

> At the same time, conservation efforts diminished. Before deregulation, California had a number of innovative programs that provided utilities with incentives to invest in conservation in lieu of capacity expansion. In the early 1990s, these mandated comprehensive reviews of energy alternatives identified numerous cost-effective investments in energy-saving technologies and conservation programs (Mowris 1998). Utilities invested as much as $400 million a year to promote these investments and programs. In the move to a competitive environment, these programs lost their constituency and momentum, largely because regulators lost the policy levers with which they provided incentives. AB 1890 did provide for continued support of such investments, but only at a much reduced level—about $220 million per year (Harvey *et al.* 2001).
>
> (Weare 2003, pp. 25–26)

The California energy crisis can be concluded with the words of James L. Sweeney (n.d., p. 1). In his opinion, "California's experience in electricity deregulation cast a pall on movements towards deregulation throughout the United States." On the other hand, many lessons can be drawn from California's experience. Seen in this light, Paul L. Joskow (2008, pp. 11–12) offers a straightforward "textbook" architecture of desirable features for conducting regulatory reform and developing competitive markets for the electricity sector. His manual involves several key components, some of which are:

- a Privatization of state-owned electricity monopolies…
- b Vertical separation of potentially competitive segments (e.g. generation, marketing and retail supply) from segments that will continue to be regulated (distribution, transmission, system operations) either structurally (through divestiture) or functionally (with internal "Chinese" walls or "ring fencing" separating affiliates within the same corporation)…
- c Horizontal restructuring of the generation segment…
- d Horizontal integration of transmission facilities and network operations…
- e The creation of voluntary public wholesale spot energy and operating reserve market institutions…
- f The development of active "demand-side" institutions…
- g The application of regulatory rules and supporting network institutions…

h The unbundling of retail tariffs … from the regulated "delivery" charges for using distribution and transmission networks.

(Joskow 2008, pp. 12–13)

Each listed element has to improve market conditions. Some of them are disputable (for instance, privatisation of state-owned electricity monopolies can be a contentious idea if we consider it from the point of view of energy security and hostile acquisitions, on the other hand one can distinguish different types of privatisation where national funds may also be involved, e.g. division of a monopoly with use of state-owned companies, balancing the market structure with private energy companies, etc.).

Nevertheless, in general, provided solutions support competition and enhance energy markets. For example, as Joskow (2008, p. 12) indicates, recalled vertical separation prevents cross-subsidisation of competitive businesses from regulated businesses. Likewise, introducing active "demand-side" institutions allows consumers to react to changes in wholesale market prices, and application of regulatory rules assures access to the grid and facilitates competitive production and exchange (Joskow 2008, pp. 12–13).

Apart from already mentioned components of Joskow's textbook, one requires special attention. This covers:

> [t]he creation of independent regulatory agencies with good information about the costs, service quality and comparative performance of the firms supplying regulated network services, the authority to enforce regulatory requirements, and an expert staff to use this information and authority to regulate effectively the prices charged by distribution and transmission companies and the terms and conditions of access to these networks by wholesale and retail suppliers of power.
>
> (Joskow 2008, p. 13)

Joskow calls regulatory authorities "an important but underappreciated component of successful reforms". The California crisis undoubtedly proves it. Regulation and the rational conduct of public authorities could have prevented the crisis in the energy sector. This clearly highlights the place of state presence in the energy sector even in liberalised markets. Bearing in mind lessons learned from the California electricity crisis, let us move on to another point on the axis of the impact on the economy, i.e. public, state-based approach.

## Essence of the state-based approach

An approach that can be contrasted with the market-based approach is the state-based approach. It involves a much more intensive level of state influence on the economy. This requires a legal basis which enables direct actions (like orders), and which creates conditions for states' operation on the market. An extreme version of such a system is "a command economy". There the state determines primarily or almost exclusively the allocation of resources (as in Communist countries) (Thomas 1992, p. 5). However, as in the case of the market-based approach also in the state-based approach it is difficult to find a homogeneous, pure situation reflecting it in a very clear way. As a result, it is not an easy thing to define this concept by referring to a one key-term like the *laissez-faire* and liberal philosophy in terms of the market-based approach.[12]

### *Between mercantilism and interventionism*

Viner qualifies "mercantilism" as a doctrine which was "in sharp contrast with the later laissez-faire" (Sills 1968, pp. 435–443). He noticed that mercantilism

> took for granted that man was inherently self-regarding and would pursue his own interests without concern about the consequences of such behavior for the interests of the community [and] ... if individuals were in their economic behavior left free from tight regulation, the consequences for the community would be disastrous.

However, Viner rightly notes that such an explanation was virtually universal (e.g. it was known in antiquity, and therefore did not distinguish mercantilism from "premercantilist"). What was new in this notion, was:

> its systematic adjustment to the concentration of power and the monopolization of loyalty by nation-states, which in their relations with other states followed a "Machiavellian" or amoral code, and were more extensive in area of jurisdiction than the earlier city-states and feudal barons but less extensive than the empires of classical antiquity and than the universal Catholic church of the Middle Ages. Also substantially new in mercantilism were its greater concern with economic matters as one phase of the then prevalent secularization of thought and practice, the change in the specific character of the economic objectives of the political authorities, and the new administrative patterns of regulation of communal life.
>
> (Sills 1968, p. 439)

Mercantilism has often been considered a regime which, after its appearance in an established form in the sixteenth century, flourished until the late eighteenth century.[13] However, in the late nineteenth century there was a return to protectionism in the form of a new mercantilism. J.W. Horrocks (1925, p. 199) noted that it was "a natural reaction against the extreme doctrine of *laissez-faire*, and a conviction revived that far more functions were properly assignable to the State than what were allowed to it under that teaching". Furthermore, it was driven by socialism and ideas spread amongst the new industrial classes (Horrocks 1925, p. 199).

The state's involvement in the economy grew throughout the twentieth century. Graham W. Thomas (1992, p. 6) classifies as causes of this "the impact of the two world wars, the Great Depression of the inter-war years, the growing strength of socialism and the Labour parties, and the revolution in economic thought associated with John Maynard Keynes". Support for government involvement in the economy rose between 1979 and 1981, when in a majority of Western countries energy crises threatened living standards. Ole Borre and José Manuel Viegas (1995, p. 279) found this failure of capitalist economy in a line with a need for government intervention. As a result, the most Western democracies introduced the *mixed economy*. Thomas (1992, p. 6) concisely defines that "[i]n this system both private and public enterprise have a role in economic activity and both market forces and the government determine the distribution of rewards".

Another point of reference which helps in analysing the state-based approach is a policy of interventionism. It is linked with a belief that some features of the market are undesirable and in this sense need improvement. In this scope, many extensive, but critical comments were made by Ludwig von Mises. For instance, von Mises (1996, p. 4) established his definition of intervention, which he considered "a limited order by a [public] authority forcing the owners of the means of production and entrepreneurs to employ their means in a different manner than they otherwise would".

### *Forms and reasons of public activity within the economy*

David E.M. Sappington and Joseph E. Stiglitz (1987, pp. 3–4) distinguish three forms of public activity within the economy: an indirect control (taxes and subsidies), a direct control (nationalisation), and a half-way measure between those two methods – a regulation. As they write, "[g]overnment action in one of these forms generally arises from a belief that markets do not always work well". Similarly, James W. McKie (1979, p. 78), writes that "if government … is persuaded that the competitive market has 'failed' beyond redemption, its most common response is to regulate rather than to supersede the private market by ownership". This correlates with the "public choice theory" based on an assumption

> that general welfare will be maximized by the exercise of individual choices, with regulatory intervention demanded for the most part only where examples of "market failure" require to be corrected in order to ensure the "proper" operation of the market.
>
> (Feintuck 2004, p. 8)

Sappington and Stiglitz list three broad classes of market failure – a situation in which the pursuit of individual interests does not lead to the common good (Cadot, Malouche & Sáez 2012, p. 41):

i *Imperfect competition*. Under variety of circumstances the market will be not competitive. (What is required for economic efficiency is more than just a rivalry.…) This is particularly relevant where are large nonconvexities, giving the rise to natural monopolies. This provides the motivation for government intervention in utilities.

ii *Imperfect information*.... [W]hen there is imperfect information, there is always a scope for government intervention.... Imperfect information provides basis of ... government regulatory activities [*inter alia*, in the field of] consumer protection.... [L]egislation [for this need] is largely based on the presumption that individuals cannot look after themselves as well as the government, largely because they are imperfectly informed and it is costly for them to gather information.

iii *Externalities*. Whenever there are externalities, competitive market solutions will be inefficient. Government regulations aimed at controlling pollution, for example, are directed at alleviating problems posed by these externalities.

(Sappington and Stiglitz 1987, pp. 4–5)

However, the list is not of a closed nature and in literature one can find other justifications, as well as other explanations of the reasoning traced here (Dibadj 2006, pp. 8–13). For instance, apart from externalities, or inadequate information Stephen G. Breyer (1982, pp. 15–22, 32–34) discusses *monopoly power*, *excess profits*, or *unequal bargaining power*. Although, these may be included in Sappington and Stiglitz's category of the imperfect competition. Furthermore, Cass R. Sunstein points out other market failures. Besides already mentioned monopoly, inadequate information, and externalities, he identifies *coordination questions*, *transitions costs*, as well as *collective actions problems* (Sunstein 1990, pp. 48–55 cited in Ogus 2001, pp. 4–11). Regarding the latter, seen through a prism of the "free-ride problem", where individually rational private attitude may entail collective or public irrationality, "If everyone acts in his self-interest, serious harm will sometimes result. Clear cases involve here public or collective goods ... [like national defence or environment]" (Sunstein 1990, p. 49).

Using the US example, James W. McKie (1979, p. 78) recalls that the oldest and most comprehensive form of government response to market failure is regulation of the class of industries known as "public utilities".[14] As the origin of this term McKie points out the law sanctioning regulation of activities "affected with a public interest".[15] Craig (1991, p. 147), explains, "[w]here there [was] only one facility which can be used, either because there [was] only one facility licensed..., or because, factually, there [was] no other such facility available, then the facility [was] 'affected with a public interest'". These bring its two main elements: essential service offered by a company (as McKie adds, essential service refers to contemporary living standards), and operation under conditions of natural monopoly (approaching it), where "monopoly is irresistibly more efficient than competition" (McKie 1979, p. 78). Martin T. Farris and Roy J. Sampson trace legal theories advanced to justify the notion of public utilities. They list "holding-out theory" (a person providing service "hold himself out" to the public obligation to provide it at reasonable price), "government function theory" (utility operates as an agent of the state – they provide service which without utilities would be provided by the state – that is why they are subordinated to regulation), "constructive grant theory" (some types of essential business grant the general public an interest in their operation), "implied contract theory" (certain special privileges granted to a company – e.g. the right to use public properties, like city streets or power dam sites – subjects business to regulation), and "police power theory" (Farris & Sampson 1973, pp. 21–22). The last one, which is considered by Farris and Sampson (1973, p. 22) as the most acceptable, is based on a notion that any sovereign state "upholds the right ... to take whatever steps it feels necessary in order to protect and provide for the health and general welfare of its citizens".

Cited notions are based on *regulation*, or provide reasoning for it (e.g. implied contract theory, government function, police power theory, public choice theory). They form a good ground for further analysis of what is regulation, how it is linked with public law, what shape have different regulatory approaches, and how broad are their scopes.

## Notes

1 David Cooperman and Eugene Victor Walter refer briefly to the day-watchman state, noticing it in a context of a relation of individual freedom and public intervention that appeared in the liberal political tradition. See Cooperman & Walter 1962, p. 403.

2 Ferdinand Lasalle (1825–1864) was a leader of the German workers movement. In 1863, he founded the General German Workers' Association (*Allgemeiner Deutscher Arbeiterverein*), see van Suntum 2005.

3 In order to understand properly what impression would have been made by Ferdinand Lassalle's words, von Mises explained,

> one must keep in mind that the Germans of his time had not yet forgotten the state of the monarchical despots, with its vast multiplicity of administrative and regulatory functions, and that they were still very much under the influence of the philosophy of Hegel, which had elevated the state to the position of a divine entity.

Bearing this in mind

> [i]f one looked upon the state, with Hegel, as "the self-conscious moral, substance," as the "Universal in and for itself, the rationality of the will," then, of course, one had to view as blasphemous any attempt to limit the function of the state to that of serving as a night watchman.

4 See Daunton 2008, p. 4. However Daunton (2008, p. 80) claimes that "[t]he British state was more effective and stronger than often assumed, in a way not captured by the notion of a laissez-faire state".

5 Some authors indicate that Smith's words have no deeper meaning. They consider it as "an ironic but useful joke" (Rothschild 1994, p. 319), or as "Smith's casual metaphor" (Kennedy 2009, p. 240). In contrast, other researchers of his thoughts underline the conscious and deliberate nature of placing in Smith's works the motive of the invisible hand (Klein and Lucas, 2011). Of particular significance here is a dispute between Gavin Kennedy and Daniel B. Klein who, for a few years, were trying to prove unintentional (Kennedy) or intentional (Klein) action of Adam Smith in using his words about the invisible hand (Kennedy 2009; Klein 2009).

Naturally, this dispute does not limit to mentioned authors, and in its width and depth is more complex (see Klein and Lucas, 2011). Thus, Peter Minowitz (2004, p. 411) rightly concludes that "[c]enturies after Smith's death, we are still struggling to fathom a two-word phrase that stands out in a thousand-page book".

6 For example, the concept of the invisible hand was used by the libertarian movement with Robert Nozick at the forefront. Nozick (2006), in his best known book *Anarchy, State, and Utopia* beginning from a free-market Lockean "state of nature" portrayed the emergence of the state as a process driven by an invisible hand (by means of a series of invisible hands) that violates no one's rights, first, as a "dominant agency", second, as an "ultra-minimal state", and finally as a legitimate "minimal state". See Rothbard 1977, p. 45, or Childs 1977, p. 23.

7 "The doctrine of laissez-faire, as explicated in Adam Smith's Wealth of Nation, holds that market economies, when left alone, are essentially self-regulating" (Kuttner 1991, 4).

8 According to Kennedy these words have never emerged

> in any student notes that have so far been found, or in any reports of [Smith's] lectures by those who attended them (John Millar, James Woodrow, Lord Buchan, John Stuart, etc.,) or by those who knew him intimately (such as Dugald Stewart, whose father was a student at Glasgow with Smith).

9 For further discussion of this issue see Lipson 1943, pp. 648–664.

10 On the other hand, Matthew J. Lindsay (2010, p. 67) considers Shugerman's view as misreading this judicial escalation of rights. Lindsay claims that iconic *laissez-faire* constitutionalism's cases were rather an exception than the rule. As he writes,

> [v]iewed within its broader historical trajectory, rather than through the narrow lens of a few exceptional cases, the constitutionalization of individual economic rights reflected not a far-reaching constraint on the regulatory authority of the states, but rather a complement to, and even a component of, the unprecedented expansion of that authority.

11 Beckert and Zafirovski 2011, s.v. "Laissez Faire".

12 Although, as already presented, also among them other approaches and key-concepts may be distinguished, e.g. libertarianism.

13 Mercantilism is related with Jean-Baptiste Colbert (1619–1683), Controller-General of Finances under the rule of King Louis XIV, "the greatest of French mercantilists, and perhaps the most notable of all mercantilists statesmen" (Horrocks 1925, p. 118).

14 Compare US case law in this respect, see Harrison, Morgan, & Verkuil 1997.

15 He gives an example of the operation of wharves and inns, reminding that a concept of public utility derives from Elizabethan times.

## References

Art, J. 2004 "Social control in Belgium: the catholic factor" in vol. 2, *1800–2000* of *Social control in Europe*, eds C. Emsley, E. Johnson, & P. Spierenburg, Ohio State University, Columbus, OH, pp. 112–124.

Aydinonat, N.E. 2008, *The invisible hand in economics: how economists explain unintended social consequences*, Routledge, Abingdon.

Balogh, T. 1962, *Some aspects of economic growth of under-developed areas*, 2nd edn, National Council of Applied Economic Research, New Delhi.

Basu, K. 2011, *Beyond the invisible hand: groundwork for a new economics*, Princeton University Press, Princeton, NJ.

Beckert, J. & Zafirovski, M. 2011, *International encyclopedia of economic sociology*, Routledge, Abingdon.

Bishop, J.D. 2000, "Ethics and capitalism: a guide to the issues", in *Ethics and capitalism*, ed. J.D. Bishop, University of Toronto Press, Toronto, pp. 3–48.

Bjørnebye, H. 2010, *Investing in EU energy security: exploring the regulatory approach to tomorrow's electricity production*, Kluwer Law International, Alphen aan den Rijn.

Borre, O. & Viegas, J.M. 1995, "Government intervention in the economy", in *The scope of government*, eds O. Borre & E. Scarbrough, Oxford University Press, Oxford, pp. 234–280.

Braithwaite, J. 2008, *Regulatory capitalism: how it works, ideas for making it work better*, Edward Elgar Publishing, Cheltenham.

Brandes, G. 1911, *Ferdinand Lassalle*, William Heinemann, London. Available from: http://archive.org/stream/ferdinandlassall014792mbp/ferdinandlassall014792mbp_djvu.txt [21 June 2015].

Breyer, S.G. 1982, *Regulation and its reform*, Harvard University Press, Cambridge, MA.

Buchan, J. 2006, *The authentic Adam Smith: his life and ideas*, W.W. Norton & Company, New York.

Bushnell, J. 2004, "California's electricity crisis: a market apart?" *Energy Policy*, 32, pp. 1045–1052. Available from: http://lindert.econ.ucdavis.edu/bushnell/site/files-and-images/Energypolicy04.pdf [11 June 2015].

Cadot, O., Malouche, M., & Sáez, S. 2012, *Streamlining non-tariff measures: a toolkit for policy makers*. World Bank Publications, Washington, DC.

Childs, Jr R.A. 1977, "The invisible hand strikes back", *Journal of Libertarian Studies*, 1(1), pp. 23–33. Available from: http://mises.org/journals/jls/1_1/1_1_4.pdf [28 June 2015].

Clarence-Smith, W.G. 1999, "The modern colonial state and global economic integration 1815–1945", in *States and sovereignty in the global economy*, eds D.A. Smith, D.J. Solinger, & S.C. Topik, Routledge, London, pp. 120–137.

Cooperman, D. & Walter, E.V. 1963, *Power and civilization: political thought in the twentieth century*. Crowell, New York.

Cortina, A. 2002, "Welcome and introduction", in *Energy liberalization and regulation revisited*, ed. B. Mossavar-Rahmani, 4–8. *XII Repsol YPF-Harvard Seminar*, Fundación Repsol YPF, Madrid. Available from: www.hks.harvard.edu/fs/whogan/Repsol_Seminars/Repsol_Seminars_Recent/Repsol_Mallorca_2001.pdf [10 June 2015].

Corwin, E.S. 1917, "The extension of judicial review in New York: 1783–1905", *Michigan Law Review*, 15(4), pp. 281–313. Available from www.jstor.org/stable/1275992?seq=5 [21 June 2015].

Craig, P. 1991, "Constitutions, property and regulation", *Public Law*, pp. 538–554.

Daunton, M.J. 2008, *State and market in Victorian Britain: war, welfare and capitalism*, Boydell Press, Woodbridge.

de George, R. 2004, "The invisible hand and thinness of the common good", in *The invisible hand and the common good*, ed. B. Hodgson, Springer, Berlin, pp. 38–47.

Dibadj, R.R. 2006, *Rescuing regulation*, State University of New York Press, Albany, NY.

Evensky, J. 1998, "Ethics and the invisible hand", in *Economics, ethics, and public policy*, ed. C.K. Wilber, Rowman & Littlefield Publishers, Lanham, MD, pp. 7–16.

Farris, M.T. & Sampson, R.J. 1973, *Public utilities: regulation, management, and ownership*, Houghton Mifflin Company, Boston, MA.

Feintuck, M. 2004, *"The public interest" in regulation*, Oxford University Press, Oxford.

Foley, D.K. 2006, *Adam's fallacy: a guide to economic theology*, Harvard University Press, Cambridge, MA.

Grady, P., Howse, R., & Maxwell, J. 1995, *Redefining social security*, Queen's University School of Policy Studies, Kingston.

Harrison, J.L., Morgan, T.D., & Verkuil, P.R. 1997, *Regulation and deregulation: cases and materials*, West Publishing Company, St. Paul, MN.

Hill, C. 2002 (1961), *The century of revolution: 1603–1714*, Routledge, London.

Hogan, W.W. 1999, *Market-based transmission investments and competitive electricity markets*. Available from: www.hks.harvard.edu/fs/whogan/tran0899.pdf [23 June 2015].

Horrocks, J.W. 1925, *A short history of mercantilism*, Methuen & Co., London.

Hudelson, R. 1999, *Political philosophy*, M.E. Sharpe, Armonk, NY.

Joskow, P.L. 2008, "Lessons learned from electricity market liberalization", *Energy Journal, Special Issue on the Future of Electricity*, 29, pp. 9–42. Available from: http://economics.mit.edu/files/2093 [10 June 2015].

Kennedy, G. 2009, "Adam Smith and the invisible hand: from metaphor to myth", *Econ Journal Watch* 6(2), pp. 239–263. Available from: http://econjwatch.org/file_download/252/2009-05-kennedy-watchpad.pdf [12 June 2015].

Kennedy, G. 2012, *Adam Smith's lost legacy* (blog), "Adam Smith and the myth of laissez faire", 9 June. Available from: http://adamsmithslostlegacy.blogspot.com/2012/06/adam-smith-and-myth-of-laissez-faire.html [17 June 2015].

Keppler, J.H. 2010, *Adam Smith and the economy of the passions*, Routledge, Abingdon.

Klein, D.B. 2009, "In Adam Smith's invisible hands: comment on Gavin Kennedy", *Econ Journal Watch Volume* 6(2), pp. 264–279. Available from: http://econjwatch.org/file_download/254/2009-05-klein-watchpad.pdf [16 June 2015].

Klein, D.B. & Lucas, B. 2011, "In a word or two, placed in the middle: the invisible hand in Smith's tomes", *Economic Affairs*, 31(1), pp. 43–52.

Knittel, C.R. & Metaxoglou, K. 2008, *Diagnosing unilateral market power in electricity reserves market*. Available from: http://web.mit.edu/knittel/www/papers/Ancil_Serv_latest.pdf [19 June 2015].

Koslowski, P. 2004, "Public interest and self-interest in the market and the democratic process", in *The invisible hand and the common good*, ed. B. Hodgson, Springer, Berlin, pp. 13–37.

KPMG 2013, *National electricity market: a case study in successful microeconomic reform*. Available from: www.aemc.gov.au/media/docs/National-Electricity-Market--A-case-study-in-successful-microeconomic-reform-d559dbe4-764e-4644-832b-de5ecf1d91ef-0.PDF [16 June 2015].

Kuttner, R. 1991, *The end of laissez-faire: global economy and national purpose after the Cold War*, University of Pennsylvania Press, Philadelphia, PA.

Labio, C. 2006, "The solution is in the text: a survey of the recent literary turn in Adam Smith studies", *Adam Smith Review*, 2, pp. 149–176.

Leach, J. 2004, *A course in public economics*, Cambridge University Press, Cambridge.

Lee Holroyd, C. 2002, *Government, international trade, and laissez-faire capitalism: Canada, Australia, and New Zealand's relations with Japan*, McGill-Queen's University Press, Montreal.

Lindsay, M.J. 2010, "In search of 'laissez-faire constitutionalism", *Harvard Law Review Forum* 123(5), pp. 55–78. Available from: www.harvardlawreview.org/media/pdf/vol.123_forum_lindsay.pdf [22 June 2015].

Lipson, E. 1943, *The economic history of England: the age of mercantilism*, vol. 2, 3rd edn, Adam & Charles Black, London.

*Lochner v New York*, 198 U.S. 45 (1905).

MacDonald, S.B., Hughes, J.E., & Crum, D.L. 2000, *New tigers & old elephants: the development game in the 21st century*, Transaction Publishers, New Brunswick.

McKie, J.W. 1979, "Government intervention in the economy of the United States", in *Government intervention in the development economy*, ed. P. Maunder, Croom Helm, London, pp. 72–100.

Metais, R. 2013, "Ensuring energy security in Europe: the EU between a market-based and a geopolitical approach", *EU Diplomacy Paper*, 3, pp. 1–30. Available from: www.coleurope.eu/sites/default/files/uploads/page/edp_3_2013_metais.pdf [22 June 2015].

Mill, J.S. 2004 (1859) *On liberty*, Barnes & Noble Books, New York.

Minowitz, P. 2004, "Adam Smith's invisible hands", *Econ Journal Watch* 1(3), pp. 381–412. Available from: http://econjwatch.org/file_download/268/ejw_com_dec04_minowitz.pdf [16 June 2015].

Mowris, R. 1998, *California energy efficiency policy and program priorities*, California Board for Energy Efficiency, Rosemead, CA.

Myrdal, G. 1953, *Political element in the development of economic theory*, Routledge & Kegan Paul, London.

Nozick, R. 2006 (1974), *Anarchy, state, and utopia*, Blackwell Publishers, Oxford.

Ogus, A.I. 1994, *Regulation: legal form and economic theory*, Oxford University Press, Oxford.

Ogus, A.I. (ed.) 2001, *Regulation, economics and the law*, Edward Elgar Publishing, Cheltenham.

Petsoulas, C. 2001, *Hayek's liberalism and its origins: his idea of spontaneous order and the Scottish enlightment*. Routledge, Abingdon.

Pressman, S. 2014, *Fifty major economists*, 3rd edn, Routledge, Abingdon.

Rothbard, M.N. 1977, "Robert Nozick and the immaculate conception of the state", *Journal of Libertarian Studies* 1(1), pp. 45–57. Available from: http://mises.org/journals/jls/1_1/1_1_6.pdf [18 June 2015].

Rothschild, E. 1994, "Adam Smith and the invisible hand", *American Economic Review*, 84(2), pp. 319–322.

Rudkevich, A., Lazebnik, A., & Sorokin, I. 2010 "A market-based approach to power system expansion planning", presentation *Technical conference on planning models and software*, Washington, DC, 9–10 June 2010. Available from: www.ferc.gov/eventcalendar/Files/20100608191257-Rudkevich,%20Lazebnik,%20Sorokin%20Charles%20River%20Associated%20and%20EFA.pdf [24 June 2015].

Ryan, E. 2011, *Federalism and the tug of war within*, Oxford University Press, Oxford.

Samuels, W.J. 2011, *Erasing the invisible hand: essays on an elusive and misused concept in economics*, Cambridge University Press, Cambridge.

Sappington, D.E.M. & Stiglitz, J.E. 1987, "Information and regulation", in *Public regulation: new perspectives on institution and policies*, ed. E.E. Bailey, MIT Press, Cambridge, MA, pp. 3–43.

Serati, M., Manera, M., & Plotegher, M. 2008, "Modeling electricity prices: from the state of the art to a draft of a new proposal", *Fondazione Eni Enrico Mattei Note di Lavoro Series*, 9, pp. 1–49. Available from: www.feem.it/userfiles/attach/Publication/NDL2008/NDL2008-009.pdf [22 June 2015].

Shugerman, J.H. 2010, "Economic crisis and the rise of judicial elections and judicial review", *Harvard Law Review*, 123(5), pp. 1063–1115. Available from: www.harvardlawreview.org/media/pdf/123_shugerman.pdf [17 June 2015].

Sikor, T., Barlösius, E., & Scheumann, W. 2008, "Introduction", in *Public and private in natural resource governance: a false dichotomy?* ed. T. Sikor, Earthscan, London, pp. 1–20.

Sills, D.L. 1968, *International encyclopedia of the social sciences*, Macmillan, New York.

Smith, A. 1904 (1776) "Of restraints upon the importation from foreign countries of such goods as can be produced at home", chap. II, book IV in *An inquiry into the nature and causes of the wealth of nations*, 5th edn, Methuen & Co., London. Available from: www.econlib.org/library/Smith/smWN13.html#B.IV [18 June 2015].

Smith, C. 2006, *Adam Smith's political philosophy: the invisible hand and spontaneous order*, Routledge, Abingdon.

Sokołowski, M.M. 2013, "Rozważania o istocie współczesnej regulacji" [Considerations on the essence of modern regulation], in *Regulacja: innowacja w sektorze energetycznym* [Regulation: innovation in the energy sector], ed. A. Walaszek-Pyzioł, C.H. Beck, Warsaw, pp. 309–329.

Sunstein, C.R. 1990, *After the rights revolution: reconceiving the regulatory state*, Harvard University Press, Cambridge, MA.

Sweeney, J.L. n.d., *The California electricity crisis: lessons for the future*. Available from: http://web.stanford.edu/~jsweeney/paper/Lessons%20for%20the%20Future.pdf [19 June 2015].

Tanzi, V. 2011, *Government versus markets: the changing economic role of the state*, Cambridge University Press, Cambridge.

Thomas, G.P. 1992, *Government and the economy today*, Manchester University Press, Manchester.

Tobin, J. 1983, "Macroeconomics under debate", *Cowles Foundation Discussion Paper* no. 669. Available from: http://cowles.econ.yale.edu/P/cd/d06b/d0669.pdf [21 June 2015].

Turpin, P. 2011, *The moral rhetoric of political economy: justice and modern economic thought*, Routledge, Abingdon.

van Suntum, U. 2005, *The invisible hand: economic thought yesterday and today*, Springer, Berlin.

Veith, S. 2010, *The EU Emission Trading Scheme: aspects of statehood, regulation and accounting*, Peter Lang, Frankfurt am Main.

Viner, J. 1927, "Adam Smith and laissez faire", *Journal of Political Economy* 35(2), pp. 198–232. Available from: http://theme.univ-paris1.fr/M1/hpe/d06/Viner_1927.pdf [22 June 2015].

von Mises, L. 1985, *Liberalism in the classical tradition*, 3rd edn, Cobden Press, San Francisco, CA.

von Mises, L. 1996 (1976), *A critique of interventionism*, Foundation for Economic Education, Irvington-on-Hudson, NY.

Wallerstein, I. 1999, "States? Sovereignty? The dilemmas of capitalists in an age of transition", in *States and sovereignty in the global economy*, eds D.A. Smith, D.J. Solinger, & S.C. Topik, Routledge, London, pp. 20–33.

Watts, D. & Ariztía, R. n.d., *The electricity crises of California, Brazil and Chile: lessons to the Chilean market*. Available from: http://web.ing.puc.cl/power/paperspdf/wattsariztia.pdf [11 June 2015].

Weare, C. 2003, *The California electricity crisis: causes and policy options*, Public Policy Institute of California, San Francisco, CA.

Wolak, F.A. 2005, "Lessons from California electricity crisis", in *Electricity deregulation: choices and challenges*, eds J.M. Griffin & S.L. Puller, University of Chicago Press, Chicago, IL, 145–181.

# 5 Theories of public law regulation

## Space for electricity

"[R]egulation is perhaps the most classical means by which public actors aim to influence private action for the sake of public interests", write Sikor, Barlösius, and Scheumann (2008, p. 5). The state with the use of its agendas control ("try to sway") private actions, limiting them by imposing restrictions. As they write "[p]ublic actors use their coercive capacity to confine the range of actions available to private actors ... [that] retain the possibility of engaging in voluntary interactions in markets". In this respect regulation targets both public and private entities (Lane 2009, p. 92). In this view, Rafał Stankiewicz (2010, pp. 104–105), referring to the Latin roots of this word, in regulation sees an attempt of arranging reality, carried out within the regulated sphere. Marek Szydło (2005, pp. 36–38) finds a similar nature of regulation. In his opinion it is a binding determination of specific patterns of behaviour, and (where necessary), applying these patterns authoritatively. These few observations show the complexity of the issues.

### Categories, senses, and definitions of regulation

Anthony I. Ogus distinguishes two main categories of regulation, analysing their scope and form. These are *social regulation* and *economic regulation*. Social regulation covers issues as health and safety, environmental protection, and consumer protection. It derives from two types of market failure. Ogus compares them providing that in the first type "individuals in an existing, potential, contractual relationship with firms supplying goods or services often have inadequate information concerning the quality offered by the suppliers; in consequence, the unregulated market may fail to meet their preferences". Whereas in the second type "even if this information problem does not exist market transactions may have spillover effects (or externalities) which adversely affect individuals who are not involved in the transaction" (Ogus 1994, p. 4).

Marek Wierzbowski (1978, pp. 95–96), in his work on regulation and administration, notices that regulation of the public character (administrative) enables embracing of a wide range of areas. In many situations it may be for reasons of a social or economic nature or sometimes even necessary. Hence, solving the policy needs, state action is based on regulatory instruments of a different intervention scale. At the end of the spectrum of low-intervention Ogus (1994, p. 5) identifies three regulatory forms: information regulation ("forcing suppliers to disclose details concerning quality of their goods or services"), private regulation ("imposing obligations which nevertheless can be enforced only by individuals for whose benefits they have been created"), and economic instruments ("are not coercive but rather induce desirable behaviour by financial incentives"). The other end of the spectrum covers prior approval – a highly interventionist instrument which prohibits conducting activity without a licence or authorisation issued by an agency. Between these two extreme points there is the most common form of regulation – "command-and-control". In this type standards imposed on suppliers are enhanced by criminal sanctions (Ogus 1994, p. 5).

On the other hand, economic regulation has a much narrower scope, and it involves fewer activities than social regulation. Ogus (1994, p. 5) correlates application of it with industries that operate under conditions of natural monopoly. In such circumstances, "the principal function of economic regulation is ... to provide a substitute for competition". Herein, three alternatives occur:

> [f]irst, the firm can be publicly owned... the exception being that the mechanics of political direction and accountability will be sufficient to meet public interest goals. Secondly, the firm may remain in, or be transferred to, private ownership but be subjected to external constraints in the form of price and quality regulation.... Thirdly, firms desiring to obtain a monopoly right may be forced to compete for it.... As a part of their competitive bid, they are required to stipulate proposed conditions of supply, relating especially to prices and quality; and those conditions then become terms of the licence or franchise under which they exercise the monopoly right.
>
> (Ogus 1994, p. 5)

However, as Barry Barton (2006, p. 11) rightly indicates, "for all analysis of regulation, no single understanding of the term has emerged". Depending on context, it can have many meanings (Marshall 2012, p. 11). In defining regulation, Barton – as well as Tony Prosser (2010, p. 1) – distinguishes two extreme points: a narrow and a broad approach. In the first, in which regulation is understood as "a set of rules promulgated under statute", Barton finds that it "is simple, but it shouts out inquiry into the process and the actors, and it does not differentiate regulation from other bodies such as criminal law". On the other hand, regulation can be defined much more broadly. In this approach it can cover "any mechanism of social control and influence, whether or not intentional, and whether or not by state.... It includes market forces, social forces and technologies. It includes law" (Barton 2006, p. 12). In other definitions regulation is a "sustained and focused control exercised by a public agency over activities that are valued by a community" (Selznick 1985, p. 363 cited in Barton, 2006, p. 12), it "consists of public interventions which affects the operation of markets through command and control" (Prosser 1997, p. 4 cited in Barton 2006, p. 12), or "is the sustained and focused attempt to alter the behaviour of others according to defined standards or purposes with the intention of producing a broadly identified outcome or outcomes, which may involve mechanisms of standard-setting, information-gathering and behaviour modification" (Black 2002). Alan Stone (1982, p. 10) perceives it as "a state-imposed limitation on the discretion that may be exercised by individuals or organizations, which is supported by the threat of sanction". Monica Gattinger (2009, p. 203) defines regulation, as "a policy instrument" that expresses "rules of behavior backed up by sanctions of the state" (see Doern *et al.* 1999, p. 2). It can come in different forms: constitutions (or quasi-constitutional rules), statutes, delegated legislation, guidelines, standards, codes, etc. (Doern & Gattinger 2003, p. 12). Varying degrees of state sanction are attached to them (Gattinger 2009, p. 203).

Bronwen Morgan and Karen Yeung gather definitions of regulation into two groups, also of a narrow and a broad sense. Narrow sense of definitions "tend to centre on deliberate attempts by the state to influence socially valuable behaviour which may have adverse side-effects by establishing, monitoring and enforcing legal rules". On the other hand, in the broad context "regulation is seen as encompassing all forms of social control, whether intentional or not, and whether imposed by the state or other social institutions" (Morgan & Yeung 2007, pp. 3–4). Tony Prosser finds that in the narrow meaning, "regulation has often been simplistic and ... treated in a ... manner as imposing a burden, as the opposite of free markets". In this way it is a means of correcting market failures (Prosser 2010, p. 1). In the broader approach, which is showed very clearly by Julia Black in her already mentioned definition, regulation is dissociated from the economic sphere, and it includes other types of control (e.g. social). Accordingly, for Prosser (2010, p. 1) regulation is a much deeper notion which needs a multi-field analysis.[1]

Lane (2009, p. 92) distinguishes traditional public regulation, which focuses on setting "upon public enterprises or public utilities... a regime that achieves efficiency in allocation". This involves the issue of a theory of entry regulation, "meaning that government would license the firms delivering goods or services on the one hand but set their prices and quantities on the other hand". However, he finds traditional regulation no longer that relevant, and this is caused by deregulation, liberalisation, and privatisation.

> Instead, governments have adopted the regulatory stance that entry should be as free as possible, in response to the deregulation theme. Once entry regulation is dropped, and competition is forthcoming among various contenders, the regulatory focus has shifted to product regulation.
>
> (Lane 2009, p. 93)

In tracing what he calls "the new wave of public regulation" (product regulation, aimed at defining what quantity and quality of public services the population may expect), Lane presents interesting remarks on the increase of regulatory boards and their activity. In his opinion, this derives from product regulation. He sees here *a paradox of reregulation* which can be closed in a simple phrase: "the more there is liberalisation, the more there will be regulation". This gives a field for interpretation that competition is not sufficient to ensure customers' satisfaction. Thus, after deregulation, reregulation may occur – an example of such an effect is in infrastructure sectors such as water – (Lane 2009, pp. 93–94). Continuing these considerations, let us delve into different regulatory approaches and their range.

## Regulatory approaches and their scope

Further deliberation on public regulation needs additional remarks. The literature on regulation provides herein a concept of "regulatory regimes". Harris and Milkis (1989, p. 25) present it as a constellation of three dimensions: "(1) new ideas justifying governmental control over business activity, (2) new institutions that structure regulatory politics, and (3) a new set of policies impinging on business". This definition helps Mark Thatcher to propose his characterisation of five regulatory regimes. He lists three middle regimes: "semi-liberalised public-service regimes", "mixed economy competition regimes", where several companies are still public owned, as well as "protected competition regimes", where reregulation suppresses or prevents competition. Apart from them, Thatcher (2002, pp. 869–870) finds two extreme situations: "the public ownership regime", where public monopolies and governments hold rule-making power and set them, as well as "private competition regime", where all suppliers are private (supply is liberalised) and where regulation is established to ensure fair and effective competition.

According to Thatcher, the middle three regimes have the following features. First, "semi-liberalised public-service regimes", are characterised by "a continuing direct public role in the supply of services, e.g. through public ownership/franchising, limited liberalization, reregulation to maintain public service, and little regulation to ensure 'fair and effective competition'", with a weak position or lack of independent regulatory agencies. Second, "mixed economy competition" is "partially publicly owned regimes in which partially publicly owned suppliers compete with private companies in a liberalized market; reregulation is concerned with ensuring 'fair and effective competition'" which, as Thatcher notes, is administered by strong independent regulatory agencies. Third, in "protected competition" liberalisation exists "in formal legal terms, but in practice reregulation (be it for industrial policy purposes and/or public service) prevents effective competition" (Thatcher 2002, pp. 869–870). These illustrate the role of the public element within liberalisation and the position of public entities engaged in conducting it.

For comparison, Tony Prosser (2010, p. 18), in his major study on regulation and its legitimacy, proposes four models of regulation: (a) "regulation for economic efficiency and consumer choice", (b) "regulation to protect rights", (c) "regulation for social solidarity", and (d) "regulation a deliberation". They are (a) aimed at opening markets and steering them when it is possible, or establishing conditions comparable to the market, (b) they protect essential rights and services, (c) they prevent negative effects of markets, as well as enable access to public services, and (d) their role is to set procedural measures for resolving problems with the use of dialogue and compromise (Prosser 2010, p. 18).

Recalled definitions emphasise the public nature of regulation. Furthermore, they show that it is a more complex term, based on several pillars. Barry Barton (2006, pp. 19–20) distinguishes eight of them (i–viii).[2] His remarks are very useful for a further analysis of public law regulation. That is why they are quoted here more broadly. Seen in that, regulation requires:

> i an objective or set of objectives [goals]: commonly this will appear in the statute constituting the agency and conferring its powers. Sometimes the legislature can state a single clear objective, and other times it confers a general mandate to act in the public interest. For example, utilities regulators may be expected to develop competitive markets, maintain security of supply, and pursue social and distributive goals.

In this sense, public regulation has to fulfil a specific goal of a publicly valid character. Tim Marshall (2012, p. 11) finds that in infrastructure industries regulation has to enable the provision of various services (transport, heat, water, waste disposal, electricity), realising the goals (impinge from associated state-policy fields) of low prices, wide-scale availability, and minimised environmental impacts. Jan-Erik Lane (2009, p. 92) notices that public regulation "aims at controlling certain parameters of the delivery of services and goods, such as price, quantity and quality". Pierce and Gellhorn classify three goals of regulation. First, is "economic efficiency" that consists of setting prices "at a low level based on costs which are prudently incurred". Second, is the obligation that "all users be served on an equal and nondiscriminatory basis". And, finally, regulation is designed to provide "minimum service reliability, honesty and fair dealing, informed choice and full disclosure of relevant information" (Pierce & Gellhorn 1994, p. 11). In Anthony I. Ogus' definition "regulation" is used to implement the system that he calls "collectivist" (1994, p. 2).

> ii power to make rules and standards: an agency usually has power to make rules that control the conduct of persons within its jurisdiction.

This may be linked with regulatory models which Barton presents. In particular, these are: the *rules-based regulation*, where the regulator provides a bundle of rules to set in detail what a regulated entity must and must not do, however there may be a notice-and-comment procedure on draft rules, and the *principle-based regulation*, which includes setting out the general principles for behaviour, with the legal standard that must be met, or the legal test for the conduct that must be avoided (Barton 2006, pp. 19–20). By setting standards a regulator establishes minimum (or other) requirements to follow (Pierce & Gellhorn 1994, pp. 13–14).

iii authorizations and permits: sometimes but not always an agency has discretionary power to grant authorizations, permits, or licenses to do something that would otherwise be prohibited by a statutory rule or by one of the agency's own rules. Occasional dispensations may only be incidental, but power to issue operating licenses subject to conditions may be central to the work of an electricity or natural gas regulator.

This corresponds with the *discretionary regulation*. In this model the regulator is authorised to approve certain activities, or to refuse them, or to allow them subject to conditions, sometimes executing this power on the basis of guidance with the objectives and interests that are to be pursued in the course of regulatory decision-making (Barton 2006, p. 20). Moreover, it may be linked with what Pierce and Gellhorn call the *public standard model* in which the regulator focuses not on product or service but on the regulated entity. By granting a licence, a regulator chooses among competing applicants the best qualified (Pierce & Gellhorn 1994, pp. 11–12).

iv procedure: an agency's procedure may be set by statute or it may have power to determine its own procedure for the different parts of its work. Procedure can vary widely, from in-house, to notice-and-comment procedures, through to formal hearings with all the trappings of a courtroom – and all the time and cost. Some procedures encourage deliberative interchange between parties instead of formal arm's length interaction.

Regulation has a legal orientation (Lane 2009, p. 92). Ogus (1994, p. 2) highlights its public character. "[I]t is *public* law in the sense that in general it is for the state (or its agents) to enforce obligations which cannot be overreached by private agreements between the parties occurred." Pierce and Gellhorn (1994, pp. 7, 10) link it with the judgement of regulators, and describe it as relied on for its enforcement on administrative agencies' decisions. In a similar manner the regulation is perceived by Baldwin, Scott, and Hood (1998, p. 3) who refer "to the promulgation of an authoritative set of rules, accompanied by some mechanism, typically a public agency, for monitoring and promoting compliance with these rules". In this respect, it correlates with next component of regulation provided by Barton.

v monitoring and surveillance: an agency may have systems in place for monitoring and surveillance of the behavior of regulated parties. In a power exchange or a stock exchange, this a complex and technical matter, but is necessary to detect misconduct, and to gather the information necessary to form judgments about effectiveness of the rules.

Ogus (1994, p. 2) writes:

> regulation contains the idea of control by a superior; it has a *directive* function. To achieve the desired ends, individuals are compelled by a superior authority – the state to behave in particular ways with a threat of sanctions if they do not comply.

Monitoring and surveillance may be considered the essence of the functions carried out by regulators. This duty of regulators is a good, pure example of their responsibilities and aims. Within them, *inter alia*, the following phases may be distinguished: establishing surveillance rules and allocating monitoring powers, collecting data, screening them to define possible abuses, as well as mitigating and sanctioning (see Glachant 2004, cited in de Hauteclocque & Perez 2012, p. 392). This links with the next feature of regulation, i.e. enforcement.

vi enforcement: an agency generally has authority to penalize misconduct. In enforcement options may be limited, or may include a wide range allowing it to respond to different misconduct with sustainable mildness of severity. Strong sanctions like prosecution or revocation of license are more difficult to use. In enforcement, agencies show widely varying practices and widely varying performance.

Richard Macrory (2008, p. 38) perceives regulatory enforcement "central to achieving compliance by signalling the threat of punishment for [those] that have offended". This "essential feature of a regulatory enforcement toolkit" enables a warning that "non-compliance will not be tolerated" and it will result in "a reprimand or consequence". Accordingly, the violator will be put in a worse position than those who complied with their regulatory obligations (Macrory 2008, p. 38). In this *legal process* model, regulation is viewed as an authoritative legal norm whose violation demands punishment. Beside it there is another way of addressing the enforcement of regulation, where it is treated more as a *social process* aimed at stimulating cooperative public–private problem-solving, which calls for remedial responses to violations (Coglianese & Kagan 2007, p. xvi).

vii accountability: provisions to keep an agency accountable can be very different. Some agencies have a judge-like independence and are able only in law by appeal or judicial review. Others are much more under the monitoring and direction of the central organs of government such a minister. In such cases, and the case of a minister who is the regulator, there is a dual accountability in law and in political terms.

The matter of accountability evokes an issue of *independence* of regulatory agency. Analysing this concept, Gilardi and Maggetti conduct a broad review of studies in this field. They note that independence requires the presence of two components: "self-determination", namely an ability to judge one's own interests and values, as well as "ownership of one's actions", i.e. the power to transform one's own interests and values preferences, into actions of an authoritative character, without external constraints. Further, Gilardi and Maggetti (2011, p. 202) establish a set of different aspects of agencies' independence, which they classify into two main categories: *formal* and de facto independence as well as their determinants.[3] Regarding the first, they distinguish independence in the field of "chairperson and management board" (e.g. term of office and its renewability, appointment, and dismissal procedure), "relationship with elected politicians" (e.g. regulators' formal obligations and overturning of their decisions), "finances and organization" (e.g. budgetary and human resources), and "regulatory competencies" (i.e. rule-making, monitoring, and sanctioning) (Gilardi & Maggetti 2011, p. 203). With regard to the latter, these authors include independence from "politicians" (*inter alia*, frequency of contacts, influence on budget, partisanship of nominations, or political vulnerability) and from "regulatees" (e.g. adequacy of budget and internal organisation as well as professional activity of regulator's chairperson/board members) (Gilardi & Maggetti 2011, p. 203).

This corresponds to models of regulatory policy-making process, linked with the regulators' position. In his work on public regulation William T. Gormley, Jr (1983, pp. 132–135) addresses four such models: "the capture model", "the interest group model", "the organizational model", and "the surrogate representation model". The *capture model* portrays regulatory agencies as subordinated to the industries they are supposed to regulate. Administrative decisions here are reactions to external pressure of the regulated industries. As a reason for this situation Gormley finds the independence of regulatory commissions and lack of political support. Regulatory commissions must reach an agreement with industries or be overwhelmed by litigation (Gormley 1983, pp. 133–134). On the other hand, in the *interest group model* competing groups exert pressure on the regulatory commissions. That is why administrative decisions are more balanced, resulting from the different interests and values (Gormley 1983, p. 34). Unlike the previous two models, which are based on external perspective, the *organizational model* uses an internal (inter-organisational) approach. In this view regulatory agencies are organisations that provide policy outputs in line with operating procedures or routines. The model emphasises the expertise of the agency, and stresses the primacy of specialisation within the administration (as opposed to commanded and centralised authority). Gormley (1983, pp. 134–135) underlines that this model "does not deny the presence of outside pressure but sees administrative expertise as a shield that reduces susceptibility to such pressure". Finally, the *surrogate representational model* also concerns government structure (mainly its officials). In this view, regulatory commissions are "the target of professional reformers (proxy advocates) who champion underrepresented interests from a government niche outside the regulatory agency" (Gormley 1983, p. 135).

viii an institution: for convenience, we can talk of an agency, but its name may be board, commission, or council. Or the regulator may be an appointed individual – it may be a minister of government who exercises the authority to regulate. Agencies differ in democratic authority, expertise, closeness to the regulated companies and independence.

Last, but not least, a mentioned *institution* and recalled in different contexts, *agency* is a necessary element of public law regulation. It is confirmed by findings concerning objectives, power to make rules and standards, authorisations and permits, procedure, monitoring and surveillance, enforcement, and accountability. An institutional core of regulation is also a key element of definitions of regulation (e.g. this is Prosser's (2010, p. 18) sense of regulation, where a range of institutions, which is counted as engaged in regulation, is its practical dimension). But the institution is not only important for this kind of approach of defining regulation. From a legal point of view, it constitutes this concept. In addition, perceived from other perspectives (economic, social), it is clearly visible that the notion of institution plays a similar role. Without an institution it is impossible to establish an effective public regulation. These show the institutionalisation of regulation.

## Institutionalisation and the tools of public law regulation

The institution is an important element of public law regulation. Properly placed within the legal system it makes it possible to realise the objectives established by the state. As that regulation is part of the public sphere, it is carried out using state administration bodies. With respect to these bodies (agencies) numerous divisions may also be made.

The diversity within the public structure was a subject of the OECD's report *Distributed Public Governance: Agencies, Authorities and other Government Bodies*. This set of bodies differs in size, function, rationale for creation, funding, legal and organisational forms, internal governance structure, accountability mechanisms, and relationships to the reporting ministry (OECD 2002, pp. 10–11). Their characteristics also vary widely. They can be created by the executive branch of government or by the legislature. They might function under public law, however private law also may be applicable (or both). Their staff may be considered as part of the civil service or come under general common employment law (OECD 2002, pp. 10–11). The scope of their names includes, *inter alia*, service agencies, public establishments, independent administrative authorities, federal agencies, bodies of public law, private law administration entities, independent administrative bodies, semi-autonomous bodies, autonomous bodies, public entities, public bodies, boards, independent agencies, regulatory independent commissions, or government corporations (OECD 2002, p. 11).

These bodies represent the national government, however they are not traditional, vertically integrated ministries. By definition, their public (governmental) character excludes from this category private companies and non-governmental organisations, as well as government companies under corporate governance, local government, and constitutional bodies (courts, audit bodies, etc.) (OECD 2002, p. 11). Their public nature is also confirmed by the regulatory tools with which they are equipped.

### *Institutional review with the regulatory characteristics*

Presented in the OECD's report (2002, pp. 17–19) regulatory bodies are gathered in three main groups: "Departmental agencies", "Public Law Administrations", and "Private Law Bodies". This was done with the use of their institutional and legal foundations, governance structure and control, financial, management, and personal rules, as well as function. On this basis, the OECD described departmental agencies as forms not separated from the state, a part of ministries without their own legal identity, which operate under public law. In general, their chief executive is appointed by the minister (who has a direct, but less formal control over agency). They are mostly funded from the state budget, some are partially user-fee financed; in terms of their function they usually deliver non-commercial services to citizens and support other public bodies (OECD 2002, pp. 17–18).

On the other hand, Public Law Administrations, are much more independent from ministries as well as their control (minister's indirect control). Regarding governance, they may have a governing board, an advisory board, or be under one-person-rule. As with departmental agencies, Public Law Administrations are financed from public funds. The OECD identifies three results that may be achieved (together or separately) with an establishment of Public Law Administrations: first, "a differentiated governance structure (governance board) – allowing more management autonomy or policy independence in some cases", second, "a differentiated control environment", and, third, "some managerial autonomy". What is worth noting is that Public Law Administrations are very broad, including action from service delivery to regulatory and quasi-judicial action (OECD 2002, p. 18).

Finally, Private Law Bodies are not companies, although they operate mostly under private law. In the field of independence, they are fully separate from the state (a governing board and the minister's indirect control). Usually Private Law Bodies are mostly sales revenue financed. With regards to their functions, they are mainly used where a service objective function requires a clear cost constraint (OECD 2002, p. 19).

In an analysis on bureaucracy and public choice Patric Dunleavy (1991, pp. 183–186) reviewed five main theoretically based agency types. These are: "delivery agencies", "transfer agencies", "contract agencies", "control agencies", and "regulatory agencies". Delivery agencies, which are classic line bureaucracies deriving from Weberian theory, are aimed at direct production of outputs and delivering services to citizens and enterprises. Transfer agencies operate governmental payments (e.g. in a form of subsidies) to individuals or companies. Contract agencies provide public procurement by setting terms for service of projects offered for private sector firms or commercially run public sector organisations (e.g. public corporations), and sign contracts with them afterwards. Control agencies transmit funds to other agencies in the public sector (e.g. in the form of grants) and supervise their spending as well as the implementation of policy by these other governmental bodies (Dunleavy 1991, pp. 183–186).

Lastly, according to Dunleavy (1991, p. 184), regulatory agencies "are to limit or control the behaviour of individuals, enterprises or other bodies using licensing systems, reporting controls, performance standards or some similar systems".

Further, Geert Bouckaert and Guy B. Peters (2004, p. 22), in their study on autonomous agencies (which they define as "more or less autonomous organizations [created by governments] to implement programs"), present different categories of activities and functions performed by them. As Bouckaert and Peters show a broader background of this matter, herein they are quoted more extensively. In this context they identify: implementation,[4] direct service delivery,[5] transfer of funds,[6] advice and policy development,[7] information,[8] research,[9] tribunal and public enquiries,[10] representation,[11] and "regulation" (Bouckaert & Peters 2004, pp. 39–40). The latter, apart from monitoring and control, covers areas included within other activities and functions outlined above. National regulatory authorities may be involved in implementing public policy (with the use of administrative decisions or guidelines), provide their expertise to government, collect information, as well as perform quasi-judicial functions.

Moreover, regulation, as a function of autonomous organisations, is correlated with one of the most crucial postulates of modern regulations, which is the already mentioned regulators' independence (Gilardi & Maggetti 2011, pp. 202–203). At this point, in view of its importance, this notion needs additional clarification. Bouckaert and Peters emphasise that regulators that are qualified as autonomous

> can be isolated from immediate, partisan political pressures, while simultaneously involving the interests affected by regulations in the process of making those regulations. This presumed strength may also be a weakness, given that the isolation from direct political control also isolates them from direct political support.
>
> (Bouckaert & Peters 2004, pp. 39–40)

Further, the cited authors see "a problem of ensuring that the organization remains faithful to the original policy directives coming from the legislature". Another aspect of this problem is adopting its own standards by the autonomous regulatory organisations (which are not in a line with those passed by the legislature). That is why Bouckaert and Peters (2004, pp. 39–40) call for balancing autonomy with some goals for which autonomous regulatory organisations were established. In this context, Paul G. Roness (2007, p. 69) rightly recalls that in 1995, the OECD initiated a programme of regulatory reforms of which key elements were: the regulation of the market, competition policy, and the establishment of independent regulatory agencies. The OECD has encouraged its member states to introduce regulatory policy. With the use of fostering competition, efficiency, and performance it has to result in the improvement of regulatory quality. As Roness (2007, p. 69) underlines "[t]he doctrine is to have regulatory agencies that are independent of the ministry, operate according to a clear regulatory policy and are staffed by experts".

The rationale for regulatory agencies is clearly addressed by Robert Baldwin and Christopher McCrudden in their study on regulation and public law. One of the reasons for the creation of these bodies is to take some workload off the more traditional branches of the government. Another is the need for expertise in such substantive matters as economy combined with new and increasingly complex forms of technology (administrative agencies are seen as experts in these fields) (Baldwin & McCrudden 1987, pp. 4–5). Agencies may enable public participation in the making of the decision. Agencies' separateness from the government linked with collegial decision-making gives various interest groups a place in government policy-making. Further, independence from changes in government means agencies ensure continuity and stability in policy-making and implementation. In addition, in dealing with controversial decisions, an agency may be used by the government as an "insulator". It takes the responsibility from the government and gives it extra time to find an alternative solution (Baldwin & McCrudden 1987, pp. 5–7).

However, these findings do not close the list of agencies' advantages offered by Baldwin and McCrudden. Among other benefits of establishing regulatory agencies there are:

> [e]conomy, speed in decision making process, ability to adapt quickly to changing conditions, and freedom from technicality in procedures... [ability] to relax the formal rules of evidence when appropriate, to avoid an over-reliance on adversarial techniques, and to avoid strict adherence on their own precedents. [Additionally] ... agencies are thought not to be as restricted to formulating policy on a case-by case basis as are the courts.
>
> (Baldwin & McCrudden 1987, p. 5)

The institutionalisation of regulation falls within a broader notion of public regulation, "which takes in all the efforts of state agencies to steer the economy" (Baldwin, Scott, & Hood 1998, p. 3). It combines both rule-making and its application through enforcement systems. It links also a wide range of public instruments based on public authority. However, as Baldwin, Scott, and Hood (1998, pp. 3–4) classify, a so-conceived regulation's disadvantage is the fact that it potentially takes in all instruments directed towards achieving certain policy goals. This makes it difficult to define this concept while setting its clear borders. Nevertheless, among these instruments there might be certain tools directly related to regulators and regulatory goals. Furthermore, regulators use an increasing number of different types of tools, and they move away from a traditional approach, in which not only binding instructions or decisions issued by the regulators can be observed. It underlines the need for compiling the tools of regulation.

### *Catalogue of regulatory tools*

To realise public interest and implement policy, the regulatory authorities are equipped with the specific *tools of regulation*. Naturally, in different legal systems their range, power, impact, applicability, appealing, etc. vary. However, by referring to some common features it is possible to provide their categorisation by highlighting several key groups of regulatory instruments. For instance, the authors of an extensive study on administration law and regulatory policy offer the following types of regulatory tools: cost-of-service rate-making, allocation in accordance with a public interest standard, "standard-setting, historically based price-settings or allocation, screening or licensing, fees or taxes, provision of information, subsidies, and no-coercive efforts (Breyer *et al.* 2002, p. 13). Cary Coglianese and Robert A. Kagan, by reviewing works of Daintith (2005), Ogus (1994, 1995), Breyer (1982), Yeung (2005), and Brownsword (2005), outline five classes of regulatory instruments. They are based on: "command" (commitment to specific conduct supported by the law of coercive sanction in case of violation), "competition" (the use of competitive forces resulting from the rivalry between competing units as a means of regulation; it covers charges, taxes, subsidies, tradable emission/property rights, or changes in liability rules), "consensus" (regulatory goals are achieved by private–public consent and cooperation that may be strengthened by legal agreement), "communication" (providing the information to enable making choices in line with regulatory objectives), and "codes" (they seek to design out the possibility for occurrence of the desirable behaviour instead of eliminating the undesirable approach) (Coglianese and Kagan 2007, pp. 80–105).

While a variety of classifications of the regulatory tools have been suggested, Arie Freiberg (2010, pp. 84–85) in his work *The Tools of Regulation* clearly determines six practical groups of instruments which the government can use for the needs of conducting its policy goals. These are: economic tools ("which involves the manipulation of the property, allocation or use of material resources such as money or property in all forms"; here he finds, *inter alia*, tenders, tradable permits and "cap and trade" schemes, price regulation, taxes, charges and levies, or bounties and subsidies), transactional regulation (based on the form of the tool – contract, procurement, grant), authorisation as regulation (Freiberg sees it as "[t]he exclusive power that governments have to confer by authorising or permitting certain forms of conduct"; e.g. licensing, registration, permission, certification, accreditation, litigation), structural regulation (the ability to influence on physical environment, e.g. with a use of physical, environmental, and process design), informational regulation (relates to access to knowledge and information; Freiberg lists herein disclosure, performance indicators, or credit ratings), and legal regulation (primary law, delegated law, quasi-legislation soft law). This last one, as he defines, is "the ability to invoke mechanisms of the legal apparatus for the purpose of applying other … tools … through a legitimated authority" (Freiberg 2010, p. 84).

Furthermore, Freiberg demonstrates in a very clear way how important role, with respect to other regulatory tools, is played by law:

> [i]n relation to economic regulation, [law] creates the rules that constitute markets; establishes agencies that can set prices or terms and conditions of

> trade; can authorise and impose taxes, levies, charges, bounties and subsidies; and it creates markets for where none previously existed (for example, the national electricity market). In relation to governmental transactions with the private and NGO sector, it can create binding rules that guide expenditures in the form of contracts or grants, and can establish guidelines for their use. Law establishes or recognises many forms of authorisation: licences, certificates, permits, accreditation systems and registration mechanisms that in turn can allow or prohibit action. It can be delegated to many state and non-state agencies, and these delegations can be given or withdrawn. Law can influence how technology is used and how the physical environment is built. Finally, and traditionally, law can provide the ultimate sanction when private systems fail.
>
> (Freiberg 2010, p. 84)

The quoted reasoning shows the complex nature of the law, which in all forms transcends the casual command and control scheme, reaching the shape and influence approach. As a result, the law becomes "a conduit, as well as a means of regulation in itself" (Freiberg 2010, p. 84). These circumstances underline the legal nature of public regulation. In this view, perceived through the prism of law, it is possible to discourse about public law regulation.

The point of this book is to analyse the electricity sector and public law regulation of the European Union within it. Earlier sections enabled provision of the theoretical considerations related to market-based and state-based approaches, liberalisation, and public regulation. The next one summarises current considerations and introduces the following, more practical chapters of this work linked with the EU's legislation on the electricity sector that was adopted in the form of legislative packages.

## Public regulation in the EU's electricity sector

Deliberation on energy regulation may be conducted in different contexts: social, economic, political, as well as legal. However, apart from common technical properties, energy regulation is based on institutional features (Fickel 2007). Because of the deep and broad character of this issue and limited nature of this book, the general remarks on regulation must finish here. Instead, in the next chapters the approach of the European Union to electricity and public law regulation within is provided. This section, acts as a link between Parts I and II, and enables us to establish concluding and introductory remarks.

Institutional market players are hard evidence that the state expresses its interest in the energy market. The state's presence in the electricity sector is inevitable. This sector is classified as strategic and sensitive for every economy. What changes is the legal form of that presence. As the postulates of *liberalisation* were introduced in the European agenda one may find that it assumes the total withdrawal of public influence from electricity (*laissez-faire*). This is in complete opposition to the state-based approach which has its roots in theories originating from *mercantilism* and other related forms (*interventionism*), and may provide a more intensive way of steering energy, which could derive from the strategic character of the sector. This was a rationale of approach to the sector before the very first liberalisation movement in the 1980s.

Although, beliefs in individualism, free and open market, even in liberalisation and a market-based approach has limits. Public force does not disappear just because of liberalisation. Liberalisation, especially conducted within the European Union, has different shapes which find a concrete sphere for public (European or national) activity. Thereby, the European Union's liberalisation cannot be simply linked with eliminating public influence.

Thus, market liberalisation (apart from far-reaching libertarianism), as presented in previous chapters, does not assume full, unlimited freedom of the market and the disappearance of the public sphere, with its laws and institutions. Further, liberalisation in European electricity, illustrated by the competitive energy market, links elements of public influence (with the use of public law regulation) with the private, market concept. However, it is steered and shaped under the provisions of European Energy Packages (public law). The EU's attitude to the electricity sector finds it necessary to create market conditions in the electricity sector through the use of public impact, although, the space for it is limited by the precondition of *market liberalisation*.

### *Public regulation as a balanced form of the state's impact on the sector: day-watchman state model*

In discussion of regulation in the energy sector with the use of public law regulation, on the basis of recalled notions on regulation, keeping in mind Barton's (2006, p. 11) remark about "no single understanding of the term" (the concept is not homogeneous), I propose to distinguish two other clarifications for the narrow and the broad sense of regulation. As regulation *sensu stricte*, I qualify the activity of national regulatory authorities conducted on the basis of public law.[12] Thus, in a narrow sense, *regulation is regulator*. In this view, the regulator is established to "protect the public interest because the market cannot" (Dugger 1989, p. 32), as well as to provide a substitute for competition (see Ogus 1994, p. 5), or, wherever possible *provide competition*, or steer market actions towards it. However, these cover goals of regulation, to which I refer in the context of the EU's public law regulation within the electricity sector.

On the other hand I perceive a broad sense of regulation as *any public mechanism of control and influence*. As it is public regulation it has to be conducted *by the state*, however in the EU it gains a broader meaning (in addition to the obligations of Member States, duties and powers of the EU's authorities emerge). Further, using the rationality principle I find it *intentional*.[13] It may include *market forces*, *social forces* and *technologies*, as well as *law* (see Barton 2006, p. 12). Law is the basis for it, as well as a concretisation of specific regulatory measures (e.g. sanctions). Moreover, distinguished by doctrine other meanings of extreme points (narrow, and broad as well) are useful for explaining the legal background of both approaches, which I now propose. Like a buckle they make it possible to include public law within my categories. Thereby, in both of them, regulation *sensu stricte* and *sensu largo* is conducted on the basis of "a set of rules promulgated under statute" (see Barton 2006, p. 12; Prosser 2010, p. 1). This grants public regulation its legal character.

These circumstances establish the grounds for public law regulation as a balanced legal form of a state's impact on the energy market. Public law regulation has a central place. We can distinguish two extreme points: total subordination and total release. In my opinion public law regulation is between them (see Sappington & Stiglitz 1987, pp. 3–4). Regulation is therefore a way in which state controls (monitors) the actions of market players. It is aimed at achieving public policy goals. In this regard, state may enforce them by imposing restrictions for non-compliance.

A necessary element of public law regulation is an institution – the authority that performs the regulatory functions. Besides the fact that it is a key element in many definitions of regulation, it has a practical dimension. It is the regulator that has its objectives, in many cases power to make rules and standards, can grant permits, monitors market behaviour, or impose sanctions. Thereby, the regulatory authority is a materialisation of public law regulation. By being an entity that conducts it, it constitutes this concept.

This practical side of regulation is confirmed by the tasks performed by regulators. The energy market regulator, with its competence in the field of promoting and enforcing orders and regulations, seems to be a clear example of this relation. The authors of a study on the EU wholesale energy markets compare the market regulator to a "watchdog" ensuring access ("effective and non-discriminatory") to transmission and distribution networks (Rademaekers, Slingenberg, & Morsy 2008).[14] Apart from this, regulators generally set tariffs and have "other tasks which relate to the efficient functioning of the market and ensuring competition, as well as the protection of consumer interests" (Rademaekers, Slingenberg, & Morsy 2008).

In a liberalised market, the existence of independent regulatory agencies is not excluded, as is proved by classic liberal philosophy. In the European legal system the energy (electricity) regulator is not just a night-watchman, limiting its activity to very few actions, treated as measures of last resort. Naturally, different regulatory approaches may also be distinguished within the electricity sector, influencing its practical dimension;[15] the EU has addressed this issue clearly. Moreover, in its way towards the internal energy market the European Union has chosen a "regulatory path". It is grounded in liberalisation, with enhanced competition and sustainability. This approach assumes establishing a regulatory framework, with independent regulatory institutions in each Member State. As proven, liberalisation finds a place for the watchman. Although, in the European legal situation this watchman-energy regulator takes the shape of a *day-watchman* linking two spheres of concepts for the economy, and the energy sector, as its part. Different trends (approaches) in European regulation, the private (regulation for competition) and the public ones (regulation for environment, climate, and energy security) confirm the status of regulation and regulator as a centrist option. Regulation fills a space between their linkage.

The *day-watchman state* model derives from the institution of the market regulator. The state plays an active role within the economy, and its strategic sectors like the energy sector. In its assumptions the day-watchman state is neither an active participant in the market, nor resigned from its participation: it takes a dualistic role. The *day-watchman* is a vigilant observer – an active observer (although not an "active participant") and becomes the market regulator (Sokołowski 2013, p. 318). The *day-watchman* creates the rules of the market game and informs all the market players, as well as ensures enforcement of them (with a use of sanctions). Furthermore, the premise of this concept is to balance the public and the private interest (Sokołowski 2013, p. 318).

Within this scope, the regulator should have full knowledge of the market and its conditions in terms of protected values and pursued objectives (Jaroszyński & Wierzbowski 2011, p. 323). Wherever necessary the regulator applies different regulatory tools established by the state for the needs of policy goals that have to be achieved by the use of regulation. These may be price regulation, licensing, registration, permission, certification, accreditation, or litigation, standardisation as well as other instruments which may be linked with controlling, monitoring mechanism, or enforcing. Naturally, this is combined with enhancing the regulator's position together with granting him independence.

### Package-way of implementing the public regulatory model

In terms of realising these assumptions, in the European Union's legal practice shaping the energy sector (that provides establishment of the rules for public regulation), the form of legislative packages – sets of interdependent or related European legal acts viewed or organised as a unit – has been used. Packages cover a broad range of public law regulation. They have established legal institutions that are crucial for reaching the European market reform's aims. This concerns establishing third party access or unbundling, as well as national regulators, enhancing their positions by granting them certain responsibilities and powers successively.

For the needs of the electricity sector, the concrete rules were adopted within the packages. They were included in the framework dedicated to Electricity Directives. This is confirmed by specific provisions of these acts. As expressed in the preamble of Directive 96/92/EC "the internal market in electricity needs to be established gradually". Thus, the market with competition ("a free market") will not exist automatically. It is a part of a bigger whole, which involves the gradual moving towards a free market mechanism. Moreover, such an approach was adopted to "enable the industry to adjust in a flexible and ordered manner to its new environment and to take account of the different ways in which electricity systems are organized at present". Thereby, the road to the common energy market, right from the beginning, assumed the continuous presence of state regulatory mechanisms, giving a place for competitive mechanisms in a stepwise manner (as liberalisation does not exclude the presence of public powers).

This "step-by-step" rule was repeated in other strategic EU documents. For example, in June 2000, the European Parliament urged the European Commission "to adopt a detailed timetable for the achievement of accurately defined objectives with a view to gradually but completely [liberalise] the energy markets". Despite the adoption of Directive 2003/54/EC that has made a significant contribution towards the creation of an electricity internal market, the EU more often expressed its concern about the level of its openness, liberalisation, or general functioning, and completion. Even complete liberalisation finds a place for public law regulation. Not only has this applied to the transitional period in which public law (in the broad and narrow sense) has been the means of attaining the Union's energy market objectives, but it also remains current in the next phase of this road towards the internal energy market.

Thereby, a market challenge in electricity has not been left alone. Competition in the energy sector has not materialised by itself. The force that has to drive it has been the EU and its institutions, with the influence on public law with the use of a set of interdependent and related legal acts organised in a form of Energy Packages as well as Climate and Energy. Obviously, it has been the Member States that had to implement the European solutions provided by EU law. Implement, and naturally assure their effective realisation. However, this simple approach is limited only to formal matter of the transposition of European law into national legislation. The more important question is to what extent, as a result of the implementation of the European Energy Packages liberalising the electricity market in the European Union, can Member States influence the energy sector? This mainly concerns the position of the state and its authorities in, as well as to, the liberalised electricity market within the EU. As Baldwin, Scott, and Hood (1998, p. 2) observe "[a]ccompanying [the] increased emphasis on regulation at [the] national level has come a parallel growth in supranational regulation – raising questions about how far regional and global markets can be steered by regulatory institutions above the level of the state".

In the European Union this issue correlates with the provision of legislative packages that strengthen the position of the national regulatory authorities (with respect to their independence from Member States), what may be linked with growth of their dependence to the European Union and its bodies. In the field of energy sector this is the Agency for the Cooperation of Energy Regulators. Moreover, the newest package, the Third Energy Package, harmonises the legal status of national regulators. Their position, duties, and powers are being unified. This demonstrates the progressive *Europeanisation* of legal regulation in the energy sector (see Watkin 1998; Snyder 2000; Jans, Prechal, & Widdershoven 2007; Walaszek-Pyzioł 2011; Szafrański 2011; Będkowski-Kozioł 2011). Its further institutionalisation remains an open question. Moreover, the

European Union legislative packages dedicated to electricity (Liberalisation Packages as well as Climate and Energy Package) has influenced the national (Member States) field of action by setting public regulation law chosen by European Union direction.

The listed considerations, arising from efforts to liberalise the European energy market, influence the scope of public law regulation at the national level. This implies the need to prove them with the use of concrete examples deriving from European law. As already mentioned the European Union applies herein a complex approach taking the form of legislative packages. In these terms, the EU's three legal acts are of particular importance, i.e. Electricity Directives. Their primary role in the process of establishing the EU's internal energy market makes it necessary to examine them in greater detail. This is complemented by the analysis of the strategic European documents influencing directly or indirectly the law-making process (namely COM documents, policy, and working papers developed by the EU and international organisations).

Seen in this light, let us move on to the next chapters concerning European Union legislation on the internal energy market (i.e. three steps of market reform: the First, the Second, and the Third Energy Package) and their influence on the scope of public law regulation in the electricity sector of the EU. As the EU sets public law regulation on a specific direction this needs additional remarks concerning these trends. The quantification of the European approach to regulation provided in the last Part of the book allows for clarification of these issues.

## Notes

1 Prosser lists some useful background for it. These are works on the legal theory of autopoiesis by Gunther Teubner (1993), governmental theories originating from Foucault (Weir, O'Malley, & Shearing 1997), and responsive regulation which he links with work of Ayres and Braithwaite (1995).

2 Order changed.

3 Listed in parentheses.

4

> The major activity of autonomous organizations in all the cases for which we have evidence is implementing public policy. The emphasis on implementation activities reflects the intentions of governments when creating agencies.... Of course... there is also policy making that goes along with the implementation. That is, first implementation is itself often making policy de facto as decisions are made about which cases meet criteria and which do not. In addition, administrative agencies are often empowered to make policies that ramify the more broadly construed policies adopted by legislatures.... Even when the agencies are designed as implementation structures their close connection to the reality of service delivery means that they may well be involved in making secondary legislation.
>
> (Bouckaert & Peters 2004, p. 38)

5

> [It is] the usual understanding of implementation through agencies.... This service-delivery role for agencies is especially evident for education, as the nominal independence of these organizations can be maintained even when they

> are funded by the State.... Also, increasingly hospitals are being organized as quasi-autonomous organizations in part to impose some market discipline on their activities, but also to provide somewhat greater autonomy from direct control by government, and with that also some capacity of politicians to insulate themselves for too direct culpability when there are problems in the health care sector, as there almost invariably are in such a complex and expensive service.
>
> (Bouckaert & Peters 2004, p. 38)

6

> [It] can be observed frequently in implementing social policy and in intergovernmental relations. A separate entity may be created to make decisions about grants and contracts as a means of insulating these decisions from direct political control. For example, the rate support grant for local governments, and the support grants for universities, are managed through quasi-autonomous organizations.... Again, this style of service delivery permits service providers to make many other decisions about the actual use of the funds, and also to match better services with local conditions.
>
> (Bouckaert & Peters 2004, p. 38)

7

> Another of the principal purposes of semi-autonomous organizations is to offer advice to government, and to provide assistance in policy development. Organizations performing this function involve a variety of experts in society in making decisions, and exist in a variety of political relationships to the government of the day. These organizations are designed to help government pursue long-range goals for the society as a whole. Of course, there is a great deal of partisan policy advice being offered within ministries and to the government as a whole, but the idea of these more autonomous advisory organizations is to create more unbiased positions on major policy issues. These organizations must find some means of balancing conflicting policy advice.
>
> (Bouckaert & Peters 2004, p. 40)

8

> [S]ome autonomous and semi-autonomous organizations are also involved in the collection and dissemination of information.... These organizations, to some extent, fall between ... policy advice ... [and] research. They are involved in doing research and in collecting research conducted by others. These organizations are also involved in advising government with the statistical information that they gather.
>
> (Bouckaert & Peters 2004, p. 41)

9 "Governments also frequently attempt to place some distance between themselves and scientific research organizations, and to provide those organizations with as much latitude as possible to make autonomous decisions about what to research and how to do that research" (Bouckaert & Peters 2004, p. 41).

10

> There are also a number of public organizations serving in a quasi-judicial function, assessing the legality of actions within specific policy areas or investigating major policy questions. In almost all countries, the level of adjudication required for a modern welfare state to deal fairly with its citizens is of such a magnitude that it could never be carried on in the regular court system. Therefore, an array of quasi-judicial organizations are created to cope with the problem of deciding about the appropriate application of laws concerning social benefits, taxes, labor markets, and the rest of the array of government programs.
>
> (Bouckaert & Peters 2004, p. 42)

11

> [A]utonomous and semi-autonomous organizations are employed as a means of providing representational and participatory opportunities for segments of the civil society. These organizations supplement the representation provided through conventional political institutions and tend to focus on particular segments of society.
>
> (Bouckaert & Peters 2004, p. 43)

12 A similar approach is offered by Marshall (2012, p. 29): "For the moment, when I refer to regulation I take the normal usage in this field, meaning the post-privatisation bodies created to manage the new industry structures and behaviours".

13 "Rationality Principle: All political behavior has a purpose". See Lowi *et al.* 2013, pp. 7–9.

14 Gormley (1983, p. 35) illustrates it providing the energy cause-and-effect sequence: "[i]f regulators allow rates to increase dramatically, they impose a terrible burden on lower-class and middle-class consumers; if they resist rate hike request, they run the risk of power failures, bankruptcies, or both".

15 For instance, William W. Hogan (2009) presents disputes on the regulation model to address immediate market failures and the challenge of improving electricity market design. He offers two approaches: "little 'r' regulation" and "big 'R' regulation". In the first, to support competitive wholesale electricity markets, Hogan finds design rules and policies as the "best mixture". Its main requirement is "to relate any proposed solution to the larger framework and to ask for alternatives that better support or are complementary to the market design". He warns that a lot of ostensibly harmless decisions occur in isolation. However their more thorough analysis shows inconsistency with the whole frame. On the other hand the "big 'R' regulation" consists of individual solutions to tackle each problem with designed ad hoc regulatory fixes. Although, according to Hogan, "[t]his creates a slippery slope problem, where one ad hoc solution creates another problem, and regulators are driven more and more to intervene in ever more ad hoc ways".

## References


Ayres, I. & Braithwaite, J. 1995, *Responsive regulation: transcending the deregulation debate*, Oxford University Press, Oxford.

Baldwin, R. & McCrudden, C. 1987, *Regulation and public law*, Weidenfeld & Nicolson, London.

Baldwin, R., Scott, C., & Hood, C. 1998, *A reader on regulation*. Oxford University Press, Oxford.

Barton, B. 2006, "The theoretical context of regulation", in *Regulating energy and natural resources*, eds B. Barton, A. Lucas, L. Barrera-Hernández, & A. Rønne, Oxford University Press, Oxford, pp. 3–10.

Będkowski-Kozioł, M. 2011, "Kilka uwag o europeizacji nadzoru regulacyjnego w sektorze energetycznym w świetle trzeciego pakietu liberalizacyjnego UE" [Some remarks on the Europeanisation of regulatory supervision in the energy sector in the light of the EU's Third Liberalisation Package], in *Europeizacja Publicznego Prawa Gospodarczego* [Europeanisation of Public Economic Law], eds H. Gronkiewicz-Waltz & K. Jaroszyński, C.H. Beck, Warsaw, pp. 15–22.

Black, J. 2002, *Critical reflections on regulation*. Available from: http://eprints.lse.ac.uk/35985/1/Disspaper4-1.pdf [23 June 2015].

Bouckaert, G. & Peters, G.B. 2004, "What is available and what is missing in the study of quangos", in *Unbundled government: a critical analysis of the global trend to agencies, quangos and contractualisation*, eds C. Pollitt & C. Talbot, Routledge, London, pp. 22–50.

Breyer, S.G. 1982, *Regulation and its reform*, Harvard University Press, Cambridge, MA.
Breyer, S.G., Stewart, R.B., Sunstein, C.R., & Vermeule, A. (eds) 2002, *Administrative law and regulatory policy: problems, text, and cases*, Aspen Law & Business, New York.
Brownsword, R. 2005, "Code, control and choice: why East is East and West is West", *Legal Studies*, 25(1), pp. 1–21.
Coglianese, C. & Kagan, R.A. (eds) 2007, "Introduction", in *Regulation and regulatory processes*, Ashgate, Aldershot, pp. xi–xxxvii.
Daintith, T. 2004, "The techniques of government", in *The changing constitution*, eds J. Jowell & D. Oliver, 5th edn, Oxford University Press, Oxford, pp. 209–236.
de Hauteclocque, A. & Perez, Y. 2012, "Electricity regulation", in *Regulation and economics*, eds R.J. van den Bergh & A.M. Paccess, vol. 9 of *Encyclopedia of law and economics*, 2nd edn, Edward Elgar, Cheltenham, pp. 377–405.
Doern, G.B. & Gattinger, M. 2003, *Power switch: energy regulatory governance in the twenty-first century*, University of Toronto Press, Toronto.
Doern, G.B., Schultz, R.J., Hill, M.M., & Prince, M.J. 1999, *Changing the rules: Canadian regulatory regimes and institutions*, University of Toronto Press, Toronto.
Dugger, W.M. 1989, Commentary to Nowotny K., "The economics of public utility regulation: an overview", in *Public utility regulation*, eds K. Nowotny, D.B. Smith, & H.M. Trebing, Kluwer Academic Publisher, Boston, MA, pp. 28–24.
Dunleavy, P. 1991, *Democracy, bureaucracy and public choice: economic explanations in political science*, Harvester Wheatsheaf, Hemel Hempstead.
European Parliament Resolution of 6 June 2000 on the Commission's second report to the Council and the European Parliament on the state of liberalisation of energy markets, OJ C 121, 24 April 2001.
Fickel, H. 2007, "IREN: International Energy Regulation Network", presentation, Madrid, 20 June 2007. Available from: www.ariae.org/download/ [13 June 2015].
Freiberg, A. 2010, *The tools of regulation*, Federation Press, Sydney.
Gattinger, M. 2009, "Multi-level energy regulatory governance in the Canadian federation: institutions, regimes, and coordination", in *Governing the energy challenge: Canada and Germany in a multi-level regional and global context*, eds B. Eberlein & G.B. Doern, University of Toronto Press, Toronto, pp. 201–225.
Gilardi, F. & Maggetti, M. 2011, "The independence of regulatory authorities", in *Handbook on the politics of regulation*, ed. D. Levi-Faur, Edward Elgar, Cheltenham, pp. 201–214.
Glachant, J.-M. 2004, *Etude comparative des pratiques de surveillance des marchés électriques étrangers: rapport pour la Commission de Régulation de l'Énergie 2004* [Comparative study of supervisory practices of foreign electricity markets: report of the Regulatory Commission of Energy 2004].
Gormley, Jr W.T. 1983. *The politics of public utility regulation*, University of Pittsburgh Press, Pittsburgh, PA.
Harris, R.A. & Milkis, S.M. 1989, *The politics of regulatory change*, Oxford University Press, Oxford.
Hogan, W.W. 2009, "Regulation and electricity markets", presentation, *Western Power Trading Forum*, New York, 16 April 2009. Available from: www.whogan.com/ [23 June 2015].
Jans, J.H., Prechal, A., & Widdershoven, R.J.G.M. 2007, *Europeanisation of public law*, Europa Law Publishing, Groningen.
Jaroszyński, K. & Wierzbowski, M. 2011, "Organy regulacyjne" [Regulatory authorities], chap. 4 in *Podmioty administrujące* [Administering entities], eds R. Hauser, A. Wróbel, & Z. Niewiadomski, vol. 6 of *System prawa administracyjnego* [System of administrative law], C.H. Beck, Warsaw, pp. 229–354.

Lane, J.-E. 2009, *State management: an enquiry into models of public administration and management*, Routledge, Abingdon.

Lowi, T.J., Ginsberg, B., Shepsle, K.A., & Ansolabehere, S. 2013, *American government: power and purpose*, 12th edn, W.W. Norton, New York.

Macrory, R. 2008. *Regulation, enforcement and governance of environmental law*, Cameron May, London.

Marshall, T. 2012. *Planning major infrastructure: a critical analysis*, Routledge, Abingdon.

Morgan, B. & Yeung, K. 2007, *An introduction to law and regulation: text and materials*, Cambridge University Press, Cambridge.

OECD 2002, *Distributed public governance: agencies, authorities and other government bodies*, OECD Publishing, Paris.

Ogus, A.I. 1994, *Regulation: legal form and economic theory*, Oxford University Press, Oxford.

Ogus, A.I. 1995, "Rethinking self-regulation", *Oxford Journal of Legal Studies*, 15(1), pp. 97–108.

Pierce, Jr R.J. & Gellhorn, E. 1994, *Regulated industries in a nutshell*, West Publishing, St. Paul, MN.

Prosser, T. 1997, *Law and regulation*, Clarendon Press, Oxford.

Prosser, T. 2010, *The regulatory enterprise: government, regulation, and legitimacy*, Oxford University Press, Oxford.

Rademaekers, K., Slingenberg, A., & Morsy, S. 2008, *Review and analysis of EU wholesale energy markets: historical and current data analysis of EU wholesale electricity, gas and CO2 markets*, ECORYS Nederland BV, Rotterdam. Available from: http://ec.europa.eu/energy/gas_electricity/studies/doc/2008_eu_wholesale_energy_market_historical.pdf [17 June 2015].

Roness, P.G. 2007, "Types of state organizations: arguments, doctrines and changes beyond new public management", in *Transcending new public management: the transformation of public sector reforms*, eds T. Christensen & P. Lægreid, Ashgate Publishing, Aldershot, pp. 65–88.

Sappington, D.E.M. & Stiglitz, J.E. 1987, "Information and regulation", in *Public regulation: new perspectives on institution and policies*, ed. E.E. Bailey, MIT Press, Cambridge, MA, pp. 3–43.

Selznick, P. 1985, "Focusing organizational research on regulation", in *Regulatory policy and the social science*, ed. R. Noll, University of California Press, Berkeley, CA, pp. 363–367.

Sikor, T., Barlösius, E., & Scheumann, W. 2008, "Introduction", in *Public and private in natural resource governance: a false dichotomy?* ed. T. Sikor, Earthscan, London, pp. 1–20.

Snyder, F.G. 2000, *The europeanisation of law: the legal effects of European integration*, Hart Publishing, Oxford and Portland, OR.

Sokołowski, M.M. 2013, "Rozważania o istocie współczesnej regulacji" [Considerations on the essence of modern regulation], in *Regulacja: innowacja w sektorze energetycznym* [Regulation: innovation in the energy sector], ed. A. Walaszek-Pyzioł, C.H. Beck, Warsaw, pp. 309–329.

Stankiewicz, R. 2010, "Kilka uwag o regulacji jako funkcji administracji gospodarczej w rozwoju sektora energetycznego" [Few remarks on regulation as the function of the economic administration in the development of the energy sector], in *Współczesne problemy prawa energetycznego* [Contemporary issues of energy law], eds M. Wierzbowski & R. Stankiewicz, LexisNexis, Warsaw, pp. 104–123.

Stone, A. 1982. *Regulation and its alternatives*, Congressional Quarterly Press, Washington, DC.

Szafrański, A. 2011, "Europeizacja prawa energetycznego" [The Europeanisation of energy law], in *Europeizacja publicznego prawa gospodarczego* [Europeanisation of public economic law], eds H. Gronkiewicz-Waltz & K. Jaroszyński, C.H. Beck, Warsaw, pp. 535–546.

Szydło, M. 2005, *Regulacja sektorów infrastrukturalnych jako rodzaj funkcji państwa wobec gospodarki* [Regulation of the infrastructure sectors as a type of state's functions within the economy], Prawo i Praktyka Gospodarcza, Warsaw.

Teubner, G. 1993, *Law as an autopoietic system*, Blackwell, Oxford.

Thatcher, M. 2002, "Analysing regulatory reform in Europe", *Journal of European Public Policy*, 9(6), pp. 859–872. Available from: www.tandfonline.com/doi/pdf/10.1080/13501760220000046391 [21 June 2015].

Walaszek-Pyzioł, A. 2011, "Europejska Agencja ds. Współpracy Organów Regulacji Energetyki: nowy wymiar europeizacji prawa energetycznego" [The European Agency for the Cooperation of Energy Regulators: the new dimension of the Europeanisation of energy law], in *Europeizacja publicznego prawa gospodarczego* [Europeanisation of public economic law], eds H. Gronkiewicz-Waltz & K. Jaroszyński, C.H. Beck, Warsaw, pp. 557–564.

Watkin, T.G. 1998, *The Europeanisation of law*, UKNCCL, London.

Weir, L., O'Malley, P. & Shearing, C. 1997, "Governmentality, criticism, politics", *Economy and Society*, 26(4), pp. 501–517.

Wierzbowski, M. 1978, "Zakres regulacji administracyjnoprawnej" [The scope of administrative law regulation], in *Zbiór studiów z zakresu nauk administracyjnych* [Collection of studies in the field of administrative sciences], eds Z. Rybicki, M. Gromadzka-Grzegorzewska, & M. Wyrzykowski, Zakład Narodowy im. Ossolińskich, Wrocław, pp. 85–96.

Yeung, K. 2005, "Government by publicity management: sunlight or spin?" *Public Law*, pp. 360–383.

# PART III

# Energy Packages

## Public tools of the liberalisation of the electricity sector

# 6 First Liberalisation Package

Traditionally, the supply of electricity in Europe has been considered a utility. Thus, the markets have been subjected to very limited competition. In principle, the general rules of EU law on free movements of goods and services also apply to electric power, but they have traditionally not been applied to these grid-bound markets (Wasenden 2008, p. 33).

In 1988, the EU launched a market reform programme of the energy sector linked with the establishment of the internal market in electricity. This led to the adoption of the Transit Directive for the electricity sector in 1990. Under provisions of its Article 3 (2), electricity exchange at the European level had to be non-discriminatory and fair for all the parties concerned, without unfair clauses or unjustified restrictions and could not endanger security of supply and quality of service. These very first rules derived from the need for a single internal market in energy and greater integration of the European energy market.

Furthermore, the Transit Directive, in its preamble, intended an internal market in the electricity sector. Achievement of it had to be done respecting the objective of economic and social cohesion, i.e. "guarantee an optimum supply of electricity to all the citizens of all the Community regions, with a view to improving and harmonizing the living conditions and development bases in particular in the least-favoured regions".

Apart from the formal basis set by the provisions of the Single European Act and the Transit Directive, which contributed to them, this movement had its economic rationale. "[E]energy is such an important component of all economic activity in the Community that the completion of the internal market is inconceivable without an integrated internal energy market", the Commission noted (Proposal for a Council Directive 1992, 548 final). Moreover, by integrating electricity markets within Europe the achievement of savings, reduction in the costs of investment in production, and growth in new entrants were assumed. Finally, as the Commission assessed in its 1992 proposal, "removing the barriers to intra-community trade will allow electricity ... users, small ones and large ones, to enjoy the benefits of a more competitive market including more freedom of choice and reduced price disparities between Member states".

Following extensive negotiations, agreement on the First Electricity Directive was reached in 1996. In that time, the United Kingdom, Sweden, and Norway had already liberalised their markets to an extent wider than required by the Directive (Wasenden 2008, pp. 33–34). Odd-Harald B. Wasenden (2008, p. 34) classifies as its basis, on the one hand, a clear distinction between monopoly functions of network operation, and, on the other, market activities as well as the included requirement for a gradual market opening (i.e. the possibility for producers and consumers to negotiate purchases and sales of electric power freely).

## Background of the First Electricity Directive

In December 1996, the European Parliament and the Council passed Directive 96/92/EC concerning common rules for the internal market in electricity. It constituted a further phase of liberalisation. As stated in its preamble "it is important to adopt measures to ensure the smooth running of the internal market" which is "to comprise an area without internal frontiers in which the free movement of goods, persons, services and capital is ensured". What is also highlighted there is the correlation between the electricity market and the internal energy market. The completion of a competitive electricity market is described in the Directive as "an important step towards completion of the internal energy market".

Seen in that light, the European Parliament and the Council found it necessary to establish common rules for electricity regarding its generation, transmission, and distribution. In the field of generation, two systems to be applied for opening up the production market were indicated. First, an authorisation procedure, or second, a tendering procedure. This simply shows that, from the very beginning, liberalisation of the energy sector has been carried out with the use of regulatory tools. In this view, where a Member State opted for the authorisation procedure, it had to establish "the criteria for the grant of authorisations for the construction of generating capacity in their territory". They could concern, *inter alia*, the safety and security of the electricity system, protection of the environment, or energy efficiency. The Directive also set provisions for refusal to grant an authorisation. This proceeding had to include applicant participation by providing reasons for the refusal, that had to be "objective and non-discriminatory", "well founded and duly substantiated", and should enable the possibility of appeal. When selecting the tendering option for the requisite capacity, Member States had to conduct an inventory of new means of production (including replacement capacity, and the need for interconnection of systems).

### *Institutional structure and non-discriminatory criteria*

Another crucial element of public law regulation covered the designation, which had to be made by Member States. It concerned indicating an authority (or a public body or a private body independent of electricity generation, transmission, and distribution activities) responsible for the organisation, monitoring, and control of the tendering procedure. Moreover, on the basis of Article 20 (3) Member States had to designate a competent authority "to settle disputes relating to the contracts and negotiations in question … and refusal of access or refusal to purchase". In terms of revoking an authority's decision it had to be "without prejudice to the exercise of rights of appeal under Community law". What should be emphasised is the fact that under the provisions of Directive 96/92/EC this authority had to be "independent of the parties". It was not a typical regulator equipped with a wide range of regulatory powers. Although, certainly the fact of this designation increased the institutional sphere created on the ground of public law.

In reference to transmission, the Directive imposed an obligation to subordinate the transmission system to central management and control. It was "to ensure the security, reliability and efficiency of the system in the interests of producers and their customers". Within the frames of Articles 7–9, to achieve this aim Member States had to establish a Transmission System Operator. The TSO should be responsible for the operation (e.g. managing energy flows, exchange with other interconnected systems, providing information to the other system operators), maintenance (ensuring a secure, reliable and efficient), as well as development of the system.[1]

As stated in the preamble of Directive 96/92/EC the TSO must "behave in an objective, transparent and non-discriminatory manner". This rule is specified in Article 7 (5). The TSO "shall not discriminate between system users or classes of system users, particularly in favour of its subsidiaries or shareholders".[2] Furthermore, the transparency obligation concerned also the technical rules for the operation of transmission systems and direct lines. Except these rules had to ensure inter-operability. Moreover, "in order to ensure transparency and non-discrimination" vertically integrated energy undertakings which were responsible for electricity transmission had to operate independently from the other activities. Another separation regarded a single buyer[3] that did not have to operate in generation and distribution activities of vertically integrated undertakings. The minimum level of the TSO's independence was "management terms", except when "the transmission system was already independent from generation and distribution activities". Moreover, the need to restrict "the flow of information between the single buyer activities and these generation and distribution activities" was noted. In this context, the accounts of all integrated electricity undertakings should provide for maximum transparency. The accounts had to be separate for each activity.[4] This was to prevent potential abuses of a dominant position. The Directive's preamble includes the examples: "abnormally high or low tariffs", or "discriminatory practices relating to equivalent transactions". The Members States were obliged to provide competent authorities with access "to the internal accounts of undertakings with due regard for confidentiality".

When it comes to electricity generation, Directive 96/92/EC obliged Member States to set "objective and non-discriminatory criteria … for the dispatching of power stations". The Member States had also the possibility of giving priority to the generation of electricity in renewable energy sources, due to reasons of environmental protection.[5] In addition, the Directive was ordered to consider the position of autoproducers and independent producers.[6]

### *Regulatory mechanisms under the First Electricity Directive*

Furthermore, on the basis of Article 3 (2), the Directive established a regulatory framework to impose on electricity *public service obligations*. This important regulatory tool was related to security (with security of supply), regularity, quality and price of supplies, as well as environmental protection. The imposition of these obligations had to be defined in a clear, transparent, non-discriminatory, and verifiable way (with a duty to notify to the Commission of any revision). To introduce them, the implementation of long-term planning[7] could be provided. In this context, Directive 96/92/EC, in Article 10 (1), allowed Member States to establish an obligation for distribution companies, which involved supplying "customers located in a given area". It was complemented by the tariff provisions that "for such supplies may be regulated, for instance to ensure equal treatment of the customers concerned".

Seen in this light, Directive 96/92/EC also set rules on the access to the system. Member States had to choose between the "negotiated access" and/or the "single buyer" procedure. As stated in Article 17, the case of negotiated access to the system required electricity producers and supply undertakings (if Member States authorised their operation), and eligible customers[8] (both, inside or outside the territory covered by the system) taking necessary measures to give them the possibility "to negotiate access to the system so as to conclude supply contracts with each other on the basis of voluntary commercial agreements". To do so (namely "to promote transparency and facilitate negotiations") system operators had to publish information about prices (their range) for use of transmission and distribution systems. As far as possible, the indicative prices published for subsequent years should be based on the average price agreed in negotiations in the previous 12-month period. Within this option, Member States could decide about implementing a "regulated system of access procedure". Here, Member States had to give eligible customers a right of access that was at least equivalent to the other procedures for access regulated in the directive by two main procedures. This right had to be based on published tariffs for the use of transmission and distribution systems. Notwithstanding, the TSO or DSO was entitled to refuse access in case of lack of necessary capacity.

When it comes to the single buyer procedure, Member States, within the territory covered by the system operator, had to designate a legal person as the single buyer. Within the procedures' scope, Member States had to take necessary measures in the field of publicly available, non-discriminatory transmission and distribution tariff, eligible customers ("free to conclude supply contracts to cover their own needs with producers and, where Member States authorize their existence, with supply undertakings outside the territory covered by the system", as well as "free to conclude supply contracts to cover their own needs with producers inside the territory covered by the system"), and independent producers who on the basis of a voluntary commercial agreement negotiated access to the system with the TSO and DSO "so as to conclude supply contracts with eligible customers outside the system". However, the Directive states an optional obligation in terms of the purchase of electricity.[9] If this purchase obligation was not introduced, Member States had to assure implementation of previously mentioned supply contracts, either with use of access to the system on the basis of the published tariff, or by negotiated access to the system based on Article 17 (in this case, with "no obligation for the single buyer to publish a non-discriminatory tariff for the use of the transmission and distribution system"). Similarly, as in the first procedure, the single buyer had the right to refuse access to the system (with a refusal to trade with eligible customers) in case of lack of necessary capacity. These provisions were strengthened by Article 19 which ensured opening electricity markets by the introduction "at least up to a significant level" of contracts under the conditions stated in Articles 17 and 18 that had to be reached. Member States were obliged to notify to the Commission the value of this level on an annual basis. Furthermore, the EU's countries had to choose customers representing the specified shares[10] who had the legal capacity to contract electricity in line with Articles 17 and 18. All final consumers consuming more than 100 GWh per year were to be included in this category. With this calculation the electricity market would be opened up by 25 per cent from 1999[11] and after six years (by the year 2005), to around 33 per cent.[12] If DSOs has not already been specified as eligible customers, they were classified to it "for the volume of electricity being consumed by their customers designated as eligible within their distribution system, in order to supply those customers".

The Directive, in Article 19 (4), obliged Member States to publish annually the criteria for the definition of eligible customers. These criteria, "together with all other appropriate information to justify the fulfilment of market opening", were sent to the Commission to be announced in the *Official Journal*. This paragraph established the right of the Commission to "request a Member State to modify its specifications ... if they create obstacles to the correct application of this directive [regarding] the smooth functioning of the internal market in electricity". In the case of not complying with the Commission's request within three months, the Commission could take other legal steps to execute its request (a final decision in accordance with Procedure I of Article 2 of Council Decision 87/373/EEC of 13 July 1987 laying down the procedures for the exercise of implementing powers conferred on the Commission).

Finally, as stated in Article 22, Member States were obliged to establish mechanisms ("appropriate and efficient") in the field of regulation, control, and transparency. Their aim was "to avoid any abuse of dominant position, in particular to the detriment of consumers, and any predatory behaviour". These mechanisms had to be in line with the provisions of the Treaty, in particular with its Article 86 (TEC).[13]

Public obligation, tariffs, duties in the field of access to the grid, eligible consumers, responsibilities for operator, etc., emphasise the role played by the regulatory regime introduced by public law (rules imposed by EU law, transposed into national law) in order to establish common rules for the internal energy market. Public law regulation and its tools, used adequately (e.g. in a clear, transparent, non-discriminatory, and verifiable way), were aimed at building a liberalised structure of the market, steered by a regulatory framework. Furthermore, in terms of European impact and coordination of Member States' steps by the European authorities, the role of the Commission should be noted (i.e. possibility to influence a Member State's specification in a situation of its non-compliance with application of the Directive and "the smooth functioning of the internal market in electricity"). This simply highlights the primacy of European activity taken for the needs of the common market of energy (instead of the national approach and national energy markets).

However, the First Package with the First Electricity Directive was just the very beginning of the liberalisation (with the use of public law) of the energy sector in Europe. These were still early assumptions; the institutions did not have a strong character. They were rather a general framework, which "engaged" rather than "forcing" undertaken actions driven by the European energy agenda.

## Aftermath of the First Package

In April 1998, the European Commission passed a Report on liberalisation of the energy markets. Within its scope, the Commission explained the basis of its legal approach to realise the aims inscribed in a postulate of an internal market. It was covered by four principles. Among them was not to "impose a rigid system on Member States, but rather a framework which Member States can fill in with arrangements best suited to their national circumstances", as well as to "avoid excessive regulation" (European Commission 1998b, p. 3). Under these terms, EU countries were to be given flexibility. Although, undue regulation was an undesirable factor, a due regulation could be in force.

The Report addressed also the main aim of the Commission in developing the internal energy market at this stage of liberalisation. It was to recognise the "greater integration of the national energy markets as a way to improve security of supply, reduce costs and improve competitiveness" (European Commission 1998b, p. 3). In the field of security, the internal market was to enable flexibility and diversification. More competition within the energy market had to increase efficiency of the European energy sector. The European Community was determined to complete the internal energy market. However, in reaching the internal market, in 1998 the Commission saw structural obstacles, especially in trade across borders as well as within borders. They emerged as an effect of the position of national utilities and the rights that were granted to them (European Commission 1998b, p. 3).

It should be noted that some Member States, even before the adoption of the Package and the First Electricity Directive, had already liberalised their energy markets (e.g. Finland, UK, Sweden). As the EC indicated:

> [o]thers have started the discussion on the necessary changes only after the adoption of the Directive. Among them there are Member States which intend to open their markets rather quickly and they have already put in place legislation such as the Netherlands, Spain and Germany, and others who have not proceeded that much in the legislative process.
>
> (European Commission 1998b, p. 15)

The Commission noted the difference in progress, but it was "clear that the restructuring of the electricity sector in line with the rules provided in the Directive is at present on the agenda of all Member States". To monitor the implementation, the Commission (1998b, p. 16) set "bilateral meetings with the Member States" as well as the Follow-up Group that met twice a year and with the objective "to prevent any inconsistencies and to ensure a coherent implementation of the Directive".

In 1999, the European Commission presented a Second Report on the harmonisation requirements of Directive 96/92/EC (Second Report). Compared to the previous Report (European Commission 1998a), the Second Report contained much more information about liberalisation.[14] The Commission explained this situation in the brief introduction to the Second Report. As one can find there it was the unclearness in several Member States' structural choices taken to implement the Directive that occurred at an early stage of the implementation phase (European Commission 1999, p. 3).

The Second Report identified barriers in the cross-border trade of electricity. Despite the finalisation of the implementation process for Directive 96/92/EC (or advanced in 1999), and physical availability of transmission capacity, for most eligible customers it was "organisationally and economically difficult ... to choose a supplier situated in another Member State, in particular if a third or fourth Member State has to be transited" (European Commission 1999, p. 14). As a result, the Commission pointed out the lack of tariff framework for cross-border transactions. This would ensure that every transaction had to be negotiated, with the necessity of paying a transmission fee to the TSO. Due to lack of coordination the double counting in transmission fees paid to different TSOs occurred. "Thus, the sum of all required transmission fees [was] in most cases [added] up to a prohibitive amount, making it cheaper for the customer to stick with local supplier" (European Commission 1999, pp. 14–15).[15]

Moreover, the Second Report highlighted the role of interconnectors, as "the bridges between the national or, in some cases, regional electricity systems ... [which] are of critical importance for the single electricity market, as capacity ... will often not be sufficient for the expected increasing power trade after liberalisation" (European Commission 1999, p. 6). Further, from the fact that Directive 96/92/EC did not deal with the rules for cross-border transactions, solving this issue was limited only to national measures. That is why in this document the combined activity at the Community level is underlined, as a method that can address in an adequate way the problems concerning cross-border trade. On the grounds of the analysis of the "available interconnector capacity" as well as of its "management", and "long term reservation" of it, the EC set the following preliminary conclusions. Among them was that:

> [t]ransparency of available transmission capacity between the TSOs is of key importance and] [t]o provide all market participants with the data they need to plan their transactions and to avoid discrimination, an information system should be established by the European TSOs [or] long term reservation of transmission capacity should be regulated and restricted to the right of priority use of the line with the obligation to make unused capacity available to the short term market.
>
> (European Commission 1999, p. 13)

To realise these considerations the Commission proposed a two-level approach. In the first level, matters from the category of "discriminatory allocation of interconnector capacity" and "long term capacity reservation over interconnectors" were "to be addressed by the Commission pursuant to the competition rules in close collaboration with national regulators on a case by case basis". It could be strengthened by the development of supportive guidelines. The second level, "a more formal approach", included amendments to the Price Transparency Directive 90/377/EEC and the Transit Directive 90/547/EEC.

Seen in that light, the Commission's role (1999, p. 25) was to ensure "the active exchange of information, experience and expertise between national regulators and competition authorities". It was to establish "a true common market" which needed the same regulatory test and standards. To do so, instead of "the harmonisation of regulatory approaches at the national level", the Commission (1999, p. 25) provided "an active policy of convergence through benchmarking". Pursuant to Article 22 of Directive 96/92/EC, the regulation was a matter of national level. As one can find there, "Member States shall create appropriate and efficient mechanisms for regulation, control and transparency so as to avoid any abuse of dominant position, in particular to the detriment of consumers, and any predatory behaviour". However, when it comes to disputes regarding network access, under the provisions of Directive 96/92/EC in principle, these were at the national level and should be resolved by national regulatory or competition authorities. "[T]he EU competition rules are applicable to such cases in the event that an appreciable effect on trade between Member States" (European Commission 1999, p. 25). Notwithstanding, even in this respect, the EC accentuated its close coordination with national authorities.

What in the Commission's opinion could not be solved by regulatory action, either on the national or European level, was the cross-border transmission tarification systems and trade related mechanisms. As the EC observed:

> [s]uch an issue cannot be dealt with properly at national level, because it is not possible for any potential single EU tarification mechanism, or indeed in due course the actual tarification levels, to be regulated by 15 different authorities, each with possibly conflicting views. EU competition policy,

> which in any event does not prevent contemporaneous national regulation, is also limited in terms of both procedure and remedies in relation to such issues.
>
> (European Commission 1999, p. 26)[16]

These conditions ensured that it became necessary to decide which European authority should be competent in the field of regulation mechanisms and the prices charged by the European TSOs regarding cross-border tariffs. Noticing the importance of this issue the EC, within the frame of the Second Report, raised two questions:

> [first,] is it acceptable to have 15 potentially conflicting decision-making processes contemporaneously treating this issue? Would such an approach not frustrate the objective of having one single EU-wide tarification system for the whole EU?
>
> [S]econdly, [i]s it possible to rely at Community level simply on EU competition rules to resolve this issue despite the fact that (i) almost all jurisdictions world-wide now accept that competition policy is an inadequate instrument to regulate transmission tariffs and (ii) the application of the competition rules does not exclude the potential conflict and multidisciplinary issues outlined above?
>
> (European Commission 1999, p. 26)

To solve this problem the Commission proposed two solutions. The first included reaching cooperation between national regulators and the Commission, with the use of the Florence Forum as a platform for this cooperation. It did not require new institutions, treaties, rules. On the other hand, it relied on the unanimous agreement of all Member States' regulatory authorities. Further, at the EU level, there was no legal authority to impose *ex ante* decided cross-border tariffs.

> In this respect, therefore it requires de facto agreement, by industry, to respect conclusions reached through this method. Equally, any decisions might only be taken once all parties had agreed, making it difficult to envisage how rapid decisions might be made.
>
> (European Commission 1999, p. 27)

The second approach covered the establishment of the new form of regulatory instrument to be administrated by the Commission, or a *European Regulator*. However, this needed a new common regulatory regime. Its advantage was "to create, at European level, a regulatory instrument equivalent to that which has been, or is in the process of being, established in almost every single EU Member State" (European Commission 1999, p. 27). In 1999, the Commission reached no conclusion regarding which of approach was appropriate. Nevertheless, it opened a debate, starting a dialogue with the Council and the European Parliament.

## Review at the turn of the century

In March 2000 in Lisbon, the European Council held a special meeting to agree to a new strategic goal for the European Union. Among topics like the EU's strengths and weaknesses, an information society for all, the establishment of the European Area of Research and Innovation, or creating a friendly environment for starting up and developing innovative businesses, during the meeting the issue of economic reforms for a complete and fully operational internal market was addressed. The European Council admitted that to complete the internal market in certain sectors, rapid work was necessary. In this context the European Council called the Commission, the Council, and the Member States to speed up liberalisation in postal services, transport, gas, and electricity. The aim was to achieve a fully operational internal market in these areas.

### *State of the very first internal energy market*

In May 2000, the EC published a communication on progress in building the internal electricity market. By this time, almost all Member States had adopted national law implementing the provisions of Directive 96/92/EC[17] establishing the minimum targets for the opening of the market (30 per cent of consumption in 2000, 35 per cent in 2003). Directive 96/92/EC created the chance for the biggest consumers to find supplies opportunities freely. As underlined in this Communication, many Member States went beyond the requirements laid down by the Directive. "As a result, implementation of the Directive opened up two thirds of the consumer market for electricity in the EU". Table 6.1 shows this in the division of each of the EU-14 (except Luxemburg).[18]

*Table 6.1* Opening of the electricity market in the EU-14 by 2000

| *Member State* | *Market opening (%)* | *Competition generation* | *Unbundling transmission* | *Grid access* |
|---|---|---|---|---|
| Austria | 30 | Authorisation | Legal | Regulated |
| Belgium | 35 | Authorisation | Legal | Regulated |
| Denmark | 90 | Authorisation | Legal | Regulated |
| Finland | 100 | Authorisation | Ownership | Regulated |
| France | 30 | Authorisation | Management | Regulated |
| Germany | 100 | Authorisation | Management | Negotiated |
| Greece | 30 | Authorisation | Management | Regulated |
| Ireland | 30 | Authorisation | Legal | Regulated |
| Italy | 30 | Authorisation | Legal | Regulated |
| Netherlands | 33 | Authorisation | Legal | Regulated |
| Portugal | 30 | Tendering | Legal | Regulated |
| Spain | 45 | Authorisation | Legal | Regulated |
| Sweden | 100 | Authorisation | Ownership | Regulated |
| UK | 100 | Authorisation | Ownership | Regulated |
| EU | 65 | | | |

Source: European Commission (2000, p. 13).

Even with most Member States implementing the provisions of the Directive, in 2000 a fully integrated market had not been achieved. Moreover, all market participants recognised that in this time two issues had to be re-examined to create an internal market of a real nature. These were, *unbundling* of operation of the network from production/distribution, as well as regulated *third-party access*. As highlighted in the Communication on recent progress, access to the market was highly correlated with access to the network, especially regarding new entrants. To make network access possible it had to be based on fairness and non-discrimination.

> Experience shows that it is very much easier to achieve this goal when operation of the transmission and distribution systems (in practice, often by incumbent, vertically integrated companies) is unbundled from the other interests of the industry, in particular production and distribution/trading.
>
> (European Commission 2000, p. 4)

Therefore, as stated in this Communication, Member States had to guarantee the complete separation of the two spheres of parent company activity: its operation of the network from production/distribution.

Furthermore, the EC (2000, p. 4) urged the Member States to "examine what measures are required to ensure that all third-party access is regulated in a transparent manner to exclude discrimination of any kind". Experience has proved that the most proper method of access to the network (in the field of non-discrimination) was the system of regulated third party access, which was based on published price. At the same time it allowed the energy companies to plan energy purchases. This was done by means of prior knowledge of their tariff rates. However, the negotiated access system required from the companies renegotiation of the price and the conditions of access, every time a contract came to an end. These circumstances resulted in the Commission expressing its belief in the fact that in 2000 the national legislation implementing the provisions of Directive 96/92/EC did not provide sufficient market opening. The EU's goal was a well-integrated energy market, "not juxtaposition of fifteen more or less liberalised [but over-fragmented] markets" (European Commission 2000, p. 4).

On this stage of energy market liberalisation, some regulatory measures aimed at facilitating the functioning of the market were proposed. These covered the "non-discriminatory cross-border transmission pricing" as well as "an effective congestion management system". The Commission (2000, p. 4) evaluated them as "two essentials to give a decisive boost to developing a European energy market". The aim was to achieve in a short way a "simple, objective, transparent, non-discriminatory trading system reflecting costs in order to create a real internal energy", with the use of "the Florence process".[19] The practical expression of the agreement between participants of the Florence Forum was reached in March 2000 on a provisional cross-border pricing mechanism, coming into force on 1 October 2000. After this date all existing national charges in the field of imports and exports had to be withdrawn.

### *Necessary measures to complete the market reform*

In 2001 the Commission announced the Communication "Completing the Internal Energy Market". It included the EC's Proposal for a Directive of the European Parliament and of the Council amending Directives 96/92/EC and 98/30/EC as well as the Proposal for a Regulation of the European Parliament and of the Council on Conditions for Access to the Network for Cross-border Exchanges in Electricity.

In addition, in the Communication the issue of market opening was evaluated and so far the effects of market opening were positive, both for the market's development as a whole, and for its impact on related policies (e.g. environmental, security of supply). Nevertheless, in 2001 the Commission found it necessary to introduce new measures to complete the internal energy market and take full advantage of its benefits. The measures concerned "the degree of market opening ('quantitative proposals')[20] and the minimum obligations regarding access to the network, consumer protection, regulation and the unbundling of the transmission and distribution function in integrated gas and electricity companies ('qualitative proposals')"[21] (European Commission 2001a, p. 2). For example, in terms of market opening, in 2000, Member States had their markets opened on different levels, varying from 30–100 per cent. Such a situation, if existing for a long time, was assessed as blocking the development of competition within the internal energy market. What should be underlined here is the fact that market opening possibility was not anticipated when Directive 96/92/EC was agreed:

> [a]t that time, it was not expected that an overwhelming majority of Member States would open their markets more than legally required, and certainly not to commit to full opening within a short fixed time scale. Thus the distortion of competition – ... between electricity ... companies, and between electricity ... users – ... was not expected. Furthermore, the reciprocity provisions of the Directive do not provide an adequate solution to this distortion.
>
> (European Commission 2001a, p. 30)

Besides this, the Commission appreciated the initial activity in terms of implementing Directive 96/92/EC. However, practical experience has shown that further developments in this field were needed to ensure the smooth functioning of the electricity market. This was confirmed by public consultations conducted by the EC.[22] As noted,

> over 70% of the respondents at the public hearing were in favour of strengthening existing unbundling provisions.... Furthermore, with respect to third party access, the system of case-by-case negotiated third party access, presently permitted by the Directive, was favoured by none of the respondents. Also in this context, many participants underlined the importance of the existence of

> an independent national regulatory authority, and indeed some insisted on the need for having a regulator at the European level.
>
> (European Commission 2001a, p. 6)

Regulators were those authorities that had

> the competence to set or approve network tariffs and intervene *ex-ante* in the market, as opposed to competition authorities, which can only deal with competition problems *ex-post* and under procedures, which are not adapted to deal with the setting of tariffs.
>
> (European Commission 2001a, p. 6)

In this view, the role of regulator was featured as "important in arriving at a truly competitive market, especially to ensure non-discriminatory access to the network" (European Commission 2001a, p. 6).

These circumstances showed that although market opening by the year 2000 had strengthened Europe's competitiveness in general, it was just a first step towards the common internal market. This early phase was characterised by imperfections in the regulatory framework. They had to be modified if a well-functioning internal electricity market had to be reached. Moreover, the analytical work conducted during this stage of energy market reform provided interesting findings for public law regulation in the EU. In particular this concerns remarks on regulatory tools and the idea of the establishment of a common regulator at the European level.

## Towards complex revision

Besides assessment of the state-of-the-art in the European energy sector conducted in the Communication "Completing the Internal Energy Market" (2001), the Commission established the first version of the Proposal for a Directive of the European Parliament and of the Council amending the Electricity and Gas Directives of the 1990s. On the basis of arguments for amending Directive 96/92/EC set out in the Communication, the Commission added to the reasons for necessary changes, the need for clarification (within the accounting unbundling requirements), and for simplification of some administrative issues, as well as the fact that certain provisions and options of the Directive "have either become redundant, or have not been selected by Member States" (European Commission 2001a, p. 34). Among them were provisions on the tendering procedure for generation[23] or on single buyer[24] – they had to be removed from the new wording of the Directive. These amendments were especially vital for the countries that were negotiating accession to the European Community (for ensuring equal terms of the structure of the electricity market).

Within the *quantitative proposals* in the first draft version, the provisions on freedom of choice for the electricity supplier were included. As stated in Recital 12 of the proposed preamble of the Directive "electricity customers should be able to choose their supplier freely". On the basis of Article 19 this concerned all non-domestic electricity customers who had to have this possibility by 1 January 2003 and, accordingly, all customers (the 100 per cent market opening formula) with this option applicable by 1 January 2005. Article 19 also provided provisions on "contracts for the supply of electricity with an eligible customer in the system of another Member State" which the Commission proposed "to avoid imbalance in the opening of electricity markets". First, it concerned the situation where the customer was eligible in both Member States' systems involved. In case of a refusal of those contracts on the grounds of the customer's eligibility in only one of the two systems, the draft Directive's provisions provided the Commission with the possibility of obliging the refusing party to "execute the requested electricity supply at the request of the Member State where the eligible customer is located".

In the field of *qualitative proposals* the Commission's proposal concerned, *inter alia*, rules for unbundling, third party access, or regulation. First, when it comes to unbundling, the Commission proposed solutions which had to ensure "a common minimum standard of unbundling throughout the internal market for electricity". This resulted in forming an independent Transmission System Operator, which, according to the preamble's Recital 5 "in order to achieve non-discriminatory access to the network", was of "paramount importance". That is why the provisions on unbundling should be strengthened. In these terms, Member States had to guarantee that electricity would be transmitted by a subsidiary company, separated, both legally and functionally, from its parent company in the field of electricity generation and sales. This was reflected in the provisions of the proposed Article 7 (6) where a much broader approach was applied. The TSO had to be fully independent "from other activities not relating to the transmission system" (in Directive 96/92/EC it was limited to generation and distribution activities), and in the field of ownership, to be independent "at least in terms of its legal form, organisation and decision making from other activities not relating to transmission" (earlier it was related only to management).[25] In this frame of reference, the draft Directive provided measures that Member States had to implement to fulfil the independent TSO standard by providing unbundling personal[26] and financial criteria[27] in the TSO's operation. Similar provisions covered unbundling of DSOs.[28]

Second, in the Commission's view, third party access for the transmission and distribution systems had to be based "on published tariffs, applicable to all eligible customers, and applied objectively and without discrimination between system users".[29] This was connected with the strengthening of the role of national regulatory authorities. As stated in the proposed Article 22 (1), Member States had to establish national regulatory authorities and guarantee them complete independence of "interests of the electricity industry". Member States had also to ensure them the necessary level of minimum competence.[30]

### *Views on public law regulation in the legislative process*

In October 2001 the proposal was reviewed by the Economic and Social Committee (ESC).[31] Apart from welcoming it as a move "towards a genuine internal market in electricity", resulting in a "greater competition between companies, lower energy prices for companies and domestic consumers, a more competitive European economy as a whole" the Committee noted the inconsistencies that appeared in the proposal (e.g. systems and procedures that were to be replaced, premises established in the preamble that were not developed). It also pointed out that

> past experience in other states, both within and outside the European Union, and showed that the market opening process and the very existence of an internal market in electricity ... give rise to a number of uncertainties and have an indirect social and/or geographical impact.

The ESC also called the Commission to ensure that the process of opening the market would not distort competition and undermine the interests of consumers, as well as would not "allow suppliers which previously had a de facto or *de jure* monopoly on their national markets to benefit unduly from the situation, or abuse their individual or collective dominant positions". On the other hand, as the ESC itself admitted, full market opening in the electricity sector would "help to put an end to the co-existence of different regulations in the Member States, which is currently causing distortions of competition and hindering the completion of the internal market". Seen in that light, the Committee warned against problems which occurred during "the California crisis" where badly planned liberalisation of the energy market caused a giant growth in final prices and led to a significant decline in the quality of services offered to energy users (see Weare 2003; Cicchetti, Dubin, & Long 2004; Sweeney 2002; Joskow 2001). Bearing this in mind, the European markets had to use the US experience "to prevent shortages and artificially high prices". The ESC welcomed the proposed measures to reduce these risks and prevent them. The proposed measures were, "giving independent regulatory authorities responsibility for monitoring the supply/demand balance, maintaining the tendering procedure for power generation plants in the event that sufficient generation capacity has not been built, and giving grid operators responsibility for maintaining and developing networks".

Further comments of the Committee concerned, *inter alia*, unbundling which did not have to "place unreasonable administrative burdens on economic agents", public service obligations, which had to be "put in place to ensure that vulnerable groups can benefit from electricity ... at a fair price", market opening's effects on the environment – an area which in the ESC's opinion seemed to be one of the most affected by this market opening process,[32] or the Community's applicant countries.[33] The Committee also referred to the establishment of national regulatory authorities. There, besides their usefulness and the need to establish them, the ESC proposed to take into consideration the possibility of providing "more transparent and democratic" national regulatory authorities' operation by "allowing the various agents involved in the electricity ... markets (i.e. consumers, workers and companies) to participate in the decision-making process". Furthermore, the ESC appraised the formation of the Council of

European Energy Regulators and – what should be stressed here – urged to "consider transforming this Council at some future date into a European Agency or similar body, with responsibility for matters relating to international transport in electricity and natural gas".

Another issue addressed in the ESC's opinion was a system for access to the grid. As Member States had different frameworks for this it could result in market imbalance in terms of mutual access of companies from different countries to different national networks. In this field Member States established "regulated access based on published tariffs", in order to assure free access as well as to avoid distortions of competition, or abuses of dominant position. Nevertheless, the Committee drew attention to the need to develop an assessment of Member States' operating capacity of existing systems or actual competition. What is worth noting, the ESC expressed its approval for the Commission's project on establishment of "a single system for access to the grid based on published tariffs" and evaluated it as "a step towards harmonising the sector"; however it should be strengthened by specific measures "needed to effectively guarantee non-discriminatory access, such as, setting a deadline for replying to access requests and drawing up flexible dispute settlement mechanisms".

These remarks are connected with the ESC's general observation on competition. As the Committee noted, completing the internal energy market, except from causes like the end of national monopolies as well as sector deregulation, could result in "a process of concentration in which small companies – many of them local authority-owned – will gradually disappear". This could lead to a situation in which the European energy market would be controlled by a limited number of large companies that operated in the various market spheres, distort competition, and abuse their market power. The Committee warned that even in the open and deregulated market situation, such states are "equivalent to a monopoly" and may encourage large companies to "maximise profits at the expense of lower quality services and higher prices, and to the detriment of the European market's competitiveness and consumers in general". To avoid this possibility the ESC suggested higher activity by the competition authorities at national and Community levels.

In December 2001, the Commission's proposal was discussed by the Council (Council of the European Union 2001). As a result of a policy debate, the Council underlined "the need to take account of Member States' specific situations", "the role of subsidiarity in the implementation of these Directives", as well as "the need to clarify some technical aspects further". Furthermore, the Council reached a convergence of views on: *regulatory authorities* (to leave Member States with the freedom to establish proper regulatory institutions, assuming that Member States will implement regulatory functions – monitoring, approval of methods and rules, dispute settlement – enlisted in the Directive), and *prices and tariffs* (to provide methods for setting prices and tariffs *ex ante* as a one approach that could balance efficiency and transparency). The Council's agreement also covered *independence of electricity network managers* (to combine legal requirements on access to network resources with compliance measures), cross-border electricity exchanges (to introduce a provisional mechanism – the *pilot mechanism* that would enable assessing the final mechanism better – while continuing to work on the proposal for a Regulation), *public service obligations* (to include provisions on environmental protection), as well as *interconnections between networks* (to pay attention to their successful development) (Council of the European Union 2001).

What is important, in March 2002, the European Parliament called the Commission and the Council to divide the Commission's proposal into two separate legal acts on electricity and gas, and to incorporate the amendments adopted by Parliament into those two new directives. A bit earlier, at the beginning of March 2002, the European Parliament's Report on the Commission's proposal was passed. The aforementioned idea by Parliament to divide the Commission's project was justified by substantive and procedural reasons. First, the internal electricity and internal gas markets were simply different. Second, the rules for them were established in two separate Directives: 96/92/EC on electricity and 98/30/EC on gas; moreover they were in a different phase of implementation. Parenthetically, the EP's attitude confirms the importance attached in the European Union to the "package approach" to legislation on the energy sector. As demonstrated by the facts, this approach has become a permanent feature of the way in which the European Union shapes the energy market.

Furthermore, the European Parliament indicated that the debate on energy market liberalisation was concentrated on quantitative issues ("speed of market opening"). As written in the Explanatory Statement to the Revision of the Electricity Market Directive, "[a]lthough harmonised dates for full market opening are a prerequisite for a well-functioning market, qualitative aspects must be brought to the centre of the political debate if a truly functioning market is to be established". Among them was to take care of *security of supply* (e.g. the Commission's proposal omitted "the potential of energy efficiency measures to increase security of supply, which must be redressed"), to ensure a level playing field for *sustainability* (the need to establish a strategy that would aim at reducing state aid, subsidies for conventional energy, as well as internalisation of external environmental costs; by that time sustainable energy production should receive protection in the market by this new Directive), as well as to guarantee a "level playing field for market actors" (reaching a single market by integrating 15 national markets needed harmonisation; in terms of market concentration the Commission's proposal included reviewing this issue, however the Parliament stressed the need for clear guidelines),[34] to give "more market power to small customers" ("the Directive should seek to improve market power for small customers by favouring aggregation and by giving a greater role to local utilities"). Further, as stated in the Report, within the functions of the regulatory authorities there should be monitoring of contracts' transparency, maximum fees for costs of connection to the grid, as well as costs of metering. It was aimed to ensure "full disclosure of information" (the Commission's proposal needed improvements in the field of relevant information about bills for the consumer and commercial accounts; the Directive should furthermore guarantee that in every Member State an independent authority provides customers with comparative information), to prevent negative effects on electricity demand (the market failure had to be addressed – in the context of the environmental and security of supply concerns; moreover the Parliament urged including in the Directive structural measures that could improve energy efficiency),[35] to support "municipal utilities" (in the Commission's proposal, utilities supplying less than 100 000 customers could be excluded from distribution unbundling; however as stated in the Parliament's Report, this model should be better defined).[36]

These remarks were reflected in the amendments to the draft. Their nature is well illustrated by the new wording of Recital 11's second sentence: "[t]he basis for a functioning market economy is to have the same rules on subsidies, tax concessions and grants, and the same treatment for tax purposes of reserves etc. throughout Europe". Seen in that light, in Recital 5 the Parliament found it necessary to add to the main obstacles in arriving at a fully operational internal market "pricing... different national approaches to the internalisation of environmental costs and differing levels of government support for some parts of the energy sector". Especially the last one – historical and current support of government for the energy sector was assessed by Parliament as the driver for distortions in the functioning of the energy market. Moreover, the European Parliament expanded the scope of Recital 11 which set the rules for a regulatory system as a tool for assuring non-discriminatory access to the grid. The Parliament noted that "legally binding access arrangements" played herein a role equal to the need for regulatory authorities. These, in turn, had to be "independent of the interests of the electricity industry and of the governments of Member States". As a minimum standard they had to have provided the power to establish, in an independent way, a binding scheme for calculating tariffs for grid access. Furthermore, according to Parliament's version of the Directive, national regulatory authorities had to monitor the evolution of retail tariffs, to promote the setting up of transparent market based mechanisms for the supply and purchase of balancing power, to monitor the market continuously, or to impose public service obligations on electricity undertakings, or require TSOs and DSOs to modify the rules ("mechanisms, terms and conditions and procedures") for suppliers' access to the grid.

Moreover, the European Parliament proposal assumed the close cooperation of national regulatory authorities with the Commission. For example, it concerned collaboration in the reference to the Commission's recommendations to Member States on the harmonised application of the provisions. As stated in the new wording of Article 6a (1), Member States had to guarantee that national regulatory authorities "take the utmost account of those recommendations in carrying out their tasks". It was argued that to reach equal market rules in the internal electricity market, as well as a national approach, Member States need also to consider a European approach. This could be achieved by ensuring close cooperation between the Commission and national regulatory bodies.[37] The European Regulators Group for the European electricity market was designed as a suitable forum for this kind of cooperation.[38]

***Regulatory regime in the modified proposal of the next package***

In June 2002, the Commission published its modified version of the legislation on the energy market (COM (2002) 304 final). Some of the Parliament's amendments were partly or in principle accepted. For example, the EC agreed on defining in which areas obstacles of market liberalisation were still present (in grid access, as well in market opening), including a requirement for national regulators to form market based mechanisms dedicated to balancing power (when the electricity market was to be sufficiently liquid), specifying provisions on the monitoring of the security of supply in the Community, reinforcing the protection of vulnerable customers.

Others accepted by the EC proposals concerned both the Directive's preamble as well as its articles. When it comes to the preamble the Commission stressed the existence of "effective regulation" and the need for providing "legally binding methodologies" for network tariffs. Even though, as a rule, securing "effective regulation" was more important than "the institutional element" (Amended proposal for a Directive 2002, 304 final, p. 3). One thing to notice is that the Commission disapproved the obligation of providing national regulatory authorities with independence from national governments. This was reflected in the Directives' articles. In terms of the independence of the national regulatory authority, the EC proposed a model of independence from the interests of industry. The Commission broadened the tasks of the regulators, adding to them "reporting on market dominance, market concentration and predatory and anticompetitive behaviour" closed in the frameworks of Article 22, in monitoring "effective competition" by the national regulatory authorities. Moreover, the EC introduced provisions proposed by the Parliament in the field of monitoring ("that system operators do indeed publish aggregated information on interconnectors, grid usage and allocation to interested parties") as well as of "the prohibition of cross-subsidisation" (Amended proposal for a Directive 2002, 304 final, p. 9).

Naturally, some of the EP's amendments were totally rejected. From the formal point of view, one of the main criticisms of the Commission was the idea to split the proposal into two Directives, on electricity and gas. The European Commission, pointing to the growing interdependence of the gas and electricity sectors, raised the need to regulate them simultaneously. This was shown by the increasing number of new power plants fuelled with gas. Additionally, the Commission was concerned that the divided proposal might result in various dates of passing and entering into force of directives. Among other unaccepted proposals, the Commission drew attention to the proposal for exemption from the obligation to legally unbundle the distribution system operator in distribution companies which were "locally owned utilities", and assessed it as "a discriminatory distinction between companies" (Amended proposal for a Directive 2002, 304 final, p. 10). Moreover, one of the amendments levied the threshold for this exemption from 100000 to 150000 clients, what, in the Commission's opinion, would result in taking too many companies out of the system (Amended proposal for a Directive 2002, 304 final, p. 10).

Furthermore, the European Parliament called for introducing in principle ownership unbundling in electricity. The Commission proposed a formula of less intensive unbundling – the legal one. It was supported with functional unbundling's measures and measures for monitoring its implementation (like the Commission's report on the effectiveness of these provisions). The provisions proposed by the EP implied also an option for national regulators to require the release of electricity generation and capacity from long-term contracts, as well as to introduce public service obligations on electricity undertakings, and impose an annual reporting obligation to national parliaments on national regulators. In the Commission's opinion these measures had to be subject to the subsidiarity principle. In this phase of market liberalisation it was more important to monitor progress in the way to a competitive internal market than to establish programmes on electricity at the European level, as the EC stated (Amended proposal for a Directive 2002, 304 final, p. 12).

The consequence of the new Commission's proposal was further legislative work caused by the divergent positions. However, within a few months of intensive work and meetings, parties managed to reach agreement on the way forward. Finally the model proposed by the Parliament was chosen.[39] As previously, liberalisation took the form of a *package*, including two directives, one for gas and one for electricity. Loyola de Palacio, Vice-President of the European Commission responsible for transport and energy, assessed the results of the political consensus on energy liberalisation as a "radical change, with European countries moving from national monopolies to full liberalisation within a few years" (European Commission 2002). The reached agreement covered the obligation to implement legal unbundling of transmission by July 2004, and of distribution by July 2007. The electricity and gas markets had to be fully liberalised for non-household customers by July 2004, and at the latest by 1 July 2007 all customers (households) could choose their supplier. The agreement concerned also the proposal for the Regulation on Cross-border Electricity Exchanges and the Decision to Promote Interconnection, Interoperability and the Development of Trans-European Energy Networks (TEN-E), and Access to the Networks. Additionally, the Council agreed the list of priority projects of European interest.[40]

### *Impact of the First Energy Package*

In conclusion, one should note that the introduction by the First Energy Package provisions, driven by the public law regulatory regime (like public obligation or duties of energy operators), provided a very first basis for shaping the structure of the internal energy market. However, because of their general, and rather soft, character (and a lack of concrete regulatory institution) the very few years of the existence of the first rules on the electricity market with their implementation and application reveal their weaknesses. The Commission evaluated these weaknesses even as structural obstacles, linking them with the strong position of the national energy utilities.

A true internal energy market needed the same regulatory tests and standards. As a measure for achieving this, the harmonisation of regulatory approaches at the national level was proposed. This also included solving the problem of cross-border tariffs, where softer and harder solutions were proposed. A softer way covered cooperation of national regulators and the Commission on the ground of the European Electricity Regulation Forum (Florence Forum). A harder solution was based on establishing a new form of regulatory instrument. Nevertheless whichever model was better at that time, both approaches were linked with enhancing the position of regulatory authorities, i.e. institutions responsible to set or approve network tariffs and intervene *ex ante* in the market, as they were assessed as an important element of a truly competitive market, necessary to ensure non-discriminatory access to the network (European Commission 2001a).

The provisions of the First Energy Package, with Directive 96/92/EC did not allow the arrival of a fully integrated market in 2000. In this early phase certain imperfections in the regulatory framework occurred. Certain provisions needed clarification or simplification. Some options of the First Electricity Directive had to be removed. Some needed expansion. Necessary amendments were driven by the fact that at this time the European energy market was rather a juxtaposition of national more or less liberalised markets. It was still over-fragmented. To achieve a fully open market, stronger regulatory tools were necessary. The measures concerned the degree of market opening (*quantitative proposals*) and the minimum obligations regarding (*qualitative proposals*) that covered access to the network, consumer protection, the unbundling of the transmission and distribution function in integrated gas and electricity companies, and the already mentioned regulation. What has to be underlined is the fact that market opening did not exclude public regulation and existence of a market regulator. The proposed shape and scope of the Second Liberalisation Package did not include deregulation, but liberalisation with regulation, making the complex revision of the regulatory framework became possible. Complex, because the new elements of public law regulation combined with enhanced already known tools were covered by its range.

The analysed provisions of the First Energy Package as well as proposals of its revision emphasise the importance that was attached to public law and its regulatory mechanisms in the European Union between the first and the second phase of energy market reform. European Union policy-makers, bearing in mind the California crisis and consequences of unlimited liberalisation of the energy market, decided to deepen and broaden the regulatory model used for the energy market's needs, with electricity as its part. Although, as has been shown, the European Union authorities at this stage of market liberalisation differed in terms of the specific solution and shape of each provision of the traced legislation, the general direction aimed at reaching the internal energy market with the use of public law regulation included in the European Energy Packages was confirmed. Also, the formula of packages dedicated to the energy sector within the final version of proposals was retained.

To characterise the final shape of the second stage of European energy market reform and indicate the place which was given to public law regulation (and thereby how the European Union influenced its scope) it is necessary to examine the adopted provisions of the Second Energy Package with the Second Electricity Directive. The following chapter deals with these issues.

## Notes

1 Moreover, according to Article 5 (2) of Directive 96/92/EC, the Transmission System Operator was obligated to estimate regularly the generating and transmission capacity which is likely to be connected to the system, as well as identify the need for interconnectors with other systems, and potential transmission capacity and the demand for electricity. This had to be done at least every two years, with publication under state supervision. Instead of a TSO, a Member State could designate any other competent authority designated to fulfil mentioned duty.
2 The same requirement concerned the DSO. See Article 11.
3 Article 2 (22), "'single buyer' shall mean any legal person who, within the system where he is established, is responsible for the unified management of the transmission system and/or for centralized electricity purchasing and selling".
4 Article 14 (3),

> [i]ntegrated electricity undertakings shall, in their internal accounting, keep separate accounts for their generation, transmission and distribution activities, and, where appropriate, consolidated accounts for other, non-electricity activities, as they would be required to do if the activities in question were carried out by separate undertakings, with a view to avoiding discrimination, cross-subsidization and distortion of competition. They shall include a balance sheet and a profit and loss account for each activity in notes to their accounts.

5 Article 8 (3), "[a] Member State may require the system operator, when dispatching generating installations, to give priority to generating installations using renewable energy sources or waste or producing combined heat and power". The same requirement might concern the DSO. See Article 11 (3).
6 Article 20 (1) (i),

> Member States shall take the necessary measures to enable independent producers and autoproducers to negotiate access to the system so as to supply their own premises and subsidiaries in the same Member State or in another Member State by means of the interconnected system.

7 Article 2 (21), "'[l]ong-term planning' shall mean the planning of the need for investment in generation and transmission capacity on a long-term basis, with a view to meeting the demand for electricity of the system and securing supplies to customers".
8 According to Article 17 (2), "where an eligible customer is connected to the distribution system, access to the system had to be negotiated with the relevant DSO and, if necessary, with the TSO concerned".
9 Article 18 (2),

> [t]he single buyer may be obliged to purchase the electricity contracted by an eligible customer from a producer inside or outside the territory covered by the system at a price which is equal to the sale price offered by the single buyer to eligible customers minus the price of the published tariff referred to in paragraph 1 (i).

10 Article 19 (1)–(2),

> [t]he share of electricity consumed by final consumers consuming more than 40GWh per year (on a consumption site basis and including autoproduction). The average Community share shall be calculated by the Commission on the basis of information regularly provided to it by Member States. The Commission shall publish this average Community share defining the degree of market opening in the Official Journal of the European Communities before November each year, with all appropriate information clarifying the calculation. The share of the national market referred to in paragraph 1 will be increased progressively over a period of six years. This increase will be calculated by reducing the Community consumption threshold of 40GWh, referred to in paragraph 1 from 40GWh to a level of 20GWh annual electricity consumption three years after the entry into force of this directive and to a level of 9GWh annual electricity consumption six years after the entry into force of this directive.

11 The percentage of electricity in the Community consumed by users consuming more than 40 (GWh) per year.

12 When the consumption threshold has fallen to 9GWh per year. See Nomden 1997, p. 12.

13 According to Article 86 TEC

> [a]ny abuse by one or more undertakings of a dominant position within the common market or in a substantial part of it shall be prohibited as incompatible with the common market in so far as it may affect trade between Member States. Such abuse may, in particular, consist in: (a) directly or indirectly imposing unfair purchase or selling prices or other unfair trading conditions; (b) limiting production, markets or technical development to the prejudice of consumers; (c) applying dissimilar conditions to equivalent transactions with other trading parties, thereby placing them at a competitive disadvantage; (d) making the conclusion of contracts subject to acceptance by the other parties of supplementary obligations which, by their nature or according to commercial usage, have no connection with the subject of such contracts.

14 The Report of 1998 in a substantial part concerned energy from renewable sources.

15 This is referred to as full or partial "pancaking".

16

> The reason for this flows notably from the fact that, as mentioned above, the TSO owns a perfect monopoly. It is becoming increasingly recognised that, in these circumstances, the prices and conditions charged by a TSO must be fixed by a regulatory authority, and cannot simply be left to the TSO itself, subject to ex-post control by a competition authority. A competition authority can only, for example, prohibit excessive pricing once this has been proven through a judicial or administrative procedure. A competition authority cannot, therefore, require, ex-ante, a TSO to pass possible efficiencies on to consumers through lower prices. For these reasons, transmission prices are set by regulatory authorities in all EU countries save Germany which, alone, relies on the competition authority to act as a price limiting mechanism.
>
> (European Commission 1999, p. 26)

17 Only Luxembourg was an exception; however, France and Belgium were to introduce executive legislation which accompanied it, Belgium also had some problems with forming the position of TSO, the same with Ireland (European Commission 2001b, p. 9).

18 After publication of the Communication, Luxembourg joined the group of countries, noting the level of market opening in electricity at 40 per cent.

19 The Forum represents the Commission, the national administrations, and the Council of European Regulators as well as the Association of European Transmission System Operators. Producers, consumers, and operators on the market, together with the European Parliament are also represented.

> The aim of the forum is to prepare and facilitate decisions or proposals of a technical nature, for example on cross-border transmission pricing and congestion management, in an informal forum bringing together all stakeholders. The advantage of these technical measures is that they can be applied rapidly by the regulatory authorities in the Member States without waiting for a new directive.
> (European Commission 2000, pp. 4–5)

20 Percentage of the market opening.
21 Structural choices on unbundling, network access, etc.
22 In September 2000, the Commission organised a public hearing on energy market liberalisation in which nearly 120 associations and companies took part.
23 With an exception, treated as a security of supply back-up tool.
24 For access to the network.
25 New wording of Article 7 (6).
26 For example, proposed Article 7 (6) (a), "those persons responsible for the management of the transmission system may not participate in company structures of the integrated electricity undertaking responsible, directly or indirectly, for the day-to-day operation of the generation, distribution and supply of electricity"; as well as new Article 7 (6) (b), "appropriate measures must be taken to ensure that the personal interests of the persons responsible for the management of the transmission system are taken into account in a manner that ensures that they are capable of acting independently".
27 For example, new version of Article 7 (6) (c), "the system operator must exercise full control over all assets necessary to maintain and develop the network".
28 See proposed Article 10 (4).
29 Proposed wording of Article 14.
30 For example, new wording of Article 22 (1) (a), "to fix or approve terms and conditions for connection and access to national networks, including transmission and distribution tariffs"; or proposed Article 22 (1) (b) "to fix or approve tariffs, or changes in tariffs at national level, to reflect costs or revenues related to cross border transmission of electricity".
31 Mostly, the opinion of the Committee concerned the Directive, although some specific remarks covered the proposal for the Regulation. This included, *inter alia*, powers of the Commission, and the Community's action which in terms of the Regulation's scope should be rather as simple as possible, leaving a margin for national decisions.
32 Under the assumption that the open energy market would decline in energy prices, the Committee anticipated an increase in the demand for energy. An increase in efficiency was not so high to fulfil the increase in energy consumption. The ESC underlined that as a consequence an increase in primary energy consumption could occur resulting in the growth of emissions and therefore hampering attempts to meet Kyoto's commitments.
33 As stated in the Committee's opinion the electricity sector in the applicant countries enjoyed "a high degree of support and public intervention", as well as maintaining "uncompetitive infrastructures and management methods". The transposition of legislation on liberalisation could have resulted in significant job losses in energy sector companies, causing unbearable social tension. That is why the EU had to share liberalisation's experience with these countries, as well as to "provide funding to help them modernise their companies". Furthermore, opening up these new markets was not enough. The ESC called on restructurating of the energy companies from the applicant countries so they could "compete under the same conditions".

34 According to the European Parliament's Report these problems had to be addressed:

> in some Member States operators control more than 50% of the market; in other Member States the sale of and merger between electricity companies have been more guided by industrial policy interests rather than by transparent merger control; the ten largest companies control over 50% of the EU market. Further mergers of these companies are planned and it is expected that within a few years only between 5–8 companies will dominate.
>
> (Report for a Directive, A5-0077/2002)

35 "Increased demand-side management not only for retailers but also for transmission and distribution companies is also required. Funding mechanisms to finance Demand Side Management (DSM) for small customers must be provided" (Report for a Directive, A5-0077/2002).

36

> Therefore all utilities which have less than 200 000 customers should be exempt and it should also apply to all municipal and community utilities regardless of their size. However, it is essential that all distribution service operators (DSOs) which are majority owned, directly or indirectly, by another electricity company, in this regard are considered as one DSO.
>
> (Report for a Directive, A5-0077/2002)

37 According to Article 6 (1) "Member States shall designate a body, which may be the independent regulatory authority referred to in Article 22, to monitor security of supply issues."

38 The European Parliament's proposal for Article 6a (1a).

39 "2452nd Council Meeting – Transport, Telecommunications and Energy – Luxembourg, 3–4 October 2002", PRES/02/285, Luxembourg, 3 October 2002. Available from: http://europa.eu/rapid/press-release_PRES-02–285_en.htm?locale=en [21 January 2014].

40 Within the electricity sector such projects were included on this list: EL.1: France, Belgium, Netherlands, Germany: electricity networks reinforcements in order to resolve the frequent problems of congestion through Benelux; EL.2: Borders of Italy with France, Austria, and Switzerland: increasing electricity interconnection capacities; EL.3: France, Spain, Portugal: increasing electricity interconnection capacities between these countries and for the Iberian peninsula; EL.4: Greece, Balkan countries, UCTE System: development of electricity infrastructure to connect Greece to the UCTE System; EL.5: United Kingdom, continental Europe, northern Europe: establishing/increasing electricity interconnection capacities; EL.6: Ireland, Northern Ireland, United Kingdom: increasing electricity interconnection capacities; EL.7: Denmark, Germany: increasing electricity interconnection capacity (European Commission 2002).

## References

Amended proposal for a Directive of the European Parliament and of the Council amending Directives 96/92/EC and 98/30/EC concerning rules for the internal markets in electricity and natural gas, Brussels, 7 June 2002, COM (2002) 304 final.

Cicchetti, C.J., Dubin, J.A., & Long, C.M. 2004, *The California electricity crisis: what, why, and what's next*, Kluwer Academic Publishers, Norwell.

Council Decision 87/373/EEC of 13 July 1987 laying down the procedures for the exercise of implementing powers conferred on the Commission, OJ L 197, 18 July 1987.

Council Directive 90/377/EEC of 29 June 1990 concerning a community procedure to improve the transparency of gas and electricity prices charged to industrial end-users, OJ L 185, 17 July 1990.

Council Directive 90/547/EEC of 29 October 1990 on the transit of electricity through transmission grids, OJ L 313, 13 November 1990.

Council of the European Union 2001, *2394th Council Meeting – Energy/Industry – Brussels, 4 and 5 December 2001*, Brussels, 4 December 2001, PRES/01/452. Available from: http://europa.eu/rapid/press-release_PRES-01-452_en.htm?locale=en [22 June 2015].

Directive 96/92/EC of the European Parliament and of the Council of 19 December 1996 concerning common rules for the internal market in electricity, OJ L 27, 30 January 1997.

European Commission 1998a, *Report to the Council and the European Parliament on harmonization requirements: Directive 96/92/EC concerning common rules for the internal market in electricity*, Brussels, 16 March 1998, COM (98) 167 final.

European Commission 1998b, *Report from the Commission to the Council and the European Parliament on state of liberalisation of the energy markets*, Brussels, 7 April 1998, COM (1998) 212 final.

European Commission 1999, *Second report to the Council and the European Parliament on harmonisation requirements: Directive 96/92/EC concerning common rules for the internal market in electricity*, Brussels, 16 April 1999, COM (1999) 164 final.

European Commission 2000, *Communication from the Commission to the Council and the European Parliament: recent progress with building the internal electricity market*, Brussels, 16 May 2000, COM (2000) 297 final.

European Commission 2001a, *Communication from the Commission to the Council and the European Parliament: completing the Internal Energy Market*, Brussels, 13 March 2001, COM (2001) 125 final.

European Commission 2001b, *Commission Staff Working Paper: first benchmarking report on the implementation of the internal electricity and gas market*, Brussels, 3 December 2001, SEC (2001) 1957.

European Commission 2002, *Loyola de Palacio: European energy market revolutionised*, Brussels, 26 November 2002, IP/02/1733. Available from: http://europa.eu/rapid/press-release_IP-02-1733_en.htm?locale=en [25 June 2015].

European Parliament 2000, *Lisbon European Council 23 and 24 March 2000 presidency conclusions*. Available from: www.europarl.europa.eu/summits/lis1_en.htm [17 June 2015].

European Parliament Legislative Resolution on the "Proposal for a European Parliament and Council Directive amending Directives 96/92/EC and 98/30/EC concerning common rules for the internal market in electricity and natural gas", OJ C 47E, 27 February 2003.

Joskow, P.L. 2001, *California's electricity crisis*, National Bureau of Economic Research, Cambridge, MA.

Nomden, K. 1997, "Reconciling liberalization and public service obligations", *EIPASCOPE*, 1, pp. 9–14. Available from: www.eipa.eu/files/repository/eipascope/scop97_1(5).pdf [16 June 2015].

Opinion of the Economic and Social Committee on the "Proposal for a Directive of the European Parliament and of the Council amending Directives 96/92/EC and 98/30/EC concerning common rules for the internal market in electricity and natural gas", and the "Proposal for a Regulation of the European Parliament and of the Council on conditions for access to the network for cross-border exchanges in electricity", OJ C 36, 8 February 2002.

Proposal for a Council Directive concerning common rules for the internal market in electricity, Brussels, 21 February 1992, COM (91) 548 final.

Report for a Directive of the European Parliament and of the Council amending Directives 96/92/EC and 98/30/EC concerning common rules for the internal market in electricity and natural gas, PE 309.068/DEF/PART1, A5-0077/2002.

Sweeney, J.L. 2002, *The California electricity crisis*, Hoover Institution Press, Stanford, CA.

Wasenden, O.-H.B. 2008, *EU market abuse regulation in energy markets*, Cappelen, Oslo.

Weare, C. 2003, *The California electricity crisis: causes and policy options*, Public Policy Institute of California, San Francisco, CA.

# 7 Second Liberalisation Package

As a result of the legislative process initiated in 2001, in 2003 Directive 2003/54/EC was passed. Together with Directive 2003/55/EC of the European Parliament and of the Council of 26 June 2003 concerning common rules for the internal market in natural gas and repealing Directive 98/30/EC, they constitute so-called *Second Energy Package* (or Second Liberalisation Package).

Previously mentioned strategic EU documents showed the need for improving the internal market by new legislation. The reasons for this were "possibilities for improving the functioning of the market", which were recognised in generation (ensuring "a level playing field"), market behaviour (reducing "the risks of market dominance" as well as "predatory behaviour"), tarification (ensuring "non-discriminatory transmission and distribution tariffs"), and, correspondingly, access to the grid (based on tariffs), the rights of small and vulnerable customers (ensuring that they are protected and well-informed), as well as "different degrees of market opening between Member States". These were the main barriers and needs driving the European Union towards another stage of legislation that could imply the fully operational and competitive internal market.

## Complex solutions for market liberalisation

Directive 2003/54/EC laid down comprehensive rules on the liberalisation of the electricity market in the European Union. What should be emphasised is, it set new deadlines for the market opening. On the grounds of Article 21 these were already presented on 1 July 2004 for all non-household,[1] and on 1 July 2007 for all customers, when they became the *eligible customers* – customers who were "free to purchase electricity from the supplier of their choice".

As it comes to the Directive's scope, on the basis of Article 1, these were common rules on organisation and functioning of the electricity sector, as well as rules on all links in the chain of processes specific to electricity: generation, transmission, distribution, supply, and provisions concerning access to the market, the criteria and procedures for tendering and granting of authorisations, and the operation of systems. *Ipso facto*, the scope of Directive 2003/54/EC was exactly the same as the scope of the former Electricity Directive.

Directive 2003/54/EC, as did the previous one, provided Member States with an option to introduce, in general economic interest, "public service obligations" on electricity companies. These comprised requirements mentioned in Directive 96/92/EC ("security, including security of supply, regularity, quality and price of supplies and environmental protection"), however, the protection of environment was clarified in a new Directive in this way that it included "energy efficiency" and "climate protection". If the Member State decided to impose the "public service obligations" they had to be "clearly defined, transparent, non-discriminatory, verifiable", i.e. in line with the previous Directive. Nevertheless Directive 2003/54/EC deepened these obligations by adding the provisions which obliged Member States to secure equal access to national consumers for the European electricity entities. In comparison to Directive 96/92/EC the possibility of introducing long-term planning[2] was limited to security of supply, energy efficiency/demand-side management, and the fulfilment of environmental goals. In doing so Member States had to take into account "the possibility of third parties seeking access to the system".

***Enhancing the position of energy consumers and monitoring security***

The provisions of the Second Energy Package strengthened the position of household consumers[3] and small enterprises.[4] Member States had to ensure a universal service which gave them "the right to be supplied of electricity a specified quality within their territory at reasonable, easily and clearly comparable and transparent prices". In implementing this obligation Member States could decide about establishing a "supplier of last resort". Apart from these they had to protect final customers, especially the vulnerable. This required including measures to avoid disconnecting consumers, as well as ensuring consumer protection in the field of "transparency regarding contractual terms and conditions, general information and dispute settlement mechanisms", and in guaranteeing eligible customers the ability to switch to a new supplier.

Seen in this light, Directive 2003/54/EC set a minimum standard for the protection of household customers. They were listed in the Directive's Annex A. Among them there were provisions that specified electricity service contracts, giving the customer, *inter alia*, information on "the identity and address of the supplier", "the services provided", "all applicable tariffs and maintenance charges", or "the duration of the contract", as well as "conditions for renewal and termination of services and of the contract" or "the existence of any right of withdrawal". Besides, the contract conditions had to "be fair and well known in advance". Additionally, consumers had to be informed about modifications of contractual conditions and provided with information on the right of withdrawal. With regard to that, the Directive obliged Member States to guarantee free possibility to terminate the contract in the situation of rejection by the consumer of its new conditions. Measures for protecting the consumers' position (that Member States had to implement on the basis of Article 3 and correlated with it Annex A) concerned also enabling consumers to choose different payment methods, assuring that they could change supplier without being charged, or could use "transparent, simple and inexpensive procedures for dealing with their complaints".

With regard to the other obligations of the Member States, on the basis of Article 4, they were required to monitor "security of supply" (the current and future supply/demand balance, additional planned/under construction capacity, the quality and level of maintenance of the networks, measures to cover peak demand and shortfalls). To execute this, Member States could decide whether to delegate this monitoring to the regulatory authorities. The competent authorities, once every two years, were to report on the security issues to the Commission. In accordance with Article 5, Member States had to establish and notify the Commission "technical safety criteria" for the "minimum technical design and operational requirements for the connection to the system of generating installations, distribution systems, directly connected consumers' equipment, interconnector circuits and direct lines". Other criteria which the Member States had to develop, were objective, transparent, and non-discriminatory criteria for the grant of authorisations for the construction of generating capacity in their territory.[5] Another example of this tendency are criteria set under Article 7 (1) – the criteria for ensuring the possibility of providing new capacity or energy efficiency/demand-side management measures through any procedure equivalent to tendering procedure, in terms of transparency and non-discrimination, based on published criteria.

### *Strengthening regulation of the system operators*

Regarding TSOs, the Second Energy Package included more complex rules for their establishment and operation. Through illustration, each TSO was literally and directly responsible for "ensuring the long-term ability of the system to meet reasonable demands for the transmission of electricity" and "contributing to security of supply through adequate transmission capacity and system reliability". One of the main aims of Directive 2003/54/EC was to strengthen the unbundling of operators. Therefore, Article 10 set a more rigorous regime for this, but still it was not the most rigorous. In contrast to the European Parliament proposal of the *ownership unbundling*, as a minimum, the model of *legal unbundling* was adopted. Thereby, the Directive's rules on unbundling did not impose an obligation to separate the transmission system from the vertically integrated undertaking, in terms of the ownership of assets. This does not change the fact that the new formula assumed a more intense unbundling. According to the foregoing Article 10, the nature of the legal unbundling was to guarantee the TSOs independence "at least in terms of its legal form, organisation and decision making from other activities not relating to transmission", in the situation in which the TSO was part of a vertically integrated undertaking. This had its practical dimension, which influenced the application of the following minimum rules. First, a person responsible for the management of the TSO was obliged not to link it with participation "in company structures of the integrated electricity undertaking responsible, directly or indirectly, for the day-to-day operation of the generation, distribution and supply of electricity". Second, appropriate measures had to ensure that the professional interests of the persons responsible for the management of the TSO were capable of acting independently. Third, the TSO was to make decisions in an independent way (from integrated electricity undertaking) in the field of assets for the operation, maintenance, or development of the grid. This did not preclude coordination mechanisms "that the economic and management supervision rights of the parent company in respect of return on assets" were protected.[6] Finally, the TSO was to elaborate a "compliance programme". Its aim was to determine anti-discriminatory and pro-observance measures,[7] as well as the specific obligations of employees.

Naturally, the Second Energy Package also concerned the other element of network activity: distribution. Under Article 14 the DSOs, besides provisions which were a repetition of Directive 96/92/EC's obligation of DSOs,[8] were broadened. For example, as stated in paragraph 2 of Article 14, each DSO was to inform system users about the possibilities and conditions of the "efficient access to the system", or according to its paragraph 7 to consider "energy efficiency/demand-side management measures and/or distributed generation that might supplant the need to upgrade or replace electricity capacity" in the distribution grid development plans. Similarly, at TSOs' level, also in distribution, Member States under Article 15 of Directive 2003/54/EC were to implement and conduct a legal form of unbundling. It was an example of strengthening of the previous provisions of Directive 96/92/EC, where unbundling in terms of independence, according to Article 7 (6) of Directive 96/92/EC, was required at the transmission level, where TSOs had independence "at least in management terms from other activities not relating to the transmission system". Additionally, the new Directive modified (although just slightly) provisions on accounting unbundling.[9]

Turning now to grid access, with the Second Energy Package, the new measures for enhancing it were introduced. Of particular importance is that Directive 2003/54/EC combined them with the already mentioned common approach – *third party access* – and legally established by the provisions of Article 20. As explained earlier, its assumption was to provide eligible customers with access to the transmission and distribution grid grounded on published, objective, and non-discriminatory tariffs. The new Directive also expanded the rules for refusal of grid access. Barring the first two sentences, which were copied from the previous Directive,[10] the Member States were to guarantee that the TSO or DSO would inform the requesting party about needed actions for grid reinforcement. However, the operator had a possibility to demand payment by the requestor, i.e. "a reasonable fee reflecting the cost of providing such information".

## Energy regulators as the axis of the Package

What should be noted is that Directive 2003/54/EC set more complex provisions on regulation. As is apparent from the documents already presented, they were one of the most important elements of the discussion during the legislative process. In line with Article 23 of the Directive, Member States were to establish energy market regulators. They could choose between models of a *single regulatory body* or *multi regulatory bodies*. The regulators had to be "wholly independent from the interests of the electricity industry". Compared to Directive 96/92/EC, it was a broader approach. Earlier, the independence of regulators concerned merely an influence of the parties. Not only does this show that under the previous legislation the regulation was shaped in a very general (core) way. According to Article 22 of Directive 96/92/EC they had to "create appropriate and efficient mechanisms for regulation, control and transparency so as to avoid any abuse of dominant position, in particular to the detriment of consumers, and any predatory behaviour". Likewise, the regulatory authorities' other responsibilities – namely activity in the field of disputes concerning "contracts, negotiations and refusal of access or refusal to purchase" – were established in Article 20 (3)–(4) of the 1996 Directive.

Seen in this light, the national regulatory authorities' scope of action was much more complex in Directive 2003/54/EC. As a minimum, the energy regulators were "responsible for ensuring non-discrimination, effective competition and the efficient functioning of the market". Moreover, they had to particularly monitor: "the rules on the management and allocation of interconnection capacity",[11] "any mechanisms to deal with congested capacity within the national electricity system", "the time taken by transmission and distribution undertakings to make connections and repairs", "the publication of appropriate information by transmission and distribution system operators",[12] "the effective unbundling of accounts", "the terms, conditions and tariffs for connecting new producers of electricity", "the extent to which transmission and distribution system operators fulfil their tasks", and "the level of transparency and competition". The results of the described monitoring were a subject of the regulators' annual report.

The regulation was "an important factor in guaranteeing non-discriminatory access to the network". As emphasised in the preamble's Recital 15 this regulation had to be *effective*. It could be conducted by either one or more national regulatory authorities (two, three, etc.). On the national level, each Member State was obliged to establish its legal position, while guaranteeing them functions, competences, and administrative powers. What should be stressed here, the regulatory authorities in all Member States had to "share the same minimum set of competences". Among them were components raised in discussions presented during the discussion on the Directives when it was on its legislative path. In that light, the regulators were to be provided with the power to "fix or approve the tariffs", or – as a minimum standard – at least, to establish "the methodologies underlying the calculation of transmission and distribution tariffs".[13]

Besides, the national regulators had to be active market players to "ensure that balancing tariffs are non-discriminatory and cost-reflective". This was necessary to guarantee all market stakeholders an "effective market access", in the lack of a "liquid market". In principle, achieving the liquid market should be done "through the setting up of transparent market-based mechanisms for the supply and purchase of electricity needed in the framework of balancing requirements". Failure to reach it, or a temporary state, required the aforementioned active role performed by the national regulatory authorities.

Furthermore, the regulators were to fix or approve, as a minimum standard, the methodologies for calculation or establishment the terms and conditions in the field of the national grid (connection and access to it – with *pro-investment tariff policy* for TSOs and DSOs)[14] as well as balancing services. In addition, Member States were to provide them with the power to demand that TSOs and DSOs alter "the terms and conditions, tariffs, rules, mechanisms and methodologies", if necessary. Significantly, during implementation of the Directive, Member States could decide about subordinating the right to set tariffs or methodologies to the relevant bodies that would have "the power to approve or reject [with a justification] a draft decision submitted by the regulatory authority".

The provisions of the Second Energy Package developed the judicial character of the energy regulators setting a timeframe for their action. Basically, regulators had two months (exceptionally, four months, or even more)[15] after receipt of a complaint from any party against a TSO or DSO to issue its decision. If not, and until overruled on appeal, this decision was binding. Further, any party affected, which had "a right to complain concerning a decision on methodologies ... or, where the regulatory authority has a duty to consult, concerning the proposed methodologies". Such a right was to be executed maximally within two months "following publication of the decision or proposal for a decision" and it had no suspending effect. Additionally, the complaints under Article 23 (5)–(6) were "without prejudice to the exercise of rights of appeal under Community and national law".

The role of Member States in reference to the national energy regulators was determined as ensuring that regulatory authorities had the ability "to carry out their duties ... in an efficient and expeditious manner". In this context, Directive 2003/54/EC reiterated Article 22 of Directive 96/92/EC, maintaining Member States' responsibilities on "appropriate and efficient mechanisms for regulation", etc. Further, the Second Energy Package introduced an national obligation to report to the Commission on market dominance, predatory, and anti-competitive behaviour.[16]

Moreover, Directive 2003/54/EC established a general framework for regulators' collaboration. It was initiated by the Commission and shaped a form of a "European Regulators' Group for Electricity and Gas" (ERGEG). In a broader context, the emergence of ERGEG and other formal regulatory forums exerted pressure for further harmonisation, at least of regulatory practices (Tapia & Mantzari 2013, p. 600). As underlined in Recital 16 it was "a suitable advisory mechanism for encouraging cooperation and coordination of national regulatory authorities, in order to promote the development of the internal market for electricity". Energy collaboration was also emphasised in Article 23 (12). According to it, energy regulators were to "contribute to the development of the internal market and of a level playing field by cooperating with each other and with the Commission in a transparent manner". The provisions of Directive 2003/54/EC not only assumed cooperation on the line regulator–regulator, but also – with inclusion of the Commission in this process – made that it posed a much more intense and multilateral dimension.

## Second Package on the implementation path

On the grounds of Directive 2003/54/EC, the Commission was obliged to monitor the application of the Directive. As a result, at the beginning of 2005, the European Commission submitted a Report on the implementation and in November 2005, a Report on progress in creating the internal energy market.

In principle, according to Article 30, the Directive from 2003 was to be implemented not later than 1 July 2004. The practice showed that in 2005 this process was not finished, and "many aspects of implementation remain[ed] disappointing" (European Commission 2005a, p. 3). In May 2004, the EU enlarged to 25 Member States, by accessions of Cyprus, Czech Republic, Estonia, Hungary, Latvia, Lithuania, Malta, Poland, Slovakia, and Slovenia. In October 2004, 18 Member States received the Commissions' warning "that they had still not fully notified to the Commission the legal measures taken to transpose the latest Directives" (European Commission 2005a, p. 3). In this context, the Commission assessed that:

> [t]his delay is unsatisfactory since it is now clear that the provisions of the previous Directives have not been adequate to achieve the objective of competition.... However after five years of competition for electricity and over three years for gas, fewer than 50% have switched supplier in most Member States. In addition, many are unsatisfied with the range of services being offered. It is not enough just to consider the number of customers changing supplier, but also the nationality of new suppliers. In many cases, customers have only been able to change to another domestic supplier with the result that penetration of national markets by foreign companies is also disappointing in many cases, reflecting a lack of integration of markets and missing infrastructure links.
>
> (European Commission 2005a, pp. 3–4)

### *Shortcomings in reaching the objectives of the internal energy market*

In November 2005, the full, complete, and effective implementation of the Second Energy Package was still "the main immediate action" (European Commission 2005c, p. 2). Some Member States implemented it without delay, some did not transpose it until that time, and this was with damage to the European liberalisation energy plan. In this context, the EU expected to achieve well-integrated markets (within neighbouring Member States) as well as markets with a high share of privatisation (which at that time were exceptions).[17] The domination of one or two companies caused the problem of a monopoly or an oligopoly. Broadening the scope of the market from national to European level with supporting competition was aimed to change it by giving energy entities a new field of play. In 2005, in the majority of markets, this goal was not reached (European Commission 2005c, p. 2). Shortcomings influenced also cross-border competition causing inadequate capacity (European Commission 2005a, p. 4). Other factors that decreased the degree of market integration were the significant price differences prevailing and linked with the above-mentioned issue, the low level of cross-border trade (European Commission 2005c, p. 6).

What should be stressed is inadequate (or lack of) progress in the implementation of unbundling. In 2005, rules on unbundling deriving from Directive 2003/54/EC were not completely implemented. These caused delays in establishing an independent position of network operators. However, in terms of TSOs, Member States did not limit legal unbundling but decided to choose a model of far-reaching consequences – ownership unbundling (European Commission 2005c, pp. 11–12). In 2005, in this group were: Denmark, Finland, Italy, the Netherlands, Spain, Sweden, the United Kingdom, Lithuania, the Czech Republic, Hungary, and Slovenia. On the other hand, legal unbundling was chosen by Austria, Belgium, France, Germany, Greece, Ireland, Luxembourg, Portugal, Estonia, Latvia, Poland, and Slovakia.[18]

With respect to distribution, the majority of Member States fully applied possible derogations (exempting smaller distributors from legal and functional unbundling, postponing legal unbundling for larger distributors until July 2007). In general, Member States did not go beyond the minimum requirements imposed by the Directive in this field – what was assessed by the Commission as "rather unambitious national implementation of the unbundling provisions" (European Commission 2005c, p. 12). Only a couple of Member States established management unbundling (European Commission 2005b, p. 82). Additionally, in the national energy regulators' opinion, DSOs were "still too closely linked to incumbents' supply business in many countries" (European Commission 2005b, p. 82).

Apart from the realisation of unbundling, the Commission was not satisfied with the "existence of regulated end user prices for electricity … alongside the competitive market and associated long term power purchase arrangements". Regarding this, the EC justified them at the initial stage of market liberalisation (calling them a "valuable transitional measure") although found risks in this approach; for instance, stiffling competition, constraining investment, and confusing and contradicting unbundling measures (European Commission 2005c, p. 4). Seen in this light, the Commission called on the removal of cross-subsidies and basing access to the grid on published regulated prices. In 2005, network tariffs were already comparable within most of the Member States, and those that deviated from the normal range, expected analysis by the regulators. Furthermore, by reviewing liberalisation progress, the Commission (2005c, p. 5) identified concentration as "the most important obstacle to the development of more vigorous competition". In the situation of further existence of this state of market play, its participants – consumers – could lose their confidence in market forces and demanded stricter regulation. The Commission's decision (2004) on the acquisition of *Gás de Portugal*, the incumbent gas company in Portugal, by *Energias de Portugal* and Italian ENI was in line with this approach. It highlighted "an important precedent on how the Commission intends to deal with possible restructuring of the industry" (European Commission 2005c, p. 6).

Besides, it was the growth of national competition policy, "with greater transparency of the behaviour of participants in wholesale markets" that could result in positive effects for the internal energy market and for cooperation in line with national regulators, competition authorities, and the European Commission (European Commission 2005c, p. 6). It is linked with the role of independent regulatory authorities, an important driver for the introduction of competition that with decisions on network tariffs and other important market rules shaped the ongoing development of the market. That is why in 2005 the EC (2005c, p. 10) called for guaranteeing them sufficient position and necessary power.

## *Factors undermining the EU's regulatory agenda of the Second Energy Package*

Directive 2003/54/EC enabled setting of the national regulatory authority's position in a different way. For example, more than one regulator could be established, or the government (ministry) could exercise some of regulator's functions while the nominated regulator performed a "minor advisory role". This flexibility and variability made it possible to identify "shortcomings in the arrangements from the point of view of effective regulation of the electricity" (European Commission 2005b, p. 85). In this field, the EC listed the following "potentially problematic" circumstances:

- a regulators do not directly set tariffs or tariff methodologies and instead only have an advisory role to the Ministry,
- b regulators are not responsible for setting tariff methodologies for distribution companies below a certain threshold with this being done by local government,
- c regulators do not directly set balancing methodologies and instead only have an advisory role to the Ministry,
- d regulators do not have responsibilities for the surveillance of wholesale electricity markets in terms of transparency and disclosure for producers and Transmission System Operators and/or market operators/power exchanges,
- e regulators are not responsible for setting end-user regulated tariffs resulting in unrealistic levels,
- f regulators are not entitled to ask for basic information on the functioning of the market in order to fulfil their reporting duties under the Directive,

g regulators are not entitled to specify clear rules for cost allocation in the preparation of unbundled accounts,
h regulators may be unable to allow for incentives to TSOs to make available more cross border connection capacity, either through investment or operational techniques such as counter trading,
i regulators have no input into conditions applied to companies seeking to merge for example the imposition of capacity release for … electricity,
j regulators may have limited input into decisions to authorise new generation plant … and on the terms and connections for connection to the network,
k regulators may have no say on public service obligations imposed on companies especially those that give a selective obligation on an individual company that also requires compensation payments or levies,
l regulators may have insufficient ability to enforce their decisions through sanctions.

(European Commission 2005b, pp. 85–86)

As the Commission concluded, each of above-mentioned issues occurring "individually … not necessarily imply an infringement of the Directive or lead to particular problems". Their potential for detriment to realisation of the Directive's aims and creation of a single European market grew in direct proportion to an increase in their number. The "inconsistent regulation between Member States", as well as greater involvement of governmental agencies in regulatory decisions increased the risk of "inconsistencies [which were more] likely to arise and to persist", were other obstacles noticed by the EC (European Commission 2005b, p. 86).

In this context, the national regulatory authorities' opinion expressed in the "Technical annex" accompanying the Commission's Communication of 2005 is worth recalling herein. The regulators emphasised the fact that "their own independence might be compromised by facts that many energy companies are also owned by public authorities" as well as "that regulatory decisions have an impact on another branch of government activity often compromises their effectiveness in fostering competition" (European Commission 2005b, p. 86). Apart from these, in many cases public administration had the possibility to overrule the regulator's decision, take over its competences, and set the regulator's budget. Numerous regulators complained that they were deprived of the power to impose sanctions or that the penalties were low; what resulted in the profitability of non-compliance (European Commission 2005b, pp. 86–87). In this view, "[it] might imply a regular dependence of regulators on ministries' good will and therefore undermine independence" (European Commission 2005b, p. 86). Furthermore, the regulators indicated the division of competence between the sector's regulatory and competition authorities "blurred" market surveillance ("no guarantee that the whole market is covered in that system and regulatory gaps might exist"). That is why the national regulators called for "[b]etter formal co-operation on competition issues" to be established in national legislation. Among drawbacks that were noticed was also the "regulatory gap" that existed in cross-border energy exchanges. Herein as well, to fill the gap, regulators were cognisant of the need for legislative action (European Commission 2005b, p. 87).

Seen in this light, the Commission admitted that Directive 2003/54/EC did not cover all obstacles described by the national authorities. However, the Directive, in Article 3 (1), set minimum standards for the position of the regulatory authorities, and at least they were to be implemented by the Member States. In this regard, the Commission underlined that:

> [c]onsistency between regulators is of high importance in creating a real internal market. Incompatible regimes on, for example, balancing and storage, incentives to remove congestion, and on investment will clearly frustrate objectives of a coherent European market. Regulators have made this clear in their submission on "regional markets". Regulators should already possess most of the powers that they need to make these objectives a reality. They should under the legislation be in a position to deal with, directly or indirectly, network access arrangements, balancing, capacity allocation and congestion management. Regulators should make maximum use of the powers that they do have in this respect.
>
> (European Commission 2005b, p. 87)

However, it was not only the transposition of requirements on the regulatory authorities granted by Directive 2005/54/EC. It should be noted that as early as 2005, the Commission (2005b, p. 87) expressed the view according to which the regulators might "need new powers in order to operate more effectively, for example a greater scope for surveillance of wholesale markets".

## Way to the third liberalisation step

The years after the adoption of the Second Energy Package were the time used by the Commission for the needs of an extensive analytical work. During this in-between phase, the EC elaborated annual "benchmarking reports" which concerned Directive 2003/54/EC's implementation and its effects as well as conducting an inquiry for the gas and electricity sectors under competition law. The results of it were published in 2007 in the Commission's Inquiry.

As addressed there, despite the fact that "[t]he process of market opening has significantly changed the functioning of the markets … the objectives of market opening have not yet been achieved … and barriers to free competition [have remained]" (European Commission 2007c, p. 2). The analysed areas were as follows: market concentration, vertical foreclosure, market integration, transparency, price formation, downstream markets, balancing markets, and liquefied natural gas markets. With regards to circumstances related to the subject of this book, the Commission noticed that in reference to vertical foreclosure "[t]he current level of unbundling of network and supply interests has negative repercussions on market functioning and on incentives to invest in networks". Thereby, the new market players (entrants) often had problems with access to the grid. In addition, this problem was deepened by the discriminatory policy of the operators, who treated their own entities in a better way (European Commission 2007c, p. 6). The existence of vertical integration resulted in a situation of not taking into account "the interest of network/infrastructure", but being guided by the "supply interests of the integrated company (including grid connection for competing power plants)" (European Commission 2007c, p. 6). In line with it was "the integration of generation/imports and supply interests within the same group". Another detrimental to competition factor was the ownership structure of generation – where assets were "in the hand of a few incumbent suppliers" or were "indirectly controlled by them on the basis of long-term power purchase agreements (PPAs) giving the incumbents control over the essential inputs into the wholesale markets" (European Commission 2007c, p. 6). In general, these factors decreased market liquidity, refraining new entries on the electricity market. Similarly, an insufficient level of cross-border electricity exchange (or even its unavailability) was harmful to market integration. What else had a negative effect for integration was "insufficient interconnector capacity and a lack of adequate incentives to invest". This concerned "additional capacity to eliminate long-established bottlenecks" (European Commission 2007c, p. 6).

The Commission also measured transparency in the electricity trade. For example, "it was noted that rules on proper market conduct and supervision differ significantly between Member States, as there is little harmonisation at EU level of the transparency requirements" (European Commission 2007c, p. 7). On the ground of this assessment the grid users needed to have transparency requirements provided in a more extensive formula, exceeding the framework of existing EU legislation. In this context,

> [t]o ensure a level playing field, all market participants require information to be made available on an equal footing and in a timely manner. At present there is an information asymmetry between the vertically integrated incumbents and their competitors. Improved transparency would minimise risks for new market players and so reduce entry barriers and improve trust in the wholesale markets and confidence in price signals. Obviously it needs to be ensured that no collusion takes place on the basis of the published information and, although commercial confidentiality is important, this should not be allowed to undermine effective transparency by being given too wide an interpretation.
>
> (European Commission 2007c, p. 7)

The Inquiry concerned tarification measures as well. The EC identified that some Member States' regulated tariffs had a negative impact on the development of competitive markets. First, this was due to their low levels (in comparison to market prices). Second, a large share of the market was covered by them. These ultimately led to the need to reset the tariffs. The Commission noticed national efforts to reduce the financial burden of the energy intensive industry as well, which had to be in accordance with the provisions of European competition and state aid law (European Commission 2007c, pp. 7–8).

To counter these stated market obstacles, the Commission proposed a set of remedies. They were grouped into two categories: of a competition, and of a regulatory character. Within the first one, the EC announced executing its powers in a full way. The legal basis was herein: Articles 81,[19] 82,[20] and 86[21] TEC, in the field of antitrust; Regulation (EC) 139/2004,[22] on mergers; and Articles 87[23] and 88[24] of the Treaty, in terms of state aid. Apart from this, the improvement of market liquidity was needed (a situation of bad market concentration and market power of unbroken pre-liberalisation monopolies was recognised as a "major concern for the success of the liberalisation process") (European Commission 2007c, p. 9). Chances to ameliorate it were "energy release programmes" like "electricity Virtual Power Plant auctions". Besides their advantages (they were suitable competition measures, both in the field of mergers, as well as antitrust rules), it was necessary to increase the scale of their impact (European Commission 2007c, p. 10).

With respect to regulatory measures, the EC called for "a substantial strengthening of the powers of regulators and enhanced European coordination". This was to lead to transparency, stability, and non-discrimination on the energy market. The mentioned strengthening was to consist of enhancing "powers for independent national energy regulators" and "consistency of regulation in cross-border issues", as well as reinforcing "coordination between national energy regulators" and "cooperation between Transmission System Operators" (European Commission 2007c, pp. 12–13). It is worth stressing that the Commission assessed stronger coordination between national regulatory authorities "with a stronger role for Community oversight". In this assumption it was necessary to reach the internal energy market, especially in the field of cross-border exchanges. In the EC's opinion (2007c, pp. 12–13), at that moment, this "regulatory gap" could not be fulfilled with the use of available competition rules.

The findings on regulation presented by the Commission were broadly discussed in a document on prospects for the EU's energy market, which was related to the Inquiry (European Commission 2007a). In it, the EC urged Member States to transpose European legislation "to ensure that they are effectively opened up for all consumers on 1 July 2007". It launched 34 infringement proceedings against 20 Member States. At the end of 2005, 16 of them received the Commission's reasoned opinions.[25] Except lack of information provided to the Commission on public service obligations and problems in marking the origin of electricity, the objections concerned regulated prices which were blocking new market players,[26] discrimination in TPA,[27] and unbundling without independence.[28] In addition, the Commission alleged that some

Member States insufficiently established the position of energy regulator. As it was underlined:

> [i]n these types of markets which are characterised by the existence of single grids through which … electricity circulate[s], independent regulators must play a key role in the functioning of the markets and third party access to the grid. They must ensure an equal treatment to all market participants. Vested interests should not be protected. Independence is needed particularly when it is necessary e.g. to approve access tariffs to the networks, or to put in place a dispute settlement mechanisms between TSO/DSO and the suppliers in order to protect them against discrimination in access to the grid.
>
> (European Commission 2006, p. 5)

Other examples which presented the problems of the existing legal framework that referred to regulation and regulators concerned; *inter alia*, short-term national orientation of regulators, limits of regulators' action lacking powers and discretion, influence of national governments (direct or indirect) (European Commission 2007a, pp. 7–8). In particular, harassment of the internal energy market was the permanent character of listed infringements. In the EC's assessment, these circumstances revealed the "insufficiencies and shortcomings of the current EC legal framework arising from the directives". As an effect, regulators were not equipped with a position guaranteeing them powers "to ensure that open markets … function in an efficient and non-discriminatory manner" (European Commission 2007a, p. 6). Due to these, at the turn of 2006/2007 the European Union was still far from reaching a fully internal energy market.

### *Need for changing the regulatory framework*

The problems of the functioning of the European energy sector caused the EC readiness to address barriers within access to the grid, national and European regulation, sector competition, framework for investments, as well as households and smaller commercial energy customers (European Commission 2007a, pp. 9–10). In this context, the EC recommended strengthening the unbundling provisions and proposed considering two alternatives for further deliberation: "fully (ownership) unbundled TSOs", and "separate system operators without ownership unbundling". In the first, the TSO would be an independent owner and operator of the transmission grid. In the second, system operation and ownership of the assets would be separated. In both models, the independence of the operator would be secured by excluding the possibility of holding a significant stake in the TSOs by supply or generation companies. However, the second model allowed for the remaining transmission assets, within a vertically integrated group (European Commission 2007a, p. 11). At the same time, in this model the "system operator would be solely responsible for operation and dispatch, being the primary interface with network users, and would exercise control over network maintenance and development decisions". Obviously, financial sources and staff not employed by a vertically integrated group, was necessary here (European Commission 2007a, p. 11).

Such a framework established the "Independent System Operator" (ISO) scheme. What complemented and supported it was "detailed regulation and permanent regulatory monitoring". For comparison, in the ownership model the regulatory burden was much lower "as the regulatory oversight could be less detailed to ensure that no discrimination takes place". These show the correlation ("balance") of the applied unbundling and regulation ("regulatory supervision") (European Commission 2007a, p. 11). In 2007, the Commission (2007a, p. 12) announced that it would examine both models on the grounds of their characteristics.

The need for improvements within the existing formal basis for liberalisation in the energy sector of the European Union involved also enhancing the role of national energy regulatory authorities. The Second Energy Package had in this respect a number of shortcomings. The implementation practice showed that its framework and introduced the solutions do not work in full:

> in many cases, experience suggests that the effectiveness of regulators is frequently constrained through a lack of independence from government and sufficient powers and discretion.... [R]egulators do not have discretionary and effective, ex-ante powers, such as establishing rules for functional unbundling or non-tariff access conditions.... [R]egulatory duties are split between the specific regulatory authority and the ministry, or the competition authority. The country reviews confirm that where insufficient powers are given to national regulators, this leads to inconsistent decision making and inadequate compliance.
>
> (European Commission 2007a, p. 12)

Also, these findings were confirmed in the analysis on regulatory entities: "Study of the Powers and Competencies of Energy and Transport Regulators" (see Europe Economics & TIS 2006). As a result, the EC found it necessary to guarantee and strengthen the regulator's discretion to act in the field of sector regulation at the national level. In the Commission's view, the regulatory authorities needed "strong ex-ante powers". These competences concerned:

> i) all aspects of third party access to networks, ii) access to gas storage, iii) balancing mechanisms, iv) market surveillance of e.g. power exchanges, v) compliance with functional and account unbundling for distribution system operators, vi) all cross border issues, vii) consumer protection including any end-user price controls viii) information gathering, ix) sanctions for non-compliance.
>
> (European Commission 2007a, p. 13)

What should be emphasised is that this range was to be the basis for strengthening European legislation, including the Directive on Electricity. Moreover, the Commission underlined the need to guarantee that decisions of national regulatory authorities were not detrimental to the European energy market. For this purpose, the EC suggested that energy regulators should notify their particular decisions (e.g. on cross-border exchange, on development of competition) to it. The Commission relied on the fact that a similar notification model existed under the provisions of Article 7 of Electricity Regulation (EC) 1228/2003 which concerned the new direct current interconnectors (European Commission 2007a, p. 13). Taking into account specific conditions (*inter alia*, an obligation to enhance competition by a new investment, the level of risk of the investment, some unbundling requirements, as well as not damaging the "competition or the effective functioning of the internal electricity market, or the efficient functioning of the regulated system to which the interconnector is linked") on the grounds of the above-mentioned Article, the new direct current interconnectors, after consultation with other Member States, could be exempted from the Second Energy Package's provisions of TPA. However, the exemption decision was to be notified to the Commission. This was accompanied with submitting to the Commission relevant information which had to enable the Commission to reach a well-founded decision. In this scope, the Member States had to inform about "detailed reasons on the basis of which the regulatory authority, or Member State, granted the exemption", "the analysis undertaken of the effect on competition and the effective functioning of the internal electricity market resulting from the grant of the exemption", or "the result of the consultation with the Member States or regulatory authorities concerned". In addition, Article 7 of Electricity Regulation (EC) 1228/2003 enabled the Commission to request amendment or withdrawal of the decision to grant an exemption (as a rule within two months after receiving a notification). Member States or regulators had four weeks to comply with the Commission's request under pain of a final decision set in accordance with Article 13 (3) of the Regulation. Seen in that light, in reference to the decisions of national regulatory authorities of potential detrimental to the European energy market nature, the Commission announced the need for analysis of criteria for decisions, which would require notification and Commission oversight (European Commission 2007a, p. 13).

Moreover, as presented in the EC's Report on prospects for the energy market, further amendments in the regulatory framework concerned strengthening the European dimension of energy regulators' collaboration. The differences in market design (e.g. in tariffs, rules for capacity allocation, or measures for security of supply) caused "market segmentation" which was not only harmful to competition but also security of supply (European Commission 2007a, p. 13).

### *Solutions for the new model of public law regulation*

One way to eliminate the presented disparities was to use existing mechanisms of ERGEG and regional initiatives for electricity. The Commission noticed "encouraging signs that significant improvements will be delivered in this way". On the other hand this was linked with regulators' approach and willingness to improve the existing situation, as well as with the scope of their powers and responsibilities. That is why the EC proposed "more detailed EU co-ordination" taking into account "[t]hree main configurations". These were as follows: "[g]radually evolving the current approach", a "European network of independent regulators (ERGEG+)", and a "new, single body at Community level" (European Commission 2007a, p. 14). The first was based on cooperation of regulators, deepened by introducing a "Community objective" in their operation. This was to be supported by the Commission's review of regulators' decisions, which had an effect on the internal energy market. The second assumed formalisation of ERGEG's role by granting it "the task to structure binding decisions for regulators and relevant market players, such as network operators, power exchanges or generators". This was to be limited to technical and cross-border. Where necessary, it would include the Commission's assistance. Finally, the third model was based on establishing a new European authority. As the EC proposed, this body "would in particular be granted the responsibility for adopting individual decisions for the EU electricity … market related to regulatory and technical issues relevant to making cross border trade work in practice" (European Commission 2007a, p. 14).

The presented options, especially the second and the third, needed amendments in existing legislation (delegations of powers in compliance with the European Community Treaty). When it came to choosing a preferable option, the Commission excluded implementing the first model. This was because of its insufficient character in which progress was to be still based on national energy regulators' consent and their different interests in the background. In this context, as the "minimum approach" the EC considered the ERGEG+ model. In the Commission's view it was more "likely to make rapid and effective progress in harmonising the technical issues necessary to make cross-border trade work effectively" (European Commission 2007a, p. 14).

The listed options and the approach towards them were repeated in a strategic EU document: "An Energy Policy for Europe" of 2007. The document highlighted the need for harmonisation of national regulatory authorities' powers and their independence. Significantly, this was to be done on "the basis of the highest, not the lowest, common denominator in the EU". Moreover, the requirement of taking into account the European perspective (not only national) by the regulators was expressed there (European Commission 2007b, p. 8). In addition, the regulation was the subject of the Commission's call on the European Council and Parliament. This concerned confirmation of the need to establish "additional measures" in the field of regulation. In the EC's opinion these were: further unbundling (in ownership or independent system operator formula, however the Commission considered ownership unbundling as the most effective measure); and effective regulation ensured by Member States. With regards to the second, the already mentioned harmonisation conducted on the ground of joint European and national direction of regulation, was a method to fulfil this assumption (European Commission 2007b, p. 21).

In 2007, the European Council invited the Commission to develop legislative proposals for further integration of the energy market. The Council addressed it in the "Action Plan (2007–2009)" attached to the March 2007 Conclusions. Apart from ensuring "timely and full implementation of ... existing Internal Market legislation relating to the opening up of ... electricity markets" the Council agreed on the need for conducting effective unbundling. It was to be "independently run" and based on "adequately regulated network operation systems". This was to be complemented by "further harmonisation of the powers and strengthening of the independence of national energy regulators", as the second element of the "Action Plan" of 2007 in this field (Presidency of the European Council Conclusion 2007).

Furthermore, in June 2007, the Commission's findings were the subject of the European Parliament assessment. In the Parliament's resolution of 10 July 2007 on prospects for the internal gas and electricity market, some significant comments (of a general and a specific character) on European regulatory measures were expressed. In terms of a broad, general Parliament approach, the correlations between the completion of the internal energy market and guaranteeing security of supply and economic efficiency in Europe, establishment of regulators of "strong and effective harmonised rules on network access together with effective unbundling" and the new market entrants were concerned. In both situations, the internal energy market and national regulators were prerequisites for energy security and new entries on the market (European Parliament Resolution 2007). Additionally, the European Parliament noticed the considerable variations within the process of implementing the existing unbundling provisions and national regulatory frameworks, while "the convergence and synchronisation of national action with regard to the unbundling provisions is the only way to proceed towards the completion of the internal energy market". Obviously, this was in line with general liberalisation and market integration, which were assessed by the Parliament equally important in completing the internal energy market in the European Union (European Parliament Resolution 2007).

In respect to the specific findings of the European Parliament, they pertained to transmission unbundling, regulators, regulated tariffs, social impact and consumer protection, interconnections, long-term contracts, electricity grid and gas networks, strategic stocks, transparency, and implementation of Community legislation. In particular, the first three of these areas have implications for this thesis. First, in reference to transmission unbundling, the European Parliament expressed its belief in ownership unbundling in transmission, as being "the most effective tool to promote investments in infrastructures in a non-discriminatory way, fair access to the grid for new entrants and transparency in the market". Seen in that light, the Parliament called on the EC to provide an analysis of ownership unbundling and of establishing independent system operators. It had to include, *inter alia*, expected costs, the benefits for the internal market and consumers, or what negative consequences would arise if no unbundling is conducted.

Second, the Commission's initiative to strengthen the EU level of cooperation between national regulators "through an EU entity", was endorsed by the Parliament, as:

> a way to promote a more European approach to regulation on cross-border issues; considers that increased convergence and harmonisation of the competences of national regulators is essential to overcome technical and regulatory differences...; emphasises that the Commission should play a determining role, whilst not undermining the independence of national regulators; believes that decisions by the regulators should be made on specifically defined technical and trade issues and on an informed basis considering, where appropriate, the views of transmission system operators (TSOs) and other relevant stakeholders, and should be legally binding.
>
> (European Parliament Resolution 2007)

In this context, only the national regulators were to take decisions affecting national markets. The Parliament supported extending their competences (e.g. in the field of investments inventory, penalising operators that do not obey regulators' decisions or TSOs that do not fulfil network maintenance obligations), which had to be "strong and ... well defined", as well as "harmonised at EU level via the establishment of common rules on transparency, disclosure and accountability" – these actions had to ensure national regulators' full independence of national governments and industry. Similarly, the idea to formalise the role of ENTSO was supported by the Parliament. Besides, the European Parliament urged strengthening of cooperation between regulators and competition authorities (both at national and European level). Finally, the European Parliament criticised the "excess interventionism of some governments in the decisions taken by national regulators".

Third, with regards to tarification, the Parliament called for ending possibilities for setting regulated tariffs (with the exception of the last resort tariffs of Directive 2003/54/EC). This was to be done gradually, ensuring protection of vulnerable customers. What is important, intervention on prices was treated as a last resort, only when the "national regulators seek to control soaring prices that are artificially stimulated, in order to prevent harm to consumers, businesses and new entrants". Even then, prices should be based on real costs and cover them (European Parliament Resolution 2007).

Furthermore, besides achieving full opening of the retail markets in July 2007 (from this date all consumers have been able to choose supplier) in the report of 2008 the EC found that, from a practical point of view, market integration was still far away, and as a rule electricity markets in the EU kept national orientation, what limited competition (European Commission 2008, p. 2). The key message of the Commission's assessment was: "[n]ot all the shortcomings can be solved within existing legislation: improved legislative measures are needed" (European Commission 2008, p. 2). For example, in 2008 the market was characterised by different prices, regional monopolies, persistent cross-border congestion between Member States, as well as the tendency towards consolidation. In addition, the EC saw lack of independence of network operators and ineffectiveness in implementing functional unbundling (European Commission 2008, pp. 3–6).

The European Commission also expressed objections on unequal levels of regulatory powers, which were shared by several regulators at national and regional levels, including the competition authority and/or ministry. In addition, in any Member State, regulators did not supervise wholesale and retail markets at a sufficient level. What is more, the Commission (2008, p. 6) noted the problem of the "regulatory gap" deriving from disintegrated and non-harmonised regulatory decisions across borders. In the EC's opinion ERGEG and the Florence Forum were able, to some extent, to improve this situation. However, voluntary cooperation could not tackle the whole problem (European Commission 2008, p. 6). Finally, with respect to public law regulation, the EC raised concerns about negative effects of regulated energy prices:

> [t]hey lead immediately to a distortion of competition and reduce liquidity in wholesale markets. In the long run, regulated prices give wrong price signals to investors and thus have a negative impact on the development of new infrastructure. By setting a price level that does not allow new entrants to supply at cost-covering prices, price regulation creates a market entry barrier for alternative suppliers and thus directly threatens security of supply.... Measures for consumer protection should not be mixed with competitive instruments, they should be addressed by separate means.
>
> (European Commission 2008, pp. 7–8)

The listed circumstances were the reasons for the overall analysis of progress on the internal market, which was rather unsatisfactory. Because of it the Commission called for improvements. In terms of public law regulation they concerned the regulators' position and further harmonisation of regulatory best practice models across borders. Further, as the EC (2008, p. 9) stated "[t]he major concerns in the various areas all share two characteristics: significant impact hampering the development of a well-functioning internal market in electricity... which cannot be solved within the existing legal framework". This resulted in the Commission's proposal, which took the form of the next legislative package: the Third Liberalisation Package. Before proceeding to examine the third phase of market liberalisation in the EU, it is necessary to conclude the main findings and the principal issues and suggestions, which have arisen through the analysis conducted above.

## Evaluation of the Second Energy Package

The European Union adopted the second step of the energy market's reform driven by, *inter alia*, the need for improving the internal energy market by ensuring a level playing field, reducing unfair market behaviour or ensuring free access to the grid, as well as protecting rights of small and vulnerable. As demonstrated earlier, even the very first works on the Proposal for a new legal framework showed that public law regulation would be an important tool used within it. This is also confirmed by the final version of this proposal, i.e. adopted Directive 2003/54/EC.

As previously, public law regulation, in its broad sense, covered "public service obligations" which Member States could impose on electricity companies. Their range was extended by clarifications in the field of energy efficiency and climate protection. Besides environment, the Package covered provisions on household consumers aimed to guarantee them several rights (e.g. the right to supply of electricity at reasonable, easily and clearly comparable and transparent prices, or to change electricity supplier). The concrete regulatory basis for this was provided by the set of minimum standards for protection of household customers. Member States were obliged to ensure its implementation and compliance.

The Second Electricity Directive created a more rigorous regime for TSOs and DSOs. Legislation strengthened the unbundling rules. A model of *legal unbundling* as a minimum was adopted. With the use of public law, the European Union imposed on entities of the energy market strict rules on their operation. Member States had to guarantee their independence from other activities not relating to transmission covering their legal form, organisation, and decision-making. This last component not only affected companies, but also its managers. It shows how deep public regulation was in this scope, and how the European Union was determined to enable equal market playing in the energy sector. It was complemented by the obligation of establishing by the operators the compliance programmes. Furthermore, public law regulation provided stricter rules for connection to the grid, where new provisions on refusal of grid access were adopted.

What should be emphasised is the fact that the Second Electricity Directive established a much more comprehensive legal dimension of regulation in its narrow sense, i.e. regarding operation of national regulatory authorities, than Directive 96/92/EC. Member States were obliged to establish an energy regulator. However, they continued to decide its institutional model (single or multi-regulatory body). The EU's countries were to provide them with independence; however, this was limited to the electricity industry, not a public sphere (e.g. government). Regulators received also a minimum range of regulatory responsibilities and powers. This way of enhancing their position had to guarantee effective regulation. Member States had to ensure it. Moreover, a priority for the European Union was achieving an equal level of regulators' position. Thereby, Directive 2003/54/EC formalised the cooperation of national regulators. This was done with the establishment of ERGEG, that together with existing regulatory forums were aimed at providing further harmonisation in regulation. In this sense, it was the very first sign of *Europeanisation* of regulation, enhanced by multilateral cooperation between line regulators and the Commission.

Nevertheless, Directive 2003/54/EC's application in practice revealed imperfections in the legal framework. Apart from delays in transposition, which impaired the European liberalisation agenda, Member States were rather choosing the necessary minimum of implementation, using possible derogations (e.g. regarding unbundling). Further, the market shaped by the Second Energy Package was still under the influence of the factors that hindered the existence of competition (e.g. high degree of market concentration, cross-subsidies, primacy of the interests of integrated companies within the same group, low market liquidity).

Furthermore, noticing the role of public law regulation and regulators, the European institutions found numerous shortfalls with respect to the regulators' position. As proved, this concerned the influence of national government (e.g. by overruling regulators' decisions, depriving powers to impose sanctions) and limits of national regulatory authorities' powers (i.e. granting them insufficient powers, in contradiction with Directive 2003/54/EC). The increasing number posed a threat to the EU's liberalisation agenda.

As Directive 2003/54/EC did not solve all problems traced in this chapter, the need for new legislation emerged. In these terms, further application of public law regulation was considered. The initial proposals and analytical work conducted in the phase prior to the next step of European legislation highlights the "regulatory direction" of the European idea for the internal energy market. It involved equipping regulators with new powers and improving those already granted, and ensuring them discretion. In addition, this approach included deepening broad public regulation's tools dedicated to energy sector (like TPA or unbundling).

Moreover, the internal energy market needed closer energy cooperation of national regulatory authorities. This stronger Community oversight had to address the cross-border exchanges that could not be covered with the use of available legislation. The aim was to decrease the level of national orientation in regulation, altering it to a more pro-European attitude (e.g. proposals in the field of notification of regulators' decisions). The proposed role of the Commission was to assist in this problem. It was complemented by the idea of establishing a new European authority, which again appeared among concepts for the European energy agenda.

This discussion proves that the shape of the Third Energy Package could have taken various shapes, steered by different notions. What combines all ideas and proposals is public law regulation and the regulatory regime that had to be strengthened. Bearing in mind these circumstances, let us move on to the next chapter of this book where the Third Liberalisation Package is addressed.

## Notes

1 As defined in Article 2 (11) of Directive 2003/54/EC "non-household customers" were "any natural or legal persons purchasing electricity which is not for their own household use and shall include producers and wholesale customers".

2 The new Directive retained the definition of the "long-term planning" adopted in the Directive of 1996; compare Article 2 (25) of Directive 2003/54/EC and Article 2 (21) of Directive 96/92/EC.
3 According to Article 2 (10) of Directive 2003/54/EC "household customers" mean "customers purchasing electricity for their own household consumption, excluding commercial or professional activities".
4 "[E]nterprises with fewer than 50 occupied persons and an annual turnover or balance sheet not exceeding EUR 10 million."
5 These criteria concerned, *inter alia*: the safety and security of the electricity system, installations, and associated equipment; protection of public health and safety; protection of the environment; land use and siting; use of public ground; energy efficiency; the nature of the primary sources; characteristics particular to the applicant, such as technical, economic, and financial capabilities. Article 5 (2) (a–h) of Directive 2003/54/EC.
6 As stated in Article 10 (2) (c),

> [i]n particular, this shall enable the parent company to approve the annual financial plan, or any equivalent instrument, of the transmission system operator and to set global limits at the levels of indebtedness of its subsidiary. It shall not permit the parent company to give instructions regarding day-to-day operations, nor with respect to individual decisions concerning the construction or upgrading of transmission lines, that do not exceed the terms of the approved financial plan, or any equivalent instrument.

7 For the adequate monitoring of the programme.
8 For example, Article 14 (1), (2), or (3) of Directive 2003/54/EC.
9 For example, in Article 19 (4), a requirement concerning audit referred to in paragraph 2 was introduced. It was to verify in particular if "the obligation to avoid discrimination and cross-subsidies referred to in paragraph 3" was respected.
10 Compare Article 20 (1) of Directive 2003/54/EC with Article 17 (5) of Directive 96/92/EC.
11 This also had an international dimension because the regulators had to conduct it "in conjunction with the regulatory authority or authorities of those Member States with which interconnection exists".
12 It concerned "interconnectors, grid usage and capacity allocation to interested parties, taking into account the need to treat non-aggregated information as commercially confidential".
13 Further, "[i]n order to avoid uncertainty and costly and time consuming disputes, these tariffs should be published prior to their entry into force".
14 As stated in Article 23 (2) (a) of Directive 2003/54/EC "[t]hese tariffs, or methodologies, shall allow the necessary investments in the networks to be carried out in a manner allowing these investments to ensure the viability of the networks".
15 When the authority needed the additional information, the time limit might be extended by two months. With the consent of the complainant this period could be further extended. The same rules were applicable when a complaint was related to "connection tariffs for major new generation facilities" – then the two-month period could be extended.
16 Until 2010, the relevant authorities of the Member States, by 31 July, had to provide an annual report and send it to the Commission. Apart from the mentioned subjects, in addition, the report was to "review the changing ownership patterns and any practical measures taken at national level to ensure a sufficient variety of market actors or practical measures taken to enhance interconnection and competition". From 2010 onwards, this report had to be elaborated every two years.
17 As the Commission admitted: "only those regions with an adequate number of players, i.e. the UK and Nordic market, have been able to deliver a really competitive market across the board" (2005c, p. 5).

18 Except Cyprus and Malta, which were granted a derogation from the unbundling obligations (van Koten & Ortmann 2007, p. 9).

19 Under Article 81 (1) "all agreements between undertakings, decisions by associations of undertakings and concerted practices which may affect trade between Member States and which have as their object or effect the prevention, restriction or distortion of competition within the common market" were forbidden, and qualified "as incompatible with the common market". Pursuant to the Treaty it covered *inter alia*, "fixing purchase or selling prices or any other trading conditions" in a direct or indirect way, limiting or controlling "production, markets, technical development, or investment", or applying "dissimilar conditions to equivalent transactions with other trading parties, thereby placing them at a competitive disadvantage".

20 As stated in Article 82,

> [a]ny abuse by one or more undertakings of a dominant position within the common market or in a substantial part of it shall be prohibited as incompatible with the common market in so far as it may affect trade between Member States. Such abuse may, in particular, consist in:
>
> a directly or indirectly imposing unfair purchase or selling prices or other unfair trading conditions;
> b limiting production, markets or technical development to the prejudice of consumers;
> c applying dissimilar conditions to equivalent transactions with other trading parties, thereby placing them at a competitive disadvantage;
> d making the conclusion of contracts subject to acceptance by the other parties of supplementary obligations which, by their nature or according to commercial usage, have no connection with the subject of such contracts.

21 For example, pursuant to Article 86 (1) "[i]n the case of public undertakings and undertakings to which Member States grant special or exclusive rights, Member States shall neither enact nor maintain in force any measure contrary to the rules contained in this Treaty".

22 The Regulation concerns concentrations with a Community dimension. On the ground of Article 1 (2) these are concentrations where: "(a) the combined aggregate worldwide turnover of all the undertakings concerned is more than EUR 5000 million", "(b) the aggregate Community-wide turnover of each of at least two of the undertakings concerned is more than EUR 250 million" – "unless each of the undertakings concerned achieves more than two-thirds of its aggregate Community-wide turnover within one and the same Member State". In addition, as stated in paragraph 3, concentration that is not within this range has a Community dimension when: "(a) the combined aggregate worldwide turnover of all the undertakings concerned is more than EUR 2500 million", "(b) in each of at least three Member States, the combined aggregate turnover of all the undertakings concerned is more than EUR 100 million", "(c) in each of at least three Member States included for the purpose of point (b), the aggregate turnover of each of at least two of the undertakings concerned is more than EUR 25 million", "(d) the aggregate Community-wide turnover of each of at least two of the undertakings concerned is more than EUR 100 million". Likewise, also in this case a rule of "two-thirds of its aggregate Community-wide turnover" was applicable.

23 On the ground of Article 87 (1) in general,

> any aid granted by a Member State or through State resources in any form whatsoever which distorts or threatens to distort competition by favouring certain undertakings or the production of certain goods shall, in so far as it affects trade between Member States, be incompatible with the common market.

24 According to Article 88 (1),

> [t]he Commission shall, in cooperation with Member States, keep under constant review all systems of aid existing in those States. It shall propose to the latter any appropriate measures required by the progressive development or by the functioning of the common market.

In addition, as stated in the paragraph 3 "[t]he Commission shall be informed, in sufficient time to enable it to submit its comments, of any plans to grant or alter aid".

25 These were: Austria, Belgium, the Czech Republic, Germany, Estonia, Spain, France, Greece, Ireland, Italy, Lithuania, Latvia, Poland, Sweden, Slovakia, and the United Kingdom (European Commission 2006).

26

> In several Member States, the regulated tariffs are of general application, and set at a level so low compared with market prices, that they fully prevent market opening in complete violation of the Directives. Regulated prices are also a strong disincentive for investment. They also prevent energy demand to adapt to price increases.
>
> (European Commission 2006)

27 "Because of the historical reservation of capacities on interconnectors, and the fact that these interconnectors are often congested, there is often no capacity left for new entrants" (European Commission 2006).

28

> Because most of the companies operating the transmission and distribution grids (TSO and DSOs) are still owned by gas and electricity suppliers (no ownership unbundling, which is not a requirement of the directives), there is a potential risk of lack of independence by these operators.
>
> (European Commission 2006)

## References

Council Regulation (EC) No 139/2004 of 20 January 2004 on the control of concentrations between undertakings (the EC Merger Regulation), OJ L 24, 29 January 2004.

Directive 2003/54/EC of the European Parliament and of the Council of 26 June 2003 concerning common rules for the internal market in electricity and repealing Directive 96/92/EC, OJ L 176, 15 July 2003.

Europe Economics & TIS 2006. *Study of the powers and competencies of energy and transport regulators.*

European Commission 2004, *Mergers: Commission prohibits acquisition of GDP by EDP and ENI*, Brussels, 9 December 2004, IP/04/1455. Available from: http://europa.eu/rapid/press-release_IP-04-1455_en.htm. [19 June 2015].

European Commission 2005a, *Annual report on the implementation of the gas and electricity internal market.* Brussels, 5 January 2005, COM (2004) 863 final.

European Commission 2005b, *Commission Staff Working Document: technical annex to the report from the Commission to the Council and the European Parliament on progress in creating the internal gas and electricity market*, Brussels, 15 November 2005, SEC (2005) 1448.

European Commission 2005c, *Communication from the Commission to the Council and the European Parliament: report on progress in creating the internal gas and electricity market*, Brussels, 15 November 2005, COM (2005) 568 final.

European Commission 2006, *The Commission to act over EU energy markets*, Brussels, 12 December 2006, MEMO/06/481. Available from: http://europa.eu/rapid/press-release_MEMO-06-481_en.htm?locale=en [15 June 2015].

European Commission 2007a, *Communication from the Commission to the Council and the European Parliament: prospects for the internal gas and electricity market*, Brussels, 10 January 2007, COM(2006) 841 final.

European Commission 2007b, *Communication from the Commission to the European Council and the European Parliament: an energy policy for Europe*, Brussels, 10 January 2007, COM (2007) 1 final.

European Commission 2007c, *Communication from the Commission: inquiry pursuant to Article 17 of Regulation (EC) No 1/2003 into the European gas and electricity sectors (final report)*, Brussels, 10 January 2007, COM (2006) 851 final.

European Commission 2008, *Report from the Commission to the Council and the European Parliament: progress in creating the internal gas and electricity market*, Brussels, 15 April 2008, COM (2008) 192 final.

European Parliament Resolution of 10 July 2007 on prospects for the internal gas and electricity market, Strasbourg, 10 July 2007, A6-0249/2007.

Presidency of the European Council Conclusion of 8–9 March 2007, Brussels, 2 May 2007, 7224/1/07, REV 1.

Tapia, J. & Mantzari, D. 2013, "The regulation/competition interaction", in *Handbook on European competition law: substantive aspects*, eds I. Lianos & D. Geradin, Edward Elgar Publishing, Cheltenham, pp. 588–628.

van Koten, S. & Ortmann, A. 2007 "The unbundling regime for electricity utilities in the EU: a case of legislative and regulatory capture?" *CERGE-EI Working Paper Series*, Charles University, Centre for Economic Research and Graduate Education, Academy of Sciences of the Czech Republic, Economics Institute, Prague. Available from: www.cerge-ei.cz/pdf/wp/Wp328.pdf [22 June 2015].

# 8 Third Liberalisation Package

In September 2007, the European Commission (EC) presented another part of a broad reform of the energy sector in the European Union, i.e. the *Third Liberalisation Package*. As previously, the package included core proposals on the electricity and gas sectors (two sectorial directives). The EC fulfilled the scope of legislation with three new regulations. These were legislation on conditions for access to the network for cross-border exchanges in electricity, and to natural gas transmission networks, and also a completely new initiative of establishing an Agency for the Cooperation of Energy Regulators.

Electricity, in the EC's opinion, was "at the heart of the Europe's well-being" (Proposal for a Directive 2007, 528 final, p. 2), and needed competition and efficiency. This was partly brought about by liberalising the electricity sector, started in the 1990s. As underlined in the Explanatory Memorandum to the proposal for a new directive on electricity, "[d]uring these 10 years, many of Europe's citizens have benefited from more choice and more competition, with improved service and security". However, as already mentioned, by 2007 full competitiveness on the energy market was not reached.[1] This was because of a lack in choice of suppliers, fragmentation along national borders, a high degree of vertical integration, or a high market concentration (Proposal for a Directive 2007, 528 final, p. 2). Seen in this light, supported by the European Council, the European Parliament, and the Council of European Energy Regulators (CEER), the Commission established a proposal for new legislation on the electricity sector. The proposal was based on six main assumptions. They referred to unbundling, powers and independence of national regulators, the ACER, TSOs' cooperation, functioning of the market, and security of supply. The first three of them in particular relate to public law regulation. Therefore, as in previous chapters, they are presented in more detail.

## Shaping the forthcoming package

With respect to unbundling, the Commission found that legal and functional unbundling had made a positive contribution to the electricity market, however the practice of implementation them, where the TSO is a legal entity within an integrated company, had shown three types of problems:

> [f]irstly, [the TSO] may treat its affiliated companies better than [competitors].... The underlying reason is that legal and functional unbundling do not solve the fundamental conflict of interest within integrated companies ... [that] is almost impossible to control by regulatory means as the independence of [the TSO] within an integrated company is impossible to monitor without an excessively burdensome and intrusive regulation.
>
> Secondly, under the current unbundling rules, non-discriminatory access to information cannot be guaranteed as there is no effective means of preventing [TSOs] releasing market sensitive information to the generation or supply branch of the integrated company.
>
> Thirdly... [v]ertically integrated network operators have no incentive for developing the network in the overall interests of the market and hence for facilitating new entry at generation or supply levels; on the contrary, they have an inherent interest to limit new investment when this will benefit its competitors and bring new competition onto the incumbent's "home market". Instead, the investment decisions made by vertically integrated companies tend to be biased to the needs of supply affiliates. Such companies seem particularly disinclined to increase interconnection ... and thereby boosting competition in the incumbent's home market to the detriment of the internal market.
>
> (Proposal for a Directive 2007, 528 final, p. 4)

To tackle these problems the EC proposed the known option of *ownership unbundling*, based on the concept that the same person cannot control a supply undertaking and, at the same time, hold any interest in or exercise any right over a TSO, and vice versa: control over a TSO excludes holding any interest in or exercising any right over a supply undertaking. An exception was a non-controlling minority interests option (Proposal for a Directive 2007, 528 final, p. 4). To preserve the interests of the shareholders of vertically integrated companies the EC proposed to divide the shares of the vertically integrated company into shares of the company owning the TSO and shares of the supply company. Afterwards, these shares might be assigned to the shareholders of the previously vertically integrated company (Proposal for a Directive 2007, 528 final, p. 4). Ownership unbundling was the preferred approach and, as a derogation, the EC provided the option of the *Independent System Operator*. Based on the assumption that vertically integrated companies retain the ownership of their network assets, obliged Member States to establish an undertaking or entity entirely which performs all the functions of a transmission network operator in a separation from the vertically integrated company. To guarantee the independence of a market operator, Member States were to provide "regulation and permanent regulatory monitoring" (Proposal for a Directive 2007, 528 final, pp. 5–6). Moreover, in some cases, the Commission assumed obligatory disposer of vertically integrated energy companies' assets. Mainly, these concerned transmission networks. Besides this derogation (or rather second possibility of shaping a legal model for TSO), the EC proposed a temporary exemption from ownership unbundling rules for investment in new energy infrastructures by supply and production companies (Proposal for a Directive 2007, 528 final, p. 6). Finally, in the case of non-compliance of unbundling rules, the Commission could intervene (Proposal for a Directive 2007, 528 final, p. 7).

Unbundling had to have a European dimension: ownership or operation of a transmission system in any Member State was impossible for a supply or production company active anywhere in the EU (Proposal for a Directive 2007, 528 final, p. 7). However, the Commission excluded the eventuality of controlling any EU transmission system by third countries, unless this was permitted by an agreement between the EU and the third country. Its rationale was to "guarantee that companies from third countries respect the same rules that apply to EU based undertakings in both letter and spirit – not to discriminate against them" (Proposal for a Directive 2007, 528 final, p. 7).

Seen in this light, the EC assessed its provisions on unbundling as a crucial action towards European market integration. Further:

> [effective unbundling] may ultimately help to create supra-national transmission system operators as the operators are no longer held back by mutual distrust. But at the same time, if supra-national transmission operators were created without ensuring their full independence, competition between affiliated supply and production companies would likely be weakened due to the risk of collusion. In the absence of effective unbundling such cooperation would therefore give rise to competition concerns.
>
> (Proposal for a Directive 2007, 528 final, p. 7)

### *Need to ensure a position of the energy regulators*

Apart from unbundling, the Commission proposed to strengthen the position of national regulators. New provisions resulted from differences in the functioning of regulators in Member States. According to the EC's opinion, some of them were "well-established bodies". To regulate the market they were equipped with substantial powers and resources. On the other hand, some regulators were of a weak position, recently established, or dispersed in the administration system. Herein, one rationale is of a particular importance:

> [t]he experience of Member States whose markets have been open for several years, and of other utility sectors open to competition, clearly indicates that strong regulators are necessary for a properly functioning market, in particular as regards the use of network infrastructures.
>
> (Proposal for a Directive 2007, 528 final, p. 8)

In the EC's assumption, a range of enhancing regulatory powers covered: monitoring (of TPA, unbundling obligations, balancing mechanisms, congestion and interconnection management, transparency obligations, the level of market opening and competition, as well as of network security and reliability), reviewing (of investment plans of TSOs and of network security and reliability rules), promoting (effective competition, together with competition authorities), and ensuring that consumer protection measures are effective (Proposal for a Directive 2007, 528 final, p. 8). To realise regulatory duties, Member States should grant them the right to use certain regulatory tools. These were powers to investigate, to request all necessary information, as well as to impose dissuasive sanctions (Proposal for a Directive 2007, 528 final, p. 9).

Furthermore, recognising the disadvantages of existing legislation on the independence of regulatory authorities (e.g. the lack of specific rules on how independence should be ensured, the lack of independence from short-term political interests), the EC proposed a far-reaching formula of independence. According to it, the regulators had to be functionally independent of any entity, public or private. The independence also had its impact on regulator's staff (e.g. could not take instruction from any government or other public or private entity). This was to be done by providing regulators with necessary legal personality, as well as financial and operational position, i.e. autonomy in budget, proper human and financial resources, and independent management (Proposal for a Directive 2007, 528 final, p. 9).

Moreover, the Commission found it necessary to give regulators "a clear mandate to cooperate at European level ... to ensure competitive, secure and environmentally sustainable internal electricity ... within the European Union, and effective market opening for all consumers and suppliers" (Proposal for a Directive 2007, 528 final, p. 9). Herein, the Commission presented a new approach. It was a proposition to establish "an independent mechanism for national regulators to cooperate and take decisions: the Agency for the Cooperation of Energy Regulators and the Commission" (Proposal for a Directive 2007, 528 final, p. 9).

### *Concept for cooperation of the energy regulatory authorities*

The idea to establish the ACER derived from the need to harmonise *grid codes* – the technical rules on electricity networks for electricity companies. Member States provided different codes, and these due to their variety did not foster market integration. To improve this situation the EC suggested using some positive experiences of earlier regulatory cooperation conducted under the auspices of self-regulatory forums (for electricity – Florence Forum) and of ERGEG. ERGEG, especially, in the Commission's view, contributed to the process of completion of the internal market by providing its independent advisory activity. However, this complex way of reaching agreements (in 2007 ERGEG consisted of 27 regulators plus more than 30 TSOs) was not producing sufficient results.[2] Due to these drawbacks the Commission did not use ERGEG as a direct solution for mentioned harmonisation.

An evaluation made by the EC indicated another solution. Harmonisation of all national grid codes required specialist expertise that could be brought only by national regulatory agencies. The Commission declared, "[i]n practice, only a body emanating from the national regulators can catalyse all the necessary resources of national regulators that is fundamental to achieving success on these issues" (Proposal for a Directive 2007, 528 final, p. 10). That is why the EC proposed a separate entity model, independent and placed outside the Commission.

In the EC's assumption the ACER's tasks were to fulfil the regulatory gap at the European level. They were coherent with the regulatory tasks performed by national regulators. The proposed structure, in which ACER, through its Regulatory Board, consisted of national regulators could closely cooperate with them and use their expertise. Apart from collaboration "[t]he structure should provide a framework for ... a regulatory review of the cooperation between transmission operators and scope for taking individual decisions concerning infrastructure in the territory of more than one Member State" (Proposal for a Directive 2007, 528 final, p. 11).

It is worth noting that besides establishing a new body, different options were analysed. One of them concerned pursuing this coordination by the Commission. However, as the EC argued "[h]armonising these issues, as well as making progress on new infrastructure, is not a task that typically falls within the Commission's sphere of activities; [t]he Commission has actually never carried out such an activity" (Proposal for a Directive 2007, 528 final, p. 10). Also, the more powerful model was taken into account. It could be comparable to the network of competition authorities created in 2004 under Council Regulation 1/2003 (although, this would require extending the EC's autonomous powers to the energy sector, as in the field of competition), or be similar to the model of European Central Banks (this would entail amendment of the Treaty) (Proposal for a Directive 2007, 528 final, p. 10).

Traced reasoning resulted in the idea of establishing the ACER as an independent body that initiates the Commission's decisions (by its proposals to the EC) and executes power to make individual binding on third parties' regulatory decisions on detailed technical issues (Proposal for a Directive 2007, 528 final, p. 11). In addition, regarding this last power, it reflected the principles defined by the EC in the draft inter-institutional agreement on the operating framework for the European regulatory agencies.

Besides the three mentioned pillars of the Commission's proposal of 2007, the legislation concerned cooperation between TSOs (e.g. strengthening their cooperation in a number of key areas, *inter alia*, in coordination of grid operation, or investment planning), functioning of the market (e.g. facilitating TPA to key infrastructures, providing guidance on the compliance of downstream bilateral long-term supply agreements with EC competition law, or guidance for the proposed obligations on the Member States and the national regulatory authorities to establish clear rules on competition in the retail market), and security of supply (e.g. strengthening Member States cooperation, or security of supply monitoring by TSOs).

## Options for the regulatory model

At the end of 2007, the legislative proposition on the internal energy market was discussed by the European Council. Several Member States expressed their doubts about the two alternatives of unbundling, requesting establishing a third option. On the other hand, the Portuguese Presidency commented on progress achieved in regulatory powers (tasks of national regulators, how to accommodate different national administrative arrangements, how to enhance their independence or define their general objectives) (Council of the European Union 2007). Nevertheless, the Council did not reach an agreement on the model of regulatory agency as the EC proposed. However, a majority accepted the principles and tasks that could underlie an independent mechanism for European regulatory coordination. Besides these points, a broad consensus was reached. It concerned such issues as investment in infrastructure, as well as planning at the national, regional, and European level (Council of the European Union 2007). Further policy debate was held during the Council meeting in February 2008.[3]

In April 2008, the Committee of Regions and the Economic and Social Committee presented their opinions on the proposal for the new energy legislative package. The CR agreed that existing legal and functional transmission unbundling is insufficient "since it does not suppress the conflict of interest that stems from vertical integration", and it supported passing additional measures. In this context, the ESC drew attention to the aspect of regional cooperation based on ownership unbundling, which should be favoured by the EC. In the field of regulatory authorities, the CR backed harmonising their activity and reinforcing their position, stressing that "[r]egulators must not focus exclusively on regulated activities, but must also ensure the proper general functioning of the market through ex-ante discretionary powers". Similarly, the ESC considered that powers of national regulators should be harmonised and their independence should increase.

What is worth emphasising is that the CR tended to strengthen the ERGEG rather than establishing the ACER. As the Committee observed

> rather than establishing a new structure, with the resulting expenses and bureaucratic burden, it would be possible to continue on the current basis with the stronger ERGEG which would have the power to deal with cross-border problems and which would also be made responsible for the other tasks which would be entrusted to the proposed agency.

According to the CR only if enhancing the ERGEG did not increase competition, would the establishment of a separate agency be justified. On the other hand, the ESC expressed its strong belief that ACER "must be given more powers to ... play an independent regulatory role".

Two months after, as a result of the Council meeting in June 2008, a broad agreement on the essential elements of the liberalisation legislative package was reached. It covered, *inter alia*, consensus on unbundling (an option allowing companies to retain ownership of transmission systems if they were managed by an independent transmission operator (ITO), was developed),[4] market functioning (provisions on extension of archiving information about transactions in supply contracts for electricity derivatives at the disposal of regulators), consumers' rights (guaranteeing the appropriate information for consumers on their energy consumption and costs), as well as the ACER (Council of the European Union 2008). With regards to the last one, as delegations concurred:

> [t]he regulatory Agency to be established will be independent from the Member States and the Commission and will have well circumscribed tasks. It will focus on issues involving more than one Member State as far as binding decision-making is concerned. Its involvement in technical matters has been strengthened, but is still of an advisory nature; it generally allows for the national levels to play their parts. In all these tasks, market participants and authorities at national level are duly consulted and due account is taken of the outcomes of regional cooperation between TSOs and between regulators.
> (Council of the European Union 2008)[5]

The EC's proposal was evaluated by the European Parliament. In its legislative resolution of 18 June 2008 on this proposal, the EP approved approximately 150 amendments to the Commission's proposal. *Inter alia*, they covered provisions on public service obligations (Article 3 (2)), regulation in the electricity sector (Article 3 (7a)), harmonisation of regulatory cooperation (Article 5a), minimum standards for the operation (Article 11), or regulation of cross-border issues (Article 22d).

It is clear that the intention of the European Parliament was strengthening the position of consumers, as well as regulators, and thus enhancing public law regulation. These three areas were gathered in the EP's amendment to Article 11 (5) of the draft of the Directive. Pursuant to it "[n]ational regulatory authorities should be given broader powers for the purpose of ensuring consumer protection within the European Union". Provisions on giving the national regulatory authorities a right of veto over decisions to appoint or dismiss persons responsible for the general management of TSOs, or right to enter into agreements with each other to foster regulatory cooperation, as well as establishing an independent energy ombudsman or a consumer body, were in line with it.

The EP's draft Directive provided strong support to ownership unbundling seen by the Commission as the best option. Although through further legislation processes, the three options for effective unbundling were approved. The Commission found proposed changes as "softening" its proposal, however they did not involve altering "the core tasks of network regulation". According to the Commission these tasks were renewables and research development policies, security of supply, and public service obligations (European Commission 2009, pp. 3–4). The Council's proposals on independence of the regulatory authorities did not cover its core principle. They concerned, *inter alia*, cooperation between other national authorities, in fields like sustainability, public service obligations, or judicial control (European Commission 2009, p. 4). In comparison to the first version of the Directive, the Council limited the number of guidelines adopted under the Comitology procedure (European Commission 2009, p. 4).

This inter-institutional debate, with the second reading of the package in the Parliament, resulted in a compromised package, which was adopted by the EC in April 2009. It included limiting certain provisions on effective unbundling of TSO, enhancing the position of regulatory authorities, as well as rules concerning Member States' obligations in the field of consumer protection, energy poverty, and the implementation of smart metering, on which the EC earlier insisted. Two months later, the package on the internal energy market – the Third Liberalisation Package – was unanimously adopted by the Council, which approved all of the EC's second-reading amendments (Council of the European Union 2009).

## Strengthening public law regulation

As a result of the traced legislative process, the Commission's proposal of 2007 became Directive 2009/72/EC. This new legal act provided a broad range of provisions on public law regulation. It was related with changes in existing institutions as well as with introducing new legal solutions. For instance, as previously, pursuant to Article 3 (2) of the Directive, Member States may introduce *public service obligations* on electricity undertakings. They have to be in the general economic interest, as well as in line with European Law (particularly Article 86 TFEU), clearly defined, transparent, non-discriminatory, and verifiable. In addition they must guarantee equality of access for electricity undertakings of the EU to national consumers. Shaped in this way under Article 3 (2), public service obligation relates to security (with security of supply),[6] regularity, quality and price of supplies, and environmental protection (with energy efficiency), energy from renewables, and climate. On the basis of Article 3 (3) Member States may appoint a *supplier of last resort*.[7]

Besides them, regarding public law regulation *sensu stricte*, the Directive not only confirms the need for designating a single national regulatory authority for energy (see Article 35), but also markedly enhances the position of regulators. The rationale for this movement derives from the need to secure competition and the supply of electricity at the most competitive price (see Recital 8 of Directive 2009/72/EC's preamble). Further, the setting up of a system operator or a transmission operator that is independent in its functions required that extensive regulatory control mechanisms are put in place.[8]

### *Comprehensive rules on unbundling*

The effective separation of the network from activities of generation and supply (effective unbundling), was needed to prevent discrimination in the operation of the network, as well as in the incentives for vertically integrated undertakings to invest adequately in their networks (Recital 9). In practice, unbundling has kept the shape proposed during the legislation process, with ownership unbundling of Article 9 as a rule. On this basis, from the beginning of March 2012, Member State had to ensure that the owner of a transmission system acts as the TSO, and this activity does not link with other fields of operation in the electricity sector: generation or supply.[9] Alternatively, Member States in which the transmission system belonged to a vertically integrated undertaking (before the beginning of September 2009) could decide about excluding themselves from the applicability of ownership unbundling. By using this exception countries had to designate an independent system operator (Article 13), or meet conditions required from setting an independent transmission operator (*inter alia*, rules on the operation,[10] or on the independence)[11] provided in Chapter V of Directive 2009/72/EC.

Naturally, the rules on unbundling are applicable to the distribution sector. Here, as well the need for executing public law, regulation in the form of regulatory authorities' presence is required. For example, pursuant to Article 26 (3) of Directive 2009/72/EC the regulatory monitoring of DSO should be entered in the situation of vertical integration of this distribution operator. To ensure realisation of unbundling rules, and hence indiscrimination in the network sector, aimed at enhancing competition and the most competitive price of electricity, the Directive provides a broad field for regulatory activity. Besides certifying undertakings as being in compliance with the provisions of an independent transmission operator, the regulatory authorities are granted several powers in this area. For example, under Article 18 (6), the TSO is obliged to store data of any commercial and financial relations between the vertically integrated undertaking and the TSO. Upon request, the TSO makes them available to the regulatory authority. In addition, the TSO submits authority on all agreements with a vertically integrated undertaking of a commercial or financial nature for its approval (Article 18 (7)). The national authority regulators participate in the process of appointing the TSO's managers. In accordance with Article 19 of the Directive, regulators must be informed with an official notification about some conditions of personal decisions of the TSO's Supervisory Body on TSO's management (e.g. the term, the duration, and the termination of office of the persons nominated by the Supervisory Body). Within three weeks, the regulator may raise objections.[12] If no objections are raised the mentioned decisions become binding.

Moreover, to secure properly conducted unbundling and exclude discriminatory conduct (Article 21 (1)), Member States have to assure that the TSO has established a compliance programme.[13] The programme does not fulfil the whole non-discrimination EU agenda expressed in the Directive. Apart from the programme, the TSO is obliged set procedures for non-discriminatory connection of new power plants to the transmission system, which regulators are entitled to approve (see Article 23).

Similarly, the compliance programme is subjected to the regulator's approval. The regulator also approves a compliance officer appointed for the programme's needs. Further, the Directive provides for close cooperation of the compliance officer and regulator. Not only shall he report regularly to the regulatory authority, but also has concrete material duties. For example, the compliance officer submits an annual report on implementation of the programme, notifies any substantial breaches regarding implementation, and reports to the regulatory authority on any commercial and financial relations between the vertically integrated undertaking and the TSO (Article 21 (4)–(5)). Moreover, it is the regulator that assures the independence of the compliance officer.[14] Under the rules established in Article 26 (2) (b), the DSOs are also obliged to elaborate a compliance programme.

### *Accelerating the development of the energy infrastructure*

Although the provisions of Directive 2009/72/EC do not only concern *public law regulation* as a measure for enhancing unbundling, it is used by the European Union to achieve other objectives which are in line with the goal of establishing the common energy market. This applies to the development of infrastructure with network development plans as an instrument for supporting it. On the basis of Article 22, the TSO is to submit annually to the regulator a ten-year network development plan. As stated in paragraph 1 of this Article, the plan "shall contain efficient measures in order to guarantee the adequacy of the system and the security of supply".[15] Furthermore, regulators play a more active role with regard to the plan. They conduct a consultation process where all actual or potential system users are invited to participate, examine coverage of all investment needs identified during the consultations, as well as ensure the plan's consistence with the non-binding Community-wide ten-year network development plan by giving regulators power to require the TSO to amend its plan (see Article 21 (4)–(5)).

Further, they monitor and evaluate its implementation. Seen in this light, the provisions of the Directive provide a catalogue of measures for ensuring realisation of investments that should be conducted by the TSO (Article 22 (7)). Because of it, Member States ensure that their regulators can use at least one of these measures (Article 22 (7)):

a to require the Transmission System Operator to execute the investments in question;
b to organise a tender procedure open to any investors for the investment in question; or
c to oblige the Transmission System Operator to accept a capital increase to finance the necessary investments and allow independent investors to participate in the capital.

The rules on organising the tender procedure entail the possibility of obliging the TSO to accept selected conditions from the following list: financing, or construction by any third party, and building, or operating the new assets concerned itself. An agreement established as a result of these requirements is subjected to the regulator's approval (see Article 22 (7)).

Parenthetically, as underlined in Recital 37 of Directive 2009/72/EC's preamble, provisions on regulatory authorities "should be without prejudice to both the Commission's powers concerning the application of competition rules including the examination of mergers with a Community dimension, and the rules on the internal market such as the free movement of capital". Despite their detailed nature, the rules on the energy market cannot affect the rules on competition laid down in EU law. Energy regulators have to interact with the EC and competition authorities. Within this scope, national regulators should (Recital 61):

> provide information on the market to permit the Commission to exercise its role of observing and monitoring the internal market in electricity and its short, medium and long-term evolution, including aspects such as generation capacity, different sources of electricity generation, transmission and distribution infrastructure, quality of service, cross-border trade, congestion management, investments, wholesale and consumer prices, market liquidity and environmental and efficiency improvements. National regulatory authorities should report to the competition authorities and the Commission those Member States in which prices impair competition and proper functioning of the market.

### *Broadening the regulators' scope of action*

In the framework of the Directive, the regulatory authority exercises a broad range of objectives. This concerns, *inter alia*, "promoting a competitive, secure and environmentally sustainable internal market in electricity within the Community", as well as an "effective market opening for all customers and suppliers", "eliminating restrictions on trade in electricity between Member States", "ensuring that customers benefit through the efficient functioning of their national market, promoting effective competition and helping to ensure consumer protection", or "helping to achieve high standards of universal and public service in electricity supply" (Article 36). The protection of consumers is an important goal of regulators which should protect their interests through promotion of effective competition, e.g. by setting virtual power plants, as the possible measures to promote competition and ensure the proper functioning of the market. Separate powers granted to regulators should enable them protection of vulnerable customers (see Recital 37 of Directive 2009/72/EC's preamble). The aim of these rules is reflected clearly in the preamble to the Directive, in its Recital 51:

> consumer interests should be at the heart of this Directive and quality of service should be a central responsibility of electricity undertakings. Existing rights of consumers need to be strengthened and guaranteed, and should include greater transparency. Consumer protection should ensure that all

consumers in the wider remit of the Community benefit from a competitive market. Consumer rights should be enforced by Member States or, where a Member State has so provided, the regulatory authorities.

The broad scope reflects broad regulatory competence, as well as the legal position of authorities. As already mentioned, the practice of introducing national regulatory authorities into the legal systems of Member States has shown that their effectiveness is decreased due to a low level of independence from governments, accompanied by insufficient powers. That is why enhancing their position required a guarantee of the ability (Recital 34):

> to take decisions in relation to all relevant regulatory issues if the internal market in electricity is to function properly, and to be fully independent from any other public or private interests. This precludes neither judicial review nor parliamentary supervision in accordance with the constitutional laws of the Member States. In addition, approval of the budget of the regulator by the national legislator does not constitute an obstacle to budgetary autonomy.

Therefore in Article 35, the Directive provides a guarantee for independence of the regulatory authority in executing their powers impartially and transparently that should be ensured by Member States. Implementation of this rule requires EU countries to form the position of regulators in line with granting them legal personality and functional independence from any public or private entity, and personal independence from the regulators' staff and management.[16] This links with an obligation to appoint the regulator's top management (the members of the board) for a once renewable, term of five to seven years (Article 35 (5) (b)). Further, Member States should give the regulators the right to take autonomous decisions, "independently from any political body", as well as provide them with the above-mentioned budgetary autonomy ("autonomy in the implementation of the allocated budget, and adequate human and financial resources to carry out its duties") (Article 35 (5) (a)).

The answer to these goals and other duties listed in Article 37,[17] are regulators' powers. Besides the already-mentioned activity in the field of unbundling or development plans, regulators should be able (Article 37 (4)):

a to issue binding decisions on electricity undertakings;

b to carry out investigations into the functioning of the electricity markets, and to decide upon and impose any necessary and proportionate measures to promote effective competition and ensure the proper functioning of the market...;[18]

c to require any information from electricity undertakings relevant for the fulfilment of its tasks, including the justification for any refusal to grant third-party access, and any information on measures necessary to reinforce the network;

d to impose effective, proportionate and dissuasive penalties on electricity undertakings not complying with their obligations…;[19]

e appropriate rights of investigations and relevant powers of instructions for dispute settlement.

Thus, with respect to electricity entities' operation, regulators are entitled to issue binding decisions, secured by dissuasive sanction (Recital 37 of Directive 2009/72/EC's preamble). This covers the power to request relevant information from electricity undertakings, make appropriate and sufficient investigations, and settle disputes (Recital 38). Additional duties and powers arise when a TSO has been designated under Chapter V of the Directive.[20]

Other powers of the regulator are linked with facilitating access to the network. For this need, the Third Electricity Directive keeps the basis for a concrete regulatory tool: tariffs (or methodologies for calculating them). These powers should be granted to national regulators, which in executing them "should ensure that transmission and distribution tariffs are non-discriminatory and cost-reflective, and should take account of the long-term, marginal, avoided network costs from distributed generation and demand-side management measures" (Recital 36 of Directive 2009/72/EC's preamble). As stated in Article 32 of the Directive published, applicable to all eligible customers, objective and non-discriminatory tariffs are the basis for the system of TPA to the transmission and distribution systems. Within this scope, the regulatory authorities, where Member States have so provided, may take steps regarding the system operator's refusal of access, based on objective and technically and economically justified criteria. If a Member State makes such a decision, regulators guarantee that the mentioned criteria are duly applied and the system user may take advantage of a dispute settlement procedure (see Article 32 (2)). Additionally, pursuant to Article 37 (10) of the Directive, regulators have the power to require TSOs and DSOs to modify the terms and conditions, including tariffs or methodologies referred, to ensure that they are proportionate and applied in a non-discriminatory manner.[21]

Finally, besides the mentioned goals of the Directive – which, as indicated, are very broad – one of its main aims is to develop "a true internal market in electricity" (see Recital 60 of Directive 2009/72/EC's preamble). An expansion of the EU's electricity grid is one of the measures for reaching it. Therefore the regulatory authorities have to focus on this, and have granted regulatory issues on cross-border interconnections as their main tasks. Where necessary, these tasks should be conducted in close cooperation with the ACER (Recital 59). This is in line with the general provisions of Article 6, where the promotion of regional cooperation is covered,[22] as well as with Article 36, which focuses on general objectives of the regulatory authority. There, in paragraph 1 (a), the rule on close cooperation with the Agency, regulatory authorities of other Member States, and the Commission is set. It concerns:

promoting ... a competitive, secure and environmentally sustainable internal market in electricity within the Community, and effective market opening for all customers and suppliers in the Community and ensuring appropriate conditions for the effective and reliable operation of electricity networks, taking into account long-term objectives.

## The new dimension of European regulation in the electricity sector

At this point, the already recalled ACER, but briefly presented in this work needs further comments, because of the Agency's importance for current public law regulation carried out by national regulatory authorities. To outline its relevance it is enough to recall again Article 6 of Directive 2009/72/EC, which highlights its legal position and competences:

> [t]he Agency shall cooperate with national regulatory authorities and transmission system operators to ensure the compatibility of regulatory frameworks between the regions with the aim of creating a competitive internal market in electricity. Where the Agency considers that binding rules on such cooperation are required, it shall make appropriate recommendations.

The Agency was established to centralise the cooperation of national regulators, harmonising it, and creating a common framework for the needs of competition without an internal energy market. Naturally, this Article, quoted to present a general idea of the Agency's operation, does not cover all its tasks and competencies. The Agency's legal position is much more complex, not only reflected by provisions of Directive 2009/72/EC, but also by provisions of other legal acts included in the Third Legislation Package. However, Regulation (EC) No 713/2009 of the European Parliament and of the Council of 13 July 2009 establishing an Agency for the Cooperation of Energy Regulators is a legal act of fundamental importance on the analysed issue.

The provisions on enhanced EU cooperation between regulators and ACER, significantly expands the common European Union's functions and responsibilities within the energy sector (Bjørnebye 2010, pp. 177–178). To some extent, this materialises regulation at the European level. Thus, it applies, in a practical way, the theory of regulation related to its institutionalisation of regulation. Furthermore, the coordination of energy regulators conducted by ACER is tangible evidence of the European impact, through the legislative measures which established the Agency – the *Third Liberalisation Package* – on the scope of public law regulation. As a result, they broaden it on the European level, simultaneously strengthening the position of national regulators. These circumstances prove how indispensable it is to trace the assumptions and legal framework of ACER. Before moving on to this matter, some findings provided above need recapitulation.

The Third Liberalisation Package greatly expanded the scope of public law regulation performed at the European level. Formally, the mere shape of the

Package confirms the comprehensive approach of the Union to the energy market (apart from sectorial directives, three additional regulations were passed). Legislation, driven by the need for reaching full energy market competitiveness, shortcomings in choice of suppliers, national orientation in regulation, as well as an overwhelming vertical integration with market concentration, established stricter conditions for an operator's activity. As traced in this chapter, it covered unbundling, where the ownership model promoted models of Transmission System Operator, several operators' duties, public service obligations on electricity undertakings, and more comprehensive provisions on compliance programmes.

Further, not only are they elements of public law regulation but also imply further regulation conducted by national regulatory authorities (e.g. regarding operators, their independence results in extensive regulatory control mechanisms that have been involved to enable its execution). Regulation is also a measure that prevents discrimination in the operation of the network, facilitating third party access to it. Where market rules based on liberalisation do not work, regulators have to act. Although, their monitoring or other duties imposing on regulators' activity shows that they do not limit their operation just to intervention.

Seen in this light, the EU finds it crucial to secure competition and supplies of electricity at the most competitive price with the use of a regulatory framework. A liberalised energy market cannot be left unsupervised. Yet it is not just control that is needed. Monitoring is just one of the regulators' tasks. This public regulation regime is much stronger in its groundwork. For instance, on this basis, regulators participate in the development of infrastructure where they actively participate in elaborating network development plans.

The Package also narrows the implementation options that Member States could use. This concerns particularly public law regulation *sensu stricte*, i.e. position of national regulatory authorities. The national regulators could no longer be weak institutions, dispersed in the national systems of administration. Regulators in this approach have to monitor different fields, review operators' activity, as well as promote competition and protect consumers. These latter, in the situation of market opening, were especially crucial. Further, with the Third Energy Package, regulators received the European basis (resulting from EU law) for powers to investigate and request information with a right to impose sanctions, to issue binding decisions, to impose any necessary and proportionate measures to promote effective competition and ensure the proper functioning of the market, as well as to settle disputes or set tariffs. As easily identified, public law regulation is applied and strengthened in many dimensions. Aimed at achieving European public policy goals, regulation is a method in which Member States monitor actions of market players, and when non-compliance occurs impose penalties. It could be observed, that in the European legal system the regulator is not just the night-watchman. Although it performs functions of the "watchdog", it does not limit its activity to control, or any other tools treated as measures of last resort.

In this context, as the institution of regulator is extremely important for regulation, under the Third Electricity Directive national regulators have their independence assured. Political (as well as industrial) interests are rejected in favour of an expert and common approach. The scale of this autonomy is demonstrated by the fact that they are not supervised. This autonomy covers budgets and management as well. Regarding the latter, it is enhanced by a renewable term of five to seven years. Thereby, the extended regulators' obligations and powers by European legislation, made it possible to perceive them as partners for national government. The Third Energy Package made them "guarantees" of the internal market in electricity that can make decisions in regard to all relevant regulatory issues if the common market in electricity was to function properly.

Thereby, it is an another requirement of European public law imposed on Member States, influencing the scope of public law regulation, which pursuant to European legislation has to protect the position of authorities acting for the needs of the market (both at the national and the European level). It has to be combined with ensuring the financial and operational position with their independent management.

These circumstances show that in its way towards the internal energy market the European Union has chosen a path built on regulation. This approach assumes establishing the regulatory framework with national independent authorities as its axis. As already demonstrated, liberalisation does not exclude regulation. The European market challenge, based on the US experience of the California crisis, is not left alone, without any public influence. Competition is not the only force that drives the electricity sector in the EU. It is supported and supervised by the Union's institution, that with passing Energy Packages were granted duties and powers regarding the energy market.

Thereby, both in theory and in practice, the energy regulators comply with the EU's liberalisation agenda. Further, enhancing the position of energy market authorities makes it possible to discuss the *day-watchman state model*, where public forces represented by a regulator play a crucial role. The "day-watchman regulator" does not participate actively in the market. This authority also does not resign from this participation. The regulator holds a balanced position, performing a dualistic role. Day-watchman in regulation is a vigilant observer ready to enter, when and where, after his/her assessment based on expertise, it is necessary. The day-watchman regulator established rules for market behaviour: issues decisions and guidelines. With the use of sanctions, he can enforce them. Being an independent part of the public sphere (independent from interests of politics and business) provides a balance of public and private spheres. Furthermore, in the realities of EU integration, the regulator implements the European agenda in the field of adopted policy goals, performing regulatory tasks in relation to competition, consumers, environmental protection, or energy security.

In this view, the tools of public law regulation are important steps towards the European energy market. As demonstrated, the actions at the national level are correlated with the common approach performed by the ACER. The Agency has a mandate to coordinate European regulation, harmonising all national regulatory frames. It differs from the previously known institutions, like Florence Forum or ERGEG, with its legal basis, duties, and powers. The importance attached by the EU to the ACER in the fulfilment of the regulatory gap by this authority necessitates consideration of the European model of regulation seen through a prism of the Agency. This issue is discussed in the following chapter.

## Notes

1 As the EC described it in the Explanatory Memorandum "process of developing real competitive markets is far from complete".

2 The EC argued that "[i]t has led to a number of non-binding codes and efforts to reach agreement on common approaches through 'gradual convergence' but has not led to real decisions on the difficult issues that now need to be taken" (Proposal for a Directive 2007, 528 final, p. 10).

3 "2854th Council Meeting Transport, Telecommunications and Energy: Brussels, 28 February 2008", Brussels, 28 February 2008, PRES/08/45. Available from: http://europa.eu/rapid/press-release_PRES-08–45_en.htm?locale=en [6 February 2014]. The basis for a debate was a Presidency Note. It covered some objections and proposals raised by the Member States. For example, Effective and Efficient Unbundling (EEU), an alternative unbundling

> designed for both the gas and electricity sectors, is based on two pillars, one related to the organisation and governance of the undertaking and related to the assets, staff, financial resources and identity of the TSO, and the other related to grid investments, market integration and connection of new power plants,

as well as "various suggestions … regarding the role of the regulator concerning the implementation and financing of transmission investment, the organisation of regional markets and additional safeguards to ensure the effective independence of the TSOs", etc. (Note from Presidency to Delegations 2008, pp. 2–3).

4 This concerned provisions,

> to take account of cases where arrangements are in place for a transmission system that belongs to a vertically integrated undertaking, which guarantees more effective independence of the TSO. These provisions aim at balancing concerns on the scope, timeframe and enforceability of this option with keeping it workable and preserving the financial interest of the vertically integrated undertaking.
> (Council of the European Union 2008)

5 These concerned provisions,

> to take account of cases where arrangements are in place for a transmission system that belongs to a vertically integrated undertaking, which guarantees more effective independence of the TSO. These provisions aim at balancing concerns on the scope, timeframe and enforceability of this option with keeping it workable and preserving the financial interest of the vertically integrated undertaking.
> (Council of the European Union 2008)

6 As a stated in Article 3 (2) of Directive 2009/72/EC

> [i]n relation to security of supply, energy efficiency/demand-side management and for the fulfilment of environmental goals and goals for energy from renewable sources, as referred to in this paragraph, Member States may introduce the implementation of long-term planning, taking into account the possibility of third parties seeking access to the system.

7 To ensure universal service provided to all household customers, and, where Member States deem it appropriate, small enterprises (namely enterprises with fewer than 50 occupied persons and an annual turnover or balance sheet not exceeding €10 million), i.e. "the right to be supplied with electricity of a specified quality within their territory at reasonable, easily and clearly comparable, transparent and non-discriminatory prices". See Article 3 (3).

8 See Recital 16. Moreover, pursuant to Recital 19,

> [t]he full effectiveness of the independent system operator or independent transmission operator solutions should be ensured by way of specific additional rules. The rules on the independent transmission operator provide an appropriate regulatory framework to guarantee fair competition, sufficient investment, access for new market entrants and the integration of electricity markets.

9 Pursuant to Article 9 (1) (b) the same person or persons are entitled neither:

> (i) directly or indirectly to exercise control over an undertaking performing any of the functions of generation or supply, and directly or indirectly to exercise control or exercise any right over a transmission system operator or over a transmission system; nor (ii) directly or indirectly to exercise control over a transmission system operator or over a transmission system, and directly or indirectly to exercise control or exercise any right over an undertaking performing any of the functions of generation or supply.

Accordingly as stated in Article 9 (1) (b)–(c) the same person or persons are not entitled

> to appoint members of the supervisory board, the administrative board or bodies legally representing the undertaking, of a transmission system operator or a transmission system, and directly or indirectly to exercise control or exercise any right over an undertaking performing any of the functions of generation or supply

as well as "to be a member of the supervisory board, the administrative board or bodies legally representing the undertaking, of both an undertaking performing any of the functions of generation or supply and a transmission system operator or a transmission system".

10 For example, under Article 17 (1), the TSOs "shall be equipped with all human, technical, physical and financial resources necessary for fulfiling their obligations under this Directive and carrying out the activity of electricity transmission", or as stated in Article 17 (2) (e)–(f),

> [t]he activity of electricity transmission shall include at least the following [additional] tasks...: (e) the operation, maintenance and development of a secure, efficient and economic transmission system; (f) investment planning ensuring the long-term ability of the system to meet reasonable demand and guaranteeing security of supply.

11 For instance, in accordance with Article 18 (1) (a)–(b), the TSO should be able to have:

> (a) effective decision-making rights, independent from the vertically integrated undertaking, with respect to assets necessary to operate, maintain or develop the transmission system; and (b) the power to raise money on the capital market in particular through borrowing and capital increase.

Independence covers also personal matters, as in Article 19 (1),

> [d]ecisions regarding the appointment and renewal, working conditions including remuneration, and termination of the term of office of the persons responsible for

the management and/or members of the administrative bodies of the transmission system operator shall be taken by the Supervisory Body of the transmission system operator.

12 The regulator's objection may be raised in two situations which are provided by Article 19 (2). First, "doubts arise as to the professional independence of a nominated person responsible for the management and/or member of the administrative bodies", or, second, "in the case of premature termination of a term of office, doubts exist regarding the justification of such premature termination".
13 "[S]ets out the measures taken in order to ensure that discriminatory conduct is excluded ... [and] the specific obligations of employees" (Article 21 (1)).
14 See Article 21 (6). Thus, only "[a]fter prior approval by the regulatory authority, the Supervisory Body may dismiss the compliance officer". However, the Supervisory Body "shall dismiss the compliance officer for reasons of lack of independence or professional capacity upon request of the regulatory authority". See Article 21 (11).
15 A more detailed framework is set in paragraph 2. Particularly, the plan should:

> (a) indicate to market participants the main transmission infrastructure that needs to be built or upgraded over the next ten years; (b) contain all the investments already decided and identify new investments which have to be executed in the next three years; and (c) provide for a time frame for all investment projects.

16 On the basis of Article 35 (4) (b), Member States ensure that the regulatory authority's staff and management "act independently from any market interest" and "do not seek or take direct instructions from any government or other public or private entity when carrying out the regulatory tasks".
17 For instance, "monitoring the level and effectiveness of market opening and competition at wholesale and retail levels,... and bringing any relevant cases to the relevant competition authorities", "helping to ensure, together with other relevant authorities, that the consumer protection measures ... are effective and enforced", "ensuring access to customer consumption data".
18 Article 37 (4) (b) provides grounds for cooperation of energy regulators with their competition and financial counterparts, as well as the Commission in investigations relating to competition law.
19 Penalties are calculated on the basis of annual turnover (up to 10 per cent).
20 This situation requires granting the regulator extra powers. For instance it includes such powers: "to issue penalties in ... for discriminatory behaviour in favour of the vertically integrated undertaking", "to monitor communications between the transmission system operator and the vertically integrated undertaking so as to ensure compliance of the transmission system operator with its obligations", or "to act as dispute settlement authority between the vertically integrated undertaking and the transmission system operator in respect of any complaint submitted pursuant", as well as "to carry out inspections, including unannounced ones, on the premises of the vertically integrated undertaking and the transmission system operator". See Article 37 (5).
21 In case of a delay, the regulator shall have the authority "to fix or approve provisional transmission and distribution tariffs or methodologies and to decide on the appropriate compensatory measures if the final transmission and distribution tariffs or methodologies deviate from those provisional tariffs or methodologies". See Article 37 (10).
22 There, in paragraph 1, it is stated that:

> Member States as well as the regulatory authorities shall cooperate with each other for the purpose of integrating their national markets at one or more regional levels, as a first step towards the creation of a fully liberalised internal market.

## References

Bjørnebye, H. 2010, *Investing in EU energy security: exploring the regulatory approach to tomorrow's electricity production*, Kluwer Law International, Alphen aan den Rijn.

Council of the European Union 2007, *2835th Council meeting transport, telecommunications and energy*, Brussels, 29 November 2007, PRES/07/274. Available from: http://europa.eu/rapid/press-release_PRES-07-274_en.htm?locale=en [6 July 2015].

Council of the European Union 2008, *2875th Council meeting transport, telecommunications and energy*, Luxembourg, 6 June 2008, PRES/08/162. Available from: http://europa.eu/rapid/press-release_PRES-08-162_en.htm?locale=en [9 July 2015].

Council of the European Union 2009, *2953rd Council meeting environment*, Luxembourg, 25 July 2009, PRES/09/190. Available from:. http://europa.eu/rapid/press-release_PRES-09-190_en.htm?locale=en [9 July 2015].

Council Regulation (EC) No 1/2003 of 16 December 2002 on the implementation of the rules on competition laid down in Articles 81 and 82 of the Treaty, OJ L 1, 4 January 2003.

Directive 2009/72/EC of the European Parliament and of the Council of 13 July 2009 concerning common rules for the internal market in electricity and repealing Directive 2003/54/EC, OJ L 211, 14 August 2009.

European Commission 2005, *Draft interinstitutional agreement on the operating framework for the European regulatory agencies*, Brussels, 25 February 2005, COM (2005) 59 final.

European Commission 2009, *Communication from the Commission to the European Parliament pursuant to the second subparagraph of Article 251(2) of the EC Treaty concerning the common position of the Council on the adoption of a Directive of the European Parliament and of the Council concerning common rules for the Internal Market in Electricity and repealing Directive 2003/54/EC*, Brussels, 12 January 2009, COM (2008) 906 final.

European Parliament Legislative Resolution of 18 June 2008 on the proposal for a Directive of the European Parliament and of the Council amending Directive 2003/54/EC concerning common rules for the internal market in electricity, OJ C 286 E, 27 November 2009.

Note from Presidency to Delegations, Brussels, 25 February 2008, 6324/1/08 REV 1.

Opinion of the Economic and Social Committee on the "Proposal for a Directive of the European Parliament and of the Council amending Directives 96/92/EC and 98/30/EC concerning common rules for the internal market in electricity and natural gas", and the "Proposal for a Regulation of the European Parliament and of the Council on conditions for access to the network for cross-border exchanges in electricity", OJ C 36, 8 February 2002.

Opinion of the European Economic and Social Committee on the "Proposal for a Directive of the European Parliament and of the Council amending Directive 2003/54/EC concerning common rules for the internal market in electricity" and the "Proposal for a Regulation of the European Parliament and of the Council on conditions for access to the network for cross-border exchanges in electricity", OJ C 211, 19 August 2008.

Proposal for a Directive of the European Parliament and of the Council amending Directive 2003/54/EC concerning common rules for the internal market in electricity, Brussels, 19 September 2007, COM (2007) 528 final.

Proposal for a Directive of the European Parliament and of the Council amending Directive 2003/55/EC concerning common rules for the internal market in natural gas, Brussels, 19 September 2007, COM (2007) 529 final.

Proposal for a Regulation of the European Parliament and of the Council establishing an Agency for the Cooperation of Energy Regulators, Brussels, 19 September 2007, COM (2007) 530 final.

Proposal for a Regulation of the European Parliament and of the Council amending Regulation (EC) No 1228/2003 on conditions for access to the network for cross-border exchanges in electricity, Brussels, 19 September 2007, COM (2007) 531 final.

Proposal for a Regulation of the European Parliament and of the Council amending Regulation (EC) No 1775/2005 on conditions for access to the natural gas transmission networks, Brussels, 19 September 2007, COM (2007) 532 final.

Regulation (EC) No 713/2009 of the European Parliament and of the Council of 13 July 2009 establishing an Agency for the Cooperation of Energy Regulators, OJ L 211, 14 August 2009.

# PART IV

# Outcomes of European regulatory reform in the electricity sector

# 9 Institutional regulatory model of the electricity sector in the EU

The Third Liberalisation Package enabled the establishment of the entity with which public law regulation exercised in the electricity sector by the national regulators entered into a new dimension. This was done with passing the new element of the Liberalisation Packages. Besides, in the earlier two-sided approach (sectorial directives on electricity and gas) the Third Energy Package brought into EU energy law the new public regulatory measure: the Community body with legal personality,[1] the Agency for the Cooperation of Energy Regulators.

The assumptions in the establishment of ACER derive from needs widely discussed in the previous chapters. Mainly, this was a need to solve the problem of lack of coordination within the energy regulators and a regulatory gap, which occurred at the European level. By this improvement of the EU's regulatory framework,[2] the Agency was identified as "a key measure" introduced to EU law in order to "contribute towards the effective functioning of the internal markets in electricity".[3]

## ACER's position, tasks, and powers

Created as "an independent mechanism for national regulators to cooperate" (Recital 5), the main goal of the Agency's operation was to assist national regulatory authorities "in exercising, at Community level, the regulatory tasks performed in the Member States and, where necessary, to coordinate their action" (Article 1 (2) of Regulation (EC) No 713/2009). Further, the Agency supports European institutions with its expertise by elaborating opinions and recommendations.[4] This activity includes also issuing opinions and recommendations addressed to TSOs and regulatory authorities (see Articles 5 and 4 of Regulation (EC) No 713/2009). The Agency's opinions also concern network codes,[5] or the draft Community-wide network development plan. These opinions are submitted to the ENTSO for Electricity (and to the ENTSO for Gas). Furthermore, under the provisions of Article 6 (4) of Regulation (EC) No 713/2009 in accordance with Article 6 of Regulation (EC) No 714/2009,[6] the Agency participates in the development of mentioned codes for the electricity sector. Where requested, ACER submits a non-binding framework guideline to the Commission (framework guideline) which indicates principles for the development of network codes relating to the areas identified in the priority list (Article 6 (2) of Regulation (EC) No 714/2009). As stated in Article 6 (7) of Regulation (EC) No 714/2009, ACER elaborates a reasoned opinion on the network code and submits it to the ENTSO for Electricity.[7] If asked by the EC, the Agency participates in the process of certifying the TSO, by issuing its opinion on the national regulator's decision (Article 3 (1) of Regulation (EC) No 714/2009).

Another category of the Agency's tasks covers monitoring. This links with activity in the field of network codes, where the Agency, *inter alia*, monitors their implementation, analysing their effects on the Community's energy market (see Article 6 (7) of Regulation (EC) No 713/2009). In accordance with Article 11 of Regulation (EC) No 713/2009, ACER's monitoring of the internal market in electricity includes the retail prices of electricity, access to the network, and compliance with consumer rights. The Agency's monitoring also concerns projects of new interconnector capacity, Community-wide network-development plans, and regional cooperation of TSOs (see Article 6 (7)–(9)). Noteworthy, in the case of identifying inconsistencies between such a plan and its implementation, ACER will investigate their reasons and adopt recommendations for the TSO, national regulatory authorities, or other competent bodies concerned, as provided in Article 6 (8) of Regulation (EC) No 713/2009. Monitoring has to be conducted in close cooperation with the EC, the Member States, and the relevant national authorities (Article 11 (1)). This is complemented by the possibility of informing the European Parliament and the Commission with the use of annual report barriers to the completion of the internal market (see Article 11 (2)–(3)).

Important for the topic of this book, the rules on the Agency are included in the frames of Article 7 of the Regulation on ACER. This Article establishes ACER's tasks regarding regulation. Herein, ACER may adopt individual decisions on technical issues. The basis for these is the relevant provisions of other elements of the Third Liberalisation Package. Thereby, the Agency is authorised to take a binding regulatory decision on granting a new direct current interconnector an exemption from certain provisions on unbundling and TPA of Directive 2009/72/EC and Regulation (EC) No 714/2009. The decision may be adopted in the event of not reaching an agreement by regulators within a timeframe of six months from the date when the exemption was requested before the last of those regulatory authorities, or upon a joint request from the regulatory authorities (Article 17 (5) of Regulation (EC) No 714/2009). On the same principles, ACER may decide upon regulatory issues of cross-border infrastructure on access and operational security belonging to the competence of national regulators. If necessary, the decision may have an interim character (see Article 8 (1) and (3) of Regulation (EC) No 713/2009). In this context, national regulators have to comply with, and implement, any relevant legally binding decisions of the Agency, according to Article 37 (1) (d) of Directive 2009/72/EC.

Under Article 7 (2), ACER may assist regulators and market players in sharing good practices by elaborating its recommendations. The Agency also establishes opinions, if a decision taken by a regulatory authority complies with the Guidelines on the mutual cooperation of regulatory authorities, as well as cooperation with the Agency that the EC may adopt in accordance with Article 38 (5) of Directive 2009/72/EC.[8] In the case of continued non-compliance with the Agency's above-mentioned opinion, ACER shall inform the Commission and the Member State concerned about these circumstances.

Moreover, the Agency provides a framework within which national regulatory authorities can cooperate, at the regional and Community levels. As stated in Article 7 (3) "[w]here the Agency considers that binding rules on such cooperation are required, it shall make the appropriate recommendations to the Commission". Although, it is still a recommendation, it concerns "binding rules" which may be introduced. Nevertheless, a decision by ACER issued pursuant to Article 7 (7) in accordance with Article 8 certainly has a binding character. This decision applies to cross-border infrastructure, and covers the terms and conditions for access to it, as well as its operational security.

In performing its role, ACER has to ensure public access to the results of its work (Article 10 (2) of the Regulation on ACER). For example, the Agency publishes its annual report on the results of monitoring of the internal energy market. A transparency rule in ACER's operation finds also a practical application in consultations carried out during developing framework guidelines in accordance with Article 6 of Regulation (EC) No 714/2009, or proposing amendments of network codes under Article 7 of that Regulation. Pursuant to Article 10 (1) of Regulation (EC) No 713/2009,

> the Agency shall consult extensively and at an early stage with market participants, transmission system operators, consumers, end-users and, where relevant, competition authorities, without prejudice to their respective competence, in an open and transparent manner, in particular when its tasks concern transmission system operators.

## Between coordination and regulation

ACER, being the authority responsible for coordination of European regulatory authorities, in some way fulfils the regulatory space at the European level, where it has to contribute towards a real European internal market for electricity. Although, it is not a classic regulator; it does not perform principal regulatory duties. Nor does it participate in granting licences, or set tariffs, or impose sanctions for energy entities. ACER is aimed at assisting national regulatory authorities in performing their duties (e.g. on sharing good practices by elaborating its recommendations). Further, being responsible for coordination, it has to steer (but in a soft way) actions at the European level, e.g. by providing its guidelines, opinions, and recommendations, as the Agency's expertise serves not only regulators, but also the European Commission. However, this may result in binding action by the EC (see Dyl *et al.* 2011, pp. 576–577). It also includes some of ACER's opinion (e.g. concerning regulators' decisions and their compatibility with the Guidelines on the mutual cooperation of regulatory authorities), where the Agency has to inform the Commission about any non-compliance. This is in line with the Agency's duties on providing a framework within which national regulatory authorities can cooperate. Herein, ACER may inform the EC about the necessity of providing binding rules on this cooperation, and as a result they may be established.

Nevertheless, some of the Agency's duties bring it closer to the duties performed by the national regulators (with the reservation that they are performed on the European level). First, is monitoring exercises by ACER, with respect to network codes, or of the electricity market, as well as projects of new interconnector capacity. Nevertheless, herein the Agency is obliged to cooperate closely with the EC, the Member States, and national authorities.

Second, provisions of the Third Liberalisation Package allow the Agency to take binding, individual decisions. Besides the fact that it involves technical issues, the Agency is authorised to grant exemption from rules on unbundling and TPA, as well as decide on cross-border infrastructure, and on operational security. This is limited to certain situations (lack of regulators' agreement or their joint request), although it does not change the fact that the Agency is entitled to perform strict regulatory action, i.e. undertake a regulatory decision. Seen in this light, the regulators have to comply with, and implement it.

The Agency, aimed at filling the regulatory gap at the European level, performs the role of coordinator of the electricity market and its regulation. This model links two components: transnational and supranational (see Chiti 2009, p. 22). Regulators represent the first one, the Agency is an emanation of the latter. Although, in the timeline, one can see the movement from a transnational model towards a more supranational approach. The previous groups and forums were based on national cooperation and regulatory discourse rather than regulation. Currently, with the establishment of the Agency, some element of supranational authority occurred. Nevertheless, this system is still based on cooperation. However, experience shows that the tendency is to strengthen it.

By not being the energy regulator in a classic sense, ACER requires close collaboration with national regulators. Regulators, which represent concerted measures of regulation in the narrow meaning, have been mentioned in this book repeatedly. To address the issue of European impact on the scope of public law regulation in the electricity sector requires presenting how the European Energy Packages have influenced, on a very pure aspect of public law, regulation with the electricity sector: the national energy regulators.

## Legal models of electricity regulation in the EU

Directive 96/92 EC established the very first model of public law regulation within the European Union. In the Commission's opinion it was a rather common market phenomenon that occurred in "almost every sector ... [to] a certain degree". However, in the electricity sector (and gas as well), there was a "general agreement that [energy] require[s] more intense regulation than most other industries in order to ensure proper functioning of competitive markets, to protect customers and deliver other policy objectives" (European Commission 2001, p. 14). This assumption was justified on the economic ground where enabling access to the grid was more efficient than duplicating existing essential infrastructure, very often owned and operated by the incumbent vertically integrated entity. With the use of regulation and its legal measures, it was possible to enable access to the grid in a more efficient way (European Commission 2001, p. 65). In addition, the threat of the former monopoly incumbent energy companies of maintaining a dominant position, existing "even after the abolition of the former monopoly rights", caused that "certain degree of regulatory oversight and control [which was] necessary to ensure a level playing field for new entrants". Other reasons for regulation derived from the need for a "daily modern life" – electricity is a necessary product that cannot be substituted – or had an environmental background ("primary energy consumption has substantial environmental consequences in terms of emissions") (European Commission 2001, p. 65).

The Commission also depicted the most important features of an effective regulatory framework. These were dealing with disputes in a quick way[9] and without undue costs (e.g. legal costs). The EC also noted a "fundamental difference … in the extent of regulation required". A factor that determined the amount of regulation was a form of existing unbundling. When ownership unbundling was applied, regulation was less intensive. On the other hand, without unbundling, it was more severe (European Commission 2001, p. 15). Furthermore, as the Commission reviewed, the model of *ex-ante* regulated TPA resulted in fewer disputes (e.g. on access tariffs, most of them concerned connection). The regulatory body solved them in the phase of setting tariffs, or publishing fixed tariffs. Ownership unbundling had the same impact on the number of disputes (fewer complaints on the grounds of less discrimination) (European Commission 2001, p. 15).

By 2001, 14 Member States established a regulatory authority responsible for energy matters. The only one exception was Germany where a regulator was not setup. Some countries indicated more than one regulator (e.g. two regulators in the UK, one for Great Britain and one for Northern Ireland) or decided to separate the federal level and regional (Belgium) (European Commission 2001, p. 65). Not only were these conditions varying, the regulatory authorities differed in their legal position, independence, resources, and staff. In particular, former – the legal position in the system of law attracted the Commission's attention. In the majority of countries, the competent ministry and therefore the government had responsibility "for certain regulatory issues, including network access conditions in some cases". At that time, the only exceptions were Sweden and Northern Ireland. There, regulators were responsible for all regulatory issues (European Commission 2001, pp. 65–66).

In general, among the mentioned issues were decisions on licences necessary for constructing power plants, generating electricity, building, supplying, and operating the grid. In this respect, in most cases, the competent minister undertook decisions. Regarding final decisions, in most cases they were also undertaken by the competent minister (except the UK, Ireland, and Finland where it was the regulator's responsibility) (European Commission 2001, p. 66). On the other hand, with respect to grid access tariffs in the majority of Member States, the regulators played a more active role. Only in France, Luxembourg, Spain, and Greece was it the minister who decided whether to take into account the regulator's proposal (European Commission 2001, p. 66). In reference to timing, in the procedure for electricity grid access tarification, two approaches were considered.[10] First, was an *ex ante* ("open book") control of TSOs' and DSOs' turnover and profits, as well as approving a methodology for tariffs (overseeing "the whole process of deciding tariffs and conditions for network access") (European Commission 2001, p. 15). Second, was an *ex post* system of regulation. In this approach, operators notify tariffs to the regulator, which accepts or rejects them. This model was implemented in the situation of the existence of ownership unbundling, "where discrimination in favour of related suppliers is not an issue" (European Commission 2001, p. 15). In 2001 this was adopted by the Scandinavian countries, Denmark, Finland, and Sweden. Besides licences and network access (as well as dispute settlement), the energy regulators had other competences and responsibilities.[11]

The minister-model was assessed by the Commission, as one that might "dilute the effectiveness of regulation" (European Commission 2001, p. 15). However, the regulators were not subordinated to governmental instructions concerning individual decisions (e.g. in the Netherlands it was possible). Nevertheless, the government shaped "general policy objectives of regulators" (European Commission 2001, p. 67). In certain Member States, a competent minister could overrule some regulators' decisions. This is linked to the fact that in the majority of Member States the president of the regulator, or members of its board, were appointed by the government. In some cases heads of state (Italy, Luxembourg), or jointly several entities (France) were responsible for this appointment. In general, regulators had a specified term, however in Finland it was not specified (European Commission 2001, p. 67).

Finally, apart from the legal position, methods of appointment, independence and influence of the government, responsibilities, and role in disputes, regulatory authorities differed in terms of resources (budget) and staff. With this in mind, shows Table 9.1, a juxtaposition of regulatory authorities in the European Union (2001).

The listed findings clearly show that that regulators' budgets ranged from €1 million (Finland) to more than €1 million (the UK). Regarding employment, the scale of difference was similarly huge: one as a minimum (Luxembourg) and 300 the maximum of staff employed (UK). The United Kingdom significantly overstated the total results. An average for EU-14 (without the UK) ranged from around a few/several million euros with respect to budget, and tens of workers when it came to staff.

With respect to regulation of tariffs, the majority of regulatory authorities, applied *ex ante* regulation. These concerned also candidate countries (EU-10).

*Table 9.1* Competences and resources of regulators in the EU-15 (2001)

| *Member State* | *Regulation* | *Grid access* | *Dispute settlement* | *Licences issued by* | *Annual budget 2001 (€m)* | *Staff* |
|---|---|---|---|---|---|---|
| Austria | *ex ante* | R | R | Minister | 7.0 | 37 |
| Belgium | *ex ante* | R | R | Minister | 9.4 | 40 |
| Denmark | *ex post* | R | R | Minister | 2.5 | 30 |
| Finland | *ex post* | R | R | Minister | 1.2 | 15 |
| France | *ex ante* | M | R | Minister | 9.1 | 65 |
| Germany | n.a. | N | C | Minister | n.a. | n.a. |
| Greece | *ex ante* | M | R | Minister | 4.4 | 10 |
| Ireland | *ex ante* | R | R | Minister/Regulator | 5.0 | 27 |
| Italy | *ex ante* | R | R | Minister | 18.0 | 63 |
| Luxemburg | *ex ante* | M | M | Minister | n.a. | 1 |
| Netherlands | *ex ante* | R | R | Minister | 4.0 | 33 |
| Portugal | *ex ante* | R | R | Minister | 4.5 | 46 |
| Spain | *ex ante* | M | R/Regional government | Minister | 16.8 | 140 |
| Sweden | *ex post* | R | R | Regulator | 3.4 | 33 |
| UK | *ex ante* | R | R | Minister/Regulator | 103.0 | 340 |

Source: European Commission (2001, p. 69).

Notes
R – regulator responsible, M – minister responsible, C – competition authority, N – not regulated, n.a. – not applicable.

As a rule, in Nordic countries the *ex post* model linked with ownership unbundling prevailed (European Commission 2003, p. 12). Differences in the regulator's powers also covered collection and scrutiny of information. The Commission (2003, p. 12) emphasised that insufficient powers in this area were "likely to leave it over-dependent on the industry and damage its effectiveness". Further, in the 2000s, in reference to the regulatory legal structure, the EC noticed some cases of a minister's influence over a regulatory authority's decision (e.g. decisions on network tariffs). This gave a reflection that in certain Member States regulators were still in the process of establishment (European Commission 2003, p. 12).

In the second phase of liberalisation of the EU's electricity sector, shaped by the provision of the Second Electricity Directive, the structure of national regulatory authorities for the EU-25 was shown in Table 9.2.

The vast majority of Member States chose the *ex ante* model of regulation. With respect to grid access and dispute settlement, an option for a regulator decision was established as a rule. Other possibilities (where a minister or a competition authority was responsible for these matters) were an exception. At this stage of liberalisation almost all European regulators had a strong position with regard to information powers (apart from Slovakia, and Germany where separate regulatory authority was not established by that time).

Although, except regulators' staff and budget which, as indicated in the previous period, varied greatly, the significant differences existed in the field of a minister's involvement in regulation conducted by the regulatory authorities. Herein, such situations might be distinguished: a general subordination to the minister, obligation to obey general guidelines or instructions passed by the minister, as well as being under ministerial supervision, or approving tariff by the minister. Besides them, certain Member States granted their regulator an independent position at that time. Further, some Member States had plans to strengthen their role (DG TREN 2004, p. 5).

As already presented, adopted in 2009 the Third Energy Package broadened national regulators' powers and enhanced their independence. In the CEER's opinion (2009, p. 11) this energy legislation was "essential to ensure that regulatory decisions are removed from political and economic interests, which is necessary to create a stable and predictable investment climate". It provided a firm basis for national regulatory authorities' autonomous decisions (independent from any political influence), as well as budget allocations (independence in field disposal of adequate human and financial resources) (CEER 2010, p. 57). To demonstrate this influence of European legislation on public law regulation within EU countries, remarks on the situation of Member States are necessary. Thereby, in the next section the regulatory framework of certain EU countries is reviewed.

## Regulatory review of selected EU Member States

A deeper examination of regulatory authorities requires separation of general remarks and presenting them as individual examples of a national regulator.

*Table* 9.2 Competences and resources of regulators in the EU-25 (2003)

| *Member State* | *Regulation* | *Grid access* | *Dispute settlement* | *Minister's involvement* | *Information powers* | *Annual budget 2003 (€m)* | *Staff* |
|---|---|---|---|---|---|---|---|
| Austria | *ex ante* | R | R | General guidelines | Strong | 8.0 | 60 |
| Belgium | *ex ante* | R | R | No | Strong | 17.0 | 99 |
| Cyprus | *ex ante* | R | R | Instructions | Strong | 0.5 | 7 |
| Czech Republic | *ex ante* | R | R | No | Strong | 3.8 | 88 |
| Denmark | *ex post* | R | R | Yes | Strong | 2.5 | 30 |
| Estonia | *ex ante* | R | R | n.k. | n.k. | 0.3 | 111 |
| Finland | *ex post* | R | R | No | Strong | 1.25 | 16 |
| France | *ex ante* | M | R | Tariff approval | Strong | 12.0 | 96 |
| Germany | n.a. | N | C | n.a. | n.a. | n.a. | n.a. |
| Greece | *ex ante* | M | R | Tariff approval | Strong | 4.4 | 40 |
| Hungary | *ex ante* | M | R | Tariff approval | Strong | 6.2 | 95 |
| Ireland | *ex ante* | R | R | No | Strong | 10.0 | 39 |
| Italy | *ex ante* | R | R | General guidelines | Strong | 18.6 | 104 |
| Latvia | *ex ante* | R | R | No | Strong | 1.7 | 68 |
| Lithuania | *ex ante* | R | R | Instruction | Strong | 0.6 | 50 |
| Luxemburg | *ex ante* | M | M | n.k. | Strong | 0.3 | 2 |
| Malta | – | R | R | n.a. | – | 0.3 | 15 |
| Netherlands | *ex ante* | R | C | Instructions | Strong | 7.0 | 55 |
| Poland | *ex ante* | R | R | Supervision | Strong | 6.7 | 258 |
| Portugal | *ex ante* | R | R | No | Strong | 6.4 | 53 |
| Slovakia | *ex ante* | R | R | No | Limited | 1.5 | 57 |
| Slovenia | *ex ante* | R | R | n.a. | Strong | 1.5 | 22 |
| Spain | *ex ante* | M | R | Yes | Strong | 21.0 | 187 |
| Sweden | *ex post* | R | R | No | Strong | 3.0 | 42 |
| UK | *ex ante* | R | R | No | Strong | 57 | 302 |

Source: DG TREN (2004, p. 14).

Note

R – regulator responsible, M – minister responsible, C – competition authority, N – not regulated, n.a. – not applicable, n.k. – not known.

This enables highlighting of specific characteristics of regulatory bodies and provides a practical analysis on the range of European Union's impact on public law regulation in national legal systems.

As institutionalisation of regulation is one of the main elements of public law regulation, I propose to conduct a review of some the EU's Member States. The review covers the following countries: Denmark, Finland, France, Germany, Italy, the Netherlands, Spain, Sweden, and the United Kingdom. It is aimed to show the influence of Energy Packages and how selected Member States implemented packages' provisions. The analysis covers Western European countries because their long-term European integration and membership in the European Union correlates with uniting their activity on the internal energy market. This allows demonstration of the impact of Energy Packages on these Member States and how it influenced their legislative process.

### Denmark

In the 1990s the Danish electricity sector was based on two unconnected, vertically integrated systems (Western operated by *Eltra*, linked with Norway, Sweden, and Germany; and Eastern operated by *Elkraft*, with Sweden and Germany); the Great Belt was the line of division (European Commission 1998, p. 9). However, in 2005, the new Danish TSO, owned by the state, was established (*Energinet.dk*) (European Commission 2005, p. 44). In 2012 Energinet.dk was certified for electricity (as well as for natural gas) after the rules for ownership unbundling. Subsequently Energinet.dk bought or merged with ten regional transmission grid companies (Danish Energy Regulatory Authority n.d.b, p. 4).

In 1996 Denmark amended the Electricity Supply Act, although in 1998 there were still some gaps in the legislation and provisions, which were not in line with Directive 96/92/EC (European Commission 1998). In 2003, the Danish electricity market was fully opened, however in 2001 this was almost done (openness reaching 90 per cent) (European Commission 2001, p. 75). By October 2015 regulated end-user prices in electricity sector will be phased out. This will be done with the establishment of a supplier centric model for the electricity retail market (European Commission 2014a, p. 54).

In the first stage of market liberalisation in Denmark, there were approximately 100 companies in distribution, and eight companies in generation (European Commission 1998). In 2011, there were 77 DSOs (European Commission 2011a, pp. 1–2). At the generation level, the largest electricity producers kept their position. The largest electricity generators in Denmark are Dong Energy and Vattenfall. Together they account for about 57 per cent of total generation capacity (European Commission 2014a, p. 56).

With respect to regulatory framework, in Denmark the Danish Energy Regulatory Agency (*Energitilsynet*, DERA) has always been an independent body. Nevertheless, until 2011, its secretariat had been provided by the Danish Competition Authority. This was done with implementation of the Third Energy Package (Danish Energy Regulatory Authority n.d.a, p. 1). Currently, DERA is responsible for monitoring and regulating prices as well as terms and conditions for customers within the electricity sector. It lays down annual efficiency requirements for electricity grid companies, or monitors and regulates Energinet.dk to ensure that only necessary costs are included in its prices (Danish Energy Regulatory Authority 2012, p. 3). DERA (2012, p. 3) also monitors the price for electricity and the supply obligation, as well as monitoring wholesale markets for electricity. Additionally, it provides specialised analyses of the electricity market.

### *Finland*

In the first stage of liberalisation, the system in Finland mainly consisted of two companies IVO (public) and PVO (private). In total, they produced 80 per cent of electricity. *Fingrid* was responsible for the transmission grid (fully separated from other activities with unbundled accounts), and at the level of distribution there were more than 100 local and regional distribution companies (European Commission 1998). What is worth noting is the fact that as early as 1995 Finland liberalised the electricity sector and all customers were qualified as eligible. With regards to generation, the country established the authorisation system, and in the field of grid access the regulated TPA, with published tariffs that followed "the postage stamp system" (European Commission 1998).

In order to fulfil the requirements of the Third Energy Package, in June 2013 Finland passed legislation that covered amendments to electricity law. It included changes in the field of ownership structure of *Fingrid*. Two main electricity generators,[12] *Fortum Oyj* and *Pohjolan Voima Oy*, sold their shares to the state. As a result of this acquisition, the state of Finland acquired the majority shares in its TSO (Energy Market Authority 2013, p. 4). At the level of Finnish distribution, in July 2013 there were 83 DSOs. Approximately two-thirds of them were legally unbundled (52 of 83 operators) (Energy Market Authority 2013, p. 8). Legal unbundling does not require any special legal form. However, separate companies cannot both be public utilities, otherwise they would be part of the same legal entity (Energy Market Authority 2013, p. 20).

In Finland the Energy Market Authority was responsible for regulating distribution network operators, regional network operators, and Transmission System Operators. Since the end of 2004, under provisions of the Second Electricity Directive, for network pricing Finland has applied *ex ante* regulation. The first regulatory phase of price regulation in the electricity network covered the years 2005–2007. The second phase included 2008–2011. The third regulatory phase that began in 2012 finishes in 2015 (Energy Market Authority 2013, p. 14). During these periods, the regulatory model used is the revenue cap model. Its aim is to initiate "more innovations and investments in the networks in order to ensure viability of the networks" (Energy Market Authority 2013, p. 14). The Authority also supervised fulfilment of the unbundling requirements. It could oblige companies to correct mistakes or omissions. In cases of infringements it imposed fines or cancelled the network licence of the electricity company

(Energy Market Authority 2013, pp. 21–22). Moreover, public law regulation covered public obligations imposed on operators. These included obligation to develop the electricity network, to connect, and to transmit electricity (Energy Market Authority 2013, pp. 24–25).

In the beginning of 2014 the Energy Market Authority was renamed the "Energy Authority". It was related to the introduction of new regulator roles. They cover, *inter alia*, promoting energy efficiency, counselling and communication, ecological design, as well as energy labelling (European Commission 2014a, p. 72).

### *France*

The French energy market in the 1990s had typical monopoly characteristics. The state-owned EdF's market dominance was evident (95 per cent in generation, active role in distribution and transmission of energy). Certainly it did not remain without effect on the liberalisation process, which in 1998 was in a very early stage and the options provided in Directive 96/92/EC were deliberated by the major stakeholders (European Commission 1998). A similar, limited approach was applied in the case of market opening. In 2001, it reached only 30 per cent. The EdF's domination continued in the following years. For example, in 2005 EdF had a market share of about 87 per cent of generation capacity (European Commission 2007a, p. 63) and in 2011 EdF possessed 91 per cent of the installed capacity (European Commission 2011b, p. 2).

In 2000, the French energy regulatory authority, *Commission de Régulation de l'Énergie* (CRE) was established (European Commission 2011b, p. 1). Its duties and powers increased with the implementation of the 2010 act introducing a New Organisation of the Electricity Market and of the 2011 transposition act of the Third Energy Package (CRE 2013, p. 1). On this basis CRE guarantees the right of access to the public electricity grid, under transparent and non-discriminatory conditions. The authority proposes tariffs to the Minister of Energy and the Minister of Economy for the use of public electricity grids and related services provided under the monopoly of the system operators of these networks. Under French law the decision is deemed established unless there is opposition from one of the ministers within two months of receipt of the proposal form CRE (CRE n.d.). CRE, which has to ensure the correct operation of the electricity market (to ensure the development of competition to benefit consumers), provides dispute settlement (*inter alia*, on interpretation or enforcement of agreements and protocols for grid access), may impose sanctions (in case of a breach of system operators' duties), issues opinions (e.g. on the decisions of other authorities), ensures the independence of system operators, as well as informs energy consumers about their rights on the energy market (CRE n.d.). Additionally, CRE is involved in regulation of nuclear power. It passes an opinion (*inter alia*, based on development of competition) on the overall maximum volume of electricity produced in nuclear sources that can be sold, or sets the volume of electricity generated in nuclear sources sold to each supplier sub-annually (CRE n.d.).

### *Germany*

In the 1990s the German electricity sector consisted of about 1000 energy companies. Nine "supra-regional transmission companies" operated the transmission grid (European Commission 1998). By 2011, this amount increased to four TSOs: *Tennet*, *Amprion*, *50Hertz*, and *TransnetBW*. At the distribution level, there are more than 50 regional utilities and over 800 municipal distributors (European Commission 2011c, p. 2). Generation is dominated by four large private companies: E.ON, RWE, EnBW, and *Vattenfall* (European Commission 2011c, p. 2).

At the beginning of the twenty-first century, Germany was the only Member State without a sector energy regulator. This role was performed by the federal competent minister responsible for energy issues (e.g. granting licences, settling disputes on "an unjustified refusal of network access or discriminatory conditions and tariffs") (European Commission 2001, p. 79). It changed in 2005 when the German Federal Network Agency (*Bundesnetzagentur*) was established to regulate all network industries, including electricity, gas, telecommunication, postal, and, since January 2006, railway markets (IEA 2007, p. 31).

*Bundesnetzagentur* operates in the energy sector as a regulatory authority under provisions of the Energy Act (EnWG) and the Grid Expansion Acceleration Act (NABEG). It provides "energy regulation", i.e. the supervision of operators of energy supply networks and federal state regulatory bodies (Bundesnetzagentur 2013). The aim of *Bundesnetzagentur*'s regulation is to strengthen competition in the energy market (generation, trade, and supply). For this purpose, *Bundesnetzagentur* (2013) has power to approve grid fees for electricity transit, to prevent and remove barriers in access to the energy grid, standardises processes for switching supplier, as well as to improve the conditions for connecting new power plants to the grid. Apart from competition within the energy market, since 2011, *Bundesnetzagentur* has been given certain duties regarding expanding the electricity grid infrastructure (Bundesnetzagentur 2013).

### *Italy*

For a very long time ENEL has had the Italian state monopoly and generally covered every sub-sector of electricity: production, transmission, distribution imports, and exports. Some exceptions were in distribution (local utilities), and in generation (autoproducers) (European Commission 1998, p. 10). Pro-competition steps taken by the Italian government at the turn of the century resulted in a weakening of its position (see Soda & Carlone 2013, pp. 33–34). This was done by separating the Transmission System Operator (*Terna*) from its assets, as well as selling the distribution infrastructure in certain Italian cities (see ENEL n.d.). The liberalisation of the Italian electricity market was conducted gradually. In 2001 the electricity market was opened at 35 per cent. In 2002, this level increased by 5 per cent to 40 per cent. By 2006, only households were not yet able to choose their electricity supplier (European Commission

2007a, p. 76). Since July 2007, all Italian electricity consumers can change supplier (OECD n.d.). With regard to capacity installed, at the end of 2012 three operators held market shares greater than 5 per cent. These were ENEL (31.1 per cent), *Edipower* (6.5 per cent), and *Edison* (5.5 per cent) (AEEG 2013, p. 7).

The institution responsible for regulation in the Italian electricity sector is the Regulatory Authority for Electricity and Gas (*Autorità per l'Energia Elettrica e il Gas*, AEEG). It aims to "protect the interests of [energy] users and consumers, promote competition and ensure efficient, cost-effective and profitable nationwide services with satisfactory quality levels" (AEEG n.d.). Thus, AEEG sets basic tariffs for regulated sectors, establishes guidelines for production and distribution of services, as well as standards, monitors conditions under which services in regulated sectors are provided, conducts inspections and applies sanctions, assesses complaints and appeals or publishes information on market conditions (Bianco 2011, pp. 101–102). In addition the Authority performs an advisory role to the government and parliament. It also elaborates reports and its recommendations concerning regulated sectors (Bianco 2011, p. 100).

### *The Netherlands*

The early structure of the electricity system in the Netherlands (1990s) was based on 33 distribution companies. They owned four generation companies, which themselves owned *Samenwerkende elektriciteitsproductiebedrijven* (SEP) – the former Dutch entity responsible for the transmission grid (European Commission 1998, pp. 10–11). In 1998, SEP was replaced by *TenneT* which became a new Transmission System Operator (TenneT 2015). At that time the market opening was estimated on 32 per cent (European Commission 1998, p. 11). By 2002 this level doubled and reached 66 per cent (European Commission 2007a, p. 93). Since July 2004, the Dutch electricity market has been fully open to competition (European Commission 2011g, p. 1). Currently, there are four main electricity generators on the market (Eurostat 2015) and eight distribution system operators (Spitzley *et al.* 2011, p. 16). Market concentration in the Netherlands at retail level is high. The three largest companies covered 80.3 per cent of the retail market at the end of 2010 (European Commission 2011f, p. 3).

In the Netherlands, energy regulation is provided by the Authority for Consumers & Markets (*Autoriteit Consument & Markt*, ACM). It is the new market authority, established in 2013 as a result of consolidation of the Netherlands Consumer Authority, the Netherlands Independent Post and Telecommunication Authority, and the Netherlands Competition Authority (ACM 2013, p. 3). The ACM sets tariffs for TSOs and DSOs, it monitors wholesale and retail markets, as well as ensures compliance of operators and power companies with national legislation on energy. The ACM is aimed at creating more transparency for energy users by streamlining tariff structures and improving information on the market. Further, the Authority supervises the implementation of new market models in retail (one of its objectives is to provide better services for consumers), as well as elaborating information codes (ACM n.d.).

### *Spain*

In the first stage of liberalisation in Spain, the generation market mainly consisted of three companies: *Endesa* (state-owned company), and *Iberdrola* and *Union Fenosa* (two private entities). They were the main players in the distribution sector as well (*Endesa* group 43 per cent, *Iberdrola* 35 per cent, *Union Fenosa* 14 per cent) (European Commission 1998, pp. 10–11). In the first phase of market opening, consumers with a consumption of 15 GWh per year were qualified as eligible (30 per cent of total electricity consumption) (European Commission 1998, pp. 11–12). In 2001, liberalisation of the market was more than 50 per cent and in 2003 it reached full opening (European Commission 2007a, p. 77). In 2010 there were five major groups competing in the market at the generation level: *Iberdrola* (24.3 per cent), *Endesa* (19.6 per cent), *Gas Natural Fenosa* (15 per cent), EDP-*Hidrocantábrico* (5.3 per cent) and E.ON (3.5 per cent) (European Commission 2011d, p. 2). The transmission of electricity is provided by *Red Eléctrica de España* (founded in 1985). In 2012, the three main Spanish DSOs were *Endesa Distribución* (42 per cent), *Iberdrola Distribución* (34 per cent), and *Gas Natural Unión Fenosa Distribución* (16 per cent) (Sonvilla *et al.* 2012, p. 16).

In March 2012, the new Spanish law on electricity that implemented the Third Energy Package was passed (CNE 2013, p. 5). On this basis the National Regulatory Authority (*Comisión Nacional de Energía*, CNE) was designated as the authority at the national level in the field of electricity (regardless of the national competition authority's responsibilities)[13] (CNE 2013, p. 7). Under the new legislation duties the powers of CNE has been broadened and enhanced. This was done by strengthening the competitive functioning of energy markets, as well as fostering development of the internal energy market and competitive regional markets. Particularly, powers attributed to CNE cover: approval of methodologies concerning transmission and distribution access tariffs, balancing services, access to interconnection infrastructures, capacity allocation and congestion management procedures, law enforcement with the possibility of imposing penalties, and protection of consumers (CNE 2013, p. 7).

### *Sweden*

In Sweden in the 1990s there were approximately 300 energy companies, although, eight of them generated almost 95 per cent of total electricity (European Commission 1998, p. 12). In 2012, three main entities: *Vattenfall*, *Fortum*, and E. ON were responsible for almost 80 per cent of total electricity production in Sweden (Ei 2013b, p. 32). In 2010, there were more than 120 electricity suppliers (European Commission 2011e, p. 2). In Sweden distribution is carried out at the local level by 170 companies (Pobłocka *et al.* 2011, p. 14), and transmission is conducted by the state entity *Svenska Kraftnät* (established in 1992). In terms of market openness, Sweden liberalised its market in the beginning of 1996 selecting all energy customers as eligible (European Commission 1998, p. 12).

Swedish regulatory policy is provided by the Energy Markets Inspectorate (*Energimarknadsinspektionen*, Ei) in cooperation with other public agencies (e.g. the Swedish Competition Authority is responsible for ensuring that competition regulations are adhered to, or the Swedish Consumer Agency ensures that energy consumers are offered fair contractual terms) (Ei 2013b, p. 6). However it is Ei (2013b, p. 6) that has collective responsibility for regulation and supervision of the Swedish electricity market and the implementation of the Electricity Act. Ei operates within four areas: supervision and consideration, customer information, monitoring and analysis, and international cooperation. It supervises compliance with laws and regulations in the energy markets sector (Ei 2013a, p. 6). For example, the Energy Markets Inspectorate determines whether the charges to connect to the electricity grids are reasonable. It also analyses developments in the energy markets as well as conducting investigations on behalf of the government. Where necessary, Ei proposes legislative changes (Ei 2013a, p. 6). It monitors supply quality, as well as considering and issuing concessions for electricity (Ei 2013a, p. 10). Among its regulatory duties Ei sets electricity network companies' fees in advance (from 2012). In the Swedish regulatory model the Energy Markets Inspectorate decides on the scale of companies' revenue in a four-year period. The first regulatory period runs from 2012 to 2015 (Ei 2013a, p. 5).

### The UK

The electricity system in England and Wales was restructured and fully legally unbundled as early as 1990. An independent TSO was established on the market (European Commission 1998, pp. 12–13). Access to the network was based on an electricity pool (a type of regulated TPA), where all generators sold exclusively energy and final consumers could choose between suppliers at the distribution level (European Commission 1998, p. 12). In terms of liberalisation, in 1998, market opening in the United Kingdom reached 42 per cent. By the beginning of the twenty-first century the British energy sector was fully opened (European Commission 2007a, p. 98).

Currently, the British transmission system is operated by the National Grid Electricity Transmission (NGET), which performs the role of single System Operator. Being also the Transmission Operator for England and Wales, it cooperates with two other Transmission Operators: Scottish Power Transmission (southern Scotland) and Scottish Hydro Electric Transmission (northern Scotland and the Scottish islands) (OFGEM n.d.d). At the level of distribution within the six regional distribution services areas there are 14 licensed distribution network operators, owned by six different energy groups (OFGEM n.d.c). In terms of electricity generation, at the end of 2012, there were 33 major power producers operating in Great Britain (some of the producers were joint ventures) (Department of Energy & Climate Change 2013, p. 123).

The Office of Gas and Electricity Markets (OFGEM) is responsible for regulation within the United Kingdom.[14] In this regard, OFGEM's first priority is protection of consumers. It monitors energy markets for any signs of anti-competitive behaviour or agreements. The Office conducts investigations into the conduct of companies that may be breaching licence conditions (which OFGEM issues) or consumers' protection law as well as acting against competition (OFGEM 2012, p. 1). In such a situation, OFGEM (2012, p. 1) has the power to impose financial penalties (up to 10 per cent of the company's turnover). To ensure compliance with licence conditions it also issues enforcement orders (OFGEM n.d.b). In case of infringments of UK or EU competition law, it may (through its bodies) accept binding commitments or issue directions to stop the behaviour (OFGEM n.d.b). Decisions about enforcement action are taken by the Gas and Electricity Markets Authority which is OFGEM's governing body (OFGEM n.d.b). Further, as the regulator, the Office sets price controls for the companies that operate the British electricity networks.[15] In addition, OFGEM, *inter alia*, supports the government with its expertise (e.g. on smart metering) (OFGEM 2013a, p. 12), as well as informing energy consumers about their powers in the market (see OFGEM n.d.a).

The frame of this work requires that the review stop at this point. Another possible area of future research would be to investigate the regulatory framework of all 28 Member States. Notwithstanding these limitations, let us conclude the above remarks. Presented in this chapter overview the newest Energy Package made it possible to start closer cooperation in energy regulation at the European level. The Agency, aimed at solving the problem of the regulatory gap, is assessed as the main driver of the real internal energy market.

Nevertheless, ACER is not the classic regulatory authority. Currently it coordinates rather than regulates, recommends rather than decides, etc. Although, as proved, there are some exceptions and areas in which ACER is approaching regulatory functions. This implies speculation and makes it possible to deliberate about its future characteristics. Besides this discussion, ACER is clear evidence of institutionalisation and Europeanisation that occur in the EU's regulatory framework. Driven by public law gathered in the European Energy Packages they influence national legislation, intensifying integration and harmonisation.

This affects the position of the national regulatory authorities. Each Package steadily endeavours to guarantee regulators an independent position with respect to domestic powers, i.e. government. It is evident that the legislative path, chosen in 1990s, involving public law regulation, with every step towards the internal energy market, intensified the European impact on Member States to make the necessary changes in the competence and powers of national regulators. The field of national action with respect to government influence narrowed while the position of national regulatory authorities strengthened. Especially significant are herein the provisions of the Third Package.

The influence of European legislation can be discerned on the grounds of national regulatory frames. First, it involved the need to establish regulatory bodies. Under the influence of the EU's Packages Member States have established regulatory institutions. Second, once the institutions have been incorporated into their legal systems, the discussion on harmonisation of their duties started. As a consequence, the main scope of national regulators' responsibilities and powers was unified, by setting the minimal requirements. Although, implementation of it has demonstrated shortcomings, resulting from the transposition's timing, its accuracy (e.g. regarding regulators' independence, i.e. methods of appointment, term, and its renewal), as well as ensuring regulators' necessary resources (financial and human).

Nevertheless, the adopted legislation provided grounds for the Commission to require the correct implementation including guaranteeing that national regulatory authorities have effective regulatory powers and are independent. In light of the Energy Packages, regulators have to be autonomous in their decisions. They must act for the needs of the internal energy market and regulatory goals stemming from the European Energy Packages. This is because public law regulation performed by national regulators is not only a goal in itself. It served specific goals inscribed into the policy agenda of the common electricity market in the EU. This raises questions about the European regulatory approach, which I seek to answer in the next chapter.

## Notes

1 In terms of the Agency's legal status, according to Article 2 of Regulation (EC) No 713/2009,

> [i]n each Member State, the Agency shall enjoy the most extensive legal capacity accorded to legal persons under national law. It shall, in particular, be able to acquire or dispose of movable and immovable property and be a party to legal proceedings.

In respect to its structure, the Agency consists of an Administrative Board (Article 13), a Board of Regulators (Article 15), a Director (Article 17), and a Board of Appeal (Article 19).

2 Vassilis Hatzopoulos (2012, p. 321) perceives this process as "agencification" of a former cooperation structure between national regulators.

3 As expressed in Recital 1 of Regulation (EC) No 713/2009's preamble. See European Commission 2007b.

4 For example, an opinion to the Commission on the draft statutes, list of members, and draft rules of procedure of the ENTSO for Electricity pursuant to Article 5 (2) of the Regulation (EC) No 714/2009.

5 As explained in Recital 6 of Regulation (EC) No 713/2009's preamble network codes were introduced to

> [provide] and [manage] effective and transparent access to the transmission networks across borders, and to ensure coordinated and sufficiently forward-looking planning and sound technical evolution of the transmission system in the Community, including the creation of interconnection capacities, with due regard to the environment.

6 Respectively, for gas it is Article 6 of Regulation (EC) No 715/2009.

7 According to Article 6 (8) the ENTSO for Electricity may amend the network code using ACER's opinion. When the Agency accepts the network code ("is satisfied that the network code is in line with the relevant framework guideline") it submits it to the Commission with a recommendation to adopt it (Article 6 (9)).

8 Regulatory duties which may arise as an effect of this can only "amend non-essential elements of this Directive by supplementing it". See Article 38 (5) of Directive 2009/72/EC.

9 Some Member States had provisions for the maximum duration of dispute settlement. These were Spain, two months, and France, between three and six months. On the other hand in the negotiated access model some disputes could be settled quickly and some often prolonged to a year (European Commission 2001, p. 17).

10 Slightly different approaches were used in the gas sector. Germany and Austria had it based on negotiated access. It set "more emphasis on the need for an authority to settle disputes and, implicitly, a procedure and methodology for handling these cases". Finally, the Netherlands adopted a "hybrid system" for gas, as a combination of negotiated third party access, and regulator's activity which allowed issuing of "guidelines on how charges should be set" (European Commission 2001, p. 15).

11 These were, *inter alia*, market monitoring, advising to the government implementing policy (e.g. environmental policy; the UK, Sweden), implementing "public service obligations and/or quality standards" (e.g. France, Italy, Ireland, UK), establishing "long-term plans for supply" (e.g. Belgium), providing "market information to customers" (e.g. UK, Denmark) or having "oversight over the non-liberalised part of the market" (e.g. Portugal, Italy, Ireland, Netherlands, Greece) (European Commission 2001, p. 68).

12 In 2012 the total number of companies producing electricity reached 220 and the number of production plants was *c.*550 (Energy Market Authority 2013).

13 In October 2013, the role of the national energy regulator was attributed to a new agency, the National Authority for Markets and Competition (*Comisión Nacional de los Mercados y la Competencia*, CNMC), which was established as a result of the merger of the previous antitrust authority with six regulatory agencies (responsible for telecom, electricity and natural gas, post, airport and railway sector) (European Commission 2014a, p. 207).

14 Apart from Northern Ireland where the Northern Ireland Authority for Utility Regulation (UREGNI) operates as a regulator.

15 OFGEM developed RIIO (Revenue = Incentives + Innovation + Outputs). It is a performance based model used for setting the network companies' price controls, set for a period of eight years. There are three separate price controls that apply to the different areas of energy. Two of them, transmission (RIIO-T1) and electricity distribution (RIIO-ED1) relate to electricity (OFGEM 2013b, p. 1).

## References

ACM 2013, *National report on energy regulation in 2012*. Available from: www.ceer.eu/portal/page/portal/EER_HOME/EER_PUBLICATIONS/NATIONAL_REPORTS/National%20Reporting%202013/NR_En/C13_NR_Netherlands-EN.pdf [7 July 2015].

ACM n.d., *Market outlook: the Netherlands authority for consumers and markets*. Available from: www.acm.nl/en/download/publication/?id=11305 [7 July 2015].

AEEG 2013, *Annual report to the International Agency for Cooperation between National Energy Regulators and the European Commission on the activities and duties of the Italian regulatory authority for electricity and gas*. Available from: www.ceer.eu/portal/page/portal/EER_HOME/EER_PUBLICATIONS/NATIONAL_REPORTS/National%20Reporting%202013/NR_En/C13_NR_Italy-EN.pdf [12 July 2015].

AEEG n.d., *Autorità per l'Energia Elettrica e il Gas: about us*. Available from: www.autorita.energia.it/it/inglese/index.htm [11 July 2015].

Bianco, A. 2011, "Short notes about energy regulation and permitting", in *Public law and regulation: collected essays*, eds A. Cicchetti, J.O. Frosini, & M. Gola, Maggioli, Santarcangelo di Romagna, ch. 6.

Bundesnetzagentur 2013, *Bundesnetzagentur: about us*. Available from: www.bundesnetzagentur.de/cln_1911/EN/Areas/Energy/AboutUs/aboutus-node.html [12 July 2015].

CEER 2009, *ERGEG 2009 status review of the liberalisation and implementation of the energy regulatory framework*. Available from: www.ceer.eu/portal/page/portal/EER_HOME/EER_PUBLICATIONS/NATIONAL_REPORTS/National%20Reporting%202009/C09-URB-24-03_ReviewReport2009_10-Dec-09.pdf [9 July 2015].

CEER 2010, *ERGEG 2010 status review of the liberalisation and implementation of the energy regulatory framework*. Available from: www.ceer.eu/portal/page/portal/EER_HOME/EER_PUBLICATIONS/NATIONAL_REPORTS/National%20Reporting%202010/C10-URB-34-04_StatusReview2010_v101201.pdf [4 July 2015].

Chiti, E. 2009, "The administrative implementation of European Union Law: a taxonomy and its implications", in *Legal challenges in EU administrative law: towards an integrated administration*, eds H.C.H. Hofmann & A.H. Türk, Edward Elgar, Cheltenham, pp. 9–33.

CNE 2013, *Spanish energy regulator's national report to the European Commission 2013*. Available from: www.ceer.eu/portal/page/portal/EER_HOME/EER_PUBLICATIONS/NATIONAL_REPORTS/National%20Reporting%202013/NR_En/C13_NR_Spain-EN.pdf [11 July 2015].

CRE 2013, *2012 national report to the European Commission*. Available from: www.ceer.eu/portal/page/portal/EER_HOME/EER_PUBLICATIONS/NATIONAL_REPORTS/National%20Reporting%202013/NR_En/C13_NR_France_Summary-EN.pdf [11 July 2015].

CRE n.d., *CRE's missions*. Available from: www.cre.fr/en/presentation/missions [13 July 2015].

Danish Energy Regulatory Authority 2012, *Results and challenges 2012*. Available from: http://energitilsynet.dk/fileadmin/Filer/publikationer/R_U_2012_UK_pdfa.pdf [11 July 2015].

Danish Energy Regulatory Authority n.d.a, *2012 national report Denmark*. Available from: www.ceer.eu/portal/page/portal/EER_HOME/EER_PUBLICATIONS/NATIONAL_REPORTS/National%20Reporting%202012/NR_En/C12_NR_Denmark-EN_v2.pdf [12 July 2015].

Danish Energy Regulatory Authority n.d.b, *2013 national report Denmark*, Available from: www.ceer.eu/portal/page/portal/EER_HOME/EER_PUBLICATIONS/NATIONAL_REPORTS/National%20Reporting%202013/NR_En/C13_NR_Denmark-EN.pdf [12 July 2015].

Department of Energy & Climate Change 2013, "Electricity", in *Digest of United Kingdom energy statistics*, ch. 5. Available from: www.gov.uk/government/uploads/system/uploads/attachment_data/file/279546/DUKES_2013_Chapter_5.pdf [9 July 2015].

DG TREN 2004, *Draft working paper: third benchmarking report on the implementation of the internal electricity and gas market*, Brussels, 1 March 2004.

Dyl, M., Paczkowska-Tomaszewska, A., Stankiewicz, R., & Wierzbowsk, M. 2011, "Zarys systemu podmiotów administrujących w Unii Europejskiej" [Outline of the system of administering entities in the European Union], in *Podmioty administrujące* [Administering entities], eds R. Hauser, A. Wróbel, & Z. Niewiadomski, vol. 6 of *System prawa administracyjnego* [System of administrative law], C.H. Beck, Warsaw, ch. 9.

Ei 2013a, *Annual report 2012*. Available from: http://ei.se/Documents/Publikationer/rapporter_och_pm/Rapporter%202013/Annualreport_Ei_2012.pdf [11 July 2015].

Ei 2013b, *The Swedish electricity and natural gas markets 2012*. Available from: http://ei.se/Documents/Publikationer/rapporter_och_pm/Rapporter%202013/Ei_R2013_14.pdf. [11 July 2015].

ENEL n.d., *1999–2001: the season of change*. Available from: www.enel.com/en-GB/group/about_us/history/1999_2001/ [12 July 2015].

Energy Market Authority 2013, *2013 national report Finland*. Available from: www.ceer.eu/portal/page/portal/EER_HOME/EER_PUBLICATIONS/NATIONAL_REPORTS/National%20Reporting%202013/NR_En/C13_NR_Finland-EN.pdf [13 July 2015].

European Commission 1998, *Report from the Commission to the Council and the European Parliament on state of liberalisation of the energy markets*, Brussels, 7 April 1998, COM (1998) 212 final.

European Commission 2001, *Commission staff working paper: first benchmarking report on the implementation of the internal electricity and gas market*, Brussels, 3 December 2001, SEC (2001) 1957.

European Commission 2003, *Commission staff working paper: second benchmarking report on the implementation of the internal electricity and gas market*, Brussels, 7 April 2003, SEC (2003) 448.

European Commission 2005, *Commission staff working document: technical annex to the report from the Commission to the Council and the European Parliament on progress in creating the internal gas and electricity market*, Brussels, 15 November 2005, SEC (2005) 1448.

European Commission 2007a, *Commission staff working document accompanying document to the Communication from the Commission to the Council and the European Parliament: prospects for the internal gas and electricity market*, Brussels, 10 January 2007, SEC (2006) 1709.

European Commission 2007b, *Communication from the Commission to the European Council and the European Parliament: an energy policy for Europe*, Brussels, 10 January 2007, COM (2007) 1 final.

European Commission 2011a, *Country report: Denmark*. Available from: http://ec.europa.eu/energy/gas_electricity/doc/dk_energy_market_2011_en.pdf [18 July 2015].

European Commission 2011b, *Country report: France*. Available from: http://ec.europa.eu/energy/gas_electricity/doc/fr_energy_market_2011_en.pdf [18 July 2015].

European Commission 2011c, *Country report: Germany*. Available from http://ec.europa.eu/energy/gas_electricity/doc/de_energy_market_2011_en.pdf [18 July 2015].

European Commission 2011d, *Country report: Spain*. Available from: http://ec.europa.eu/energy/gas_electricity/doc/es_energy_market_2011_en.pdf [18 July 2015].

European Commission 2011e, *Country report: Sweden*. Available from: http://ec.europa.eu/energy/gas_electricity/doc/sv_energy_market_2011_en.pdf [18 July 2015].

European Commission 2011f, *Country report: the Netherlands*. Available from: http://ec.europa.eu/energy/gas_electricity/doc/nl_energy_market_2011_en.pdf [18 July 2015].

European Commission 2011g, *Netherlands: internal market fact sheet*. Available from: http://ec.europa.eu/energy/energy_policy/doc/factsheets/market/market_nl_en.pdf [12 July 2015].

European Commission 2014a, *Commission staff working document: country reports accompanying the document communication from the Commission to the European Parliament, the Council, the European Economic and Social Committee and the Committee of the Regions "progress towards completing the internal energy market"*, Brussels, 13 October 2014, SWD(2014) 311 final.

European Commission 2014b, *Commission staff working document: enforcement of the third internal energy market package accompanying the document communication from the Commission to the European Parliament, the Council, the European Economic and Social Committee and the Committee of the Regions "progress towards completing the internal energy market"*, Brussels, 13 October 2014, SWD(2014) 315 final.

Eurostat 2015, *Electricity market indicators, table 2: number of main electricity generating companies, 2003–2012*. Available from: http://epp.eurostat.ec.europa.eu/statistics_explained/

index.php/Electricity_market_indicators#Electricity_markets_-_generation_and_installed_capacity [11 July 2015].

Hatzopoulos, V. 2012, *Regulating services in the European Union*, Oxford University Press, Oxford.

IEA 2007, *Energy policies of IEA countries: Germany 2007 review*, OECD/IEA, Paris.

OECD n.d., *Italy: inventory of estimated budgetary support and tax expenditures for fossil-fuels*. Available from: www.oecd.org/site/tadffss/ITA.pdf [13 July 2015].

OFGEM 2012, *Protecting customers: OFGEM's enforcement powers: factsheet 113*. Available from www.ofgem.gov.uk/ofgem-publications/64011/factsheet-113-enforcement [13 July 2015].

OFGEM 2013a, *Annual report and accounts 2012–13*. Available from: www.ofgem.gov.uk/ofgem-publications/74220/ofgem-arr-201213final.pdf [13 July 2015].

OFGEM 2013b, *Price controls explained: factsheet 117*. Available from: www.ofgem.gov.uk/ofgem-publications/64003/pricecontrolexplainedmarch13web.pdf [13 July 2015].

OFGEM n.d.a, *Information for consumers*. Available from: www.ofgem.gov.uk/information-consumers [13 July 2015].

OFGEM n.d.b, *OFGEM's powers*. Available from: www.ofgem.gov.uk/investigations/ofgems-powers [13 July 2015].

OFGEM n.d.c, *The GB electricity distribution network*. Available from: www.ofgem.gov.uk/electricity/distribution-networks/gb-electricity-distribution-network [13 July 2015].

OFGEM n.d.d, *The GB electricity transmission network*. Available from: www.ofgem.gov.uk/electricity/transmission-networks/gb-electricity-transmission-network [13 July 2015].

Pobłocka, A., Brückmann, R., Herling, J., Becker, L., & Bauknech, D. 2011, *Integration of electricity from renewables to the electricity grid and to the electricity market – RES: national report: Sweden*, Berlin. Available from: www.eclareon.eu/sites/default/files/sweden_-_res_integration_national_study_nreap_final.pdf [13 July 2015].

Regulation (EC) No 713/2009 of the European Parliament and of the Council of 13 July 2009 establishing an Agency for the Cooperation of Energy Regulators, OJ L 211, 14 August 2009.

Regulation (EC) No 714/2009 of the European Parliament and of the Council of 13 July 2009 on conditions for access to the network for cross-border exchanges in electricity and repealing Regulation (EC) No 1228/2003, OJ L 211, 14 August 2009.

Regulation (EC) No 715/2009 of the European Parliament and of the Council of 13 July 2009 on conditions for access to the natural gas transmission networks and repealing Regulation (EC) No 1775/2005, OJ L 211, 14 August 2009.

Soda, G. & Carlone, A. 2013, "Cultural change, reorganization and diversification (1996–2002): the search for a new identity', in *National monopoly to successful multinational: the case of Enel*, eds M. Bergami, P.L. Celli, & G. Soda, Palgrave Macmillan, Houndmills, ch. 2.

Sonvilla, P.M., Piria, R., Bracker, J.F., & Bauknecht, D. 2012, *Integration of electricity from renewables to the electricity grid and to the electricity market – RES: national report: Spain*, Berlin. Available from: www.eclareon.eu/sites/default/files/spain_-_res_integration_national_study_nreap.pdf [13 July 2015].

Spitzley, J.-B., Binda Zane, E., Bauknecht, D., & Frank, R. 2011, *Integration of electricity from renewables to the electricity grid and to the electricity market – RES: national report: Netherlands*, Berlin. Available from: www.eclareon.eu/sites/default/files/netherlands_-_res_integration_national_study_nreap.pdf [13 July 2015].

TenneT 2015, *TenneT: history*. Available from: www.tennet.eu/nl/about-tennet/organisation/history.html [12 July 2015].

# 10 European regulatory approach to the electricity sector

Conducted by the European Union (EU), liberalisation of the electricity sector did not exclude public law regulation. The classic regulatory goals related to setting market competition, promoting it, and strengthening the EU's legislation were extended by two other directions. First, is energy security with security of supplies. Second, this concerns bringing public law regulation closer to environment issues, which in the EU are also perceived as climate matters.

For more than 20 years on the way to the EU internal energy market, the focus on these components was of a different degree. In the 1990s, the main objectives for the internal market for electricity included "free movement of products", and improving "security of supply", as well as "competitiveness" (Proposal for a Council Directive 1992, 548 final, p. 4). Protection of the environment was perceived as an additional objective to which "the completion of the internal energy market [might] yield benefits ... by encouraging greater efficiency and a more rapid adoption of 'cleaner' technologies" (Proposal for a Council Directive 1992, 548 final, p. 4). Nevertheless, it was also covered by the aim of "improving competitiveness" which covered using resources in the most efficient way, reaping the benefits of higher efficiency (Proposal for a Council Directive 1992, 548 final, p. 4).

These pillars were confirmed within the framework of the Second[1] and Third Energy Packages. In particular, the three objectives are clearly presented in the latter. As stated in the Explanatory Memorandum to the proposal for Directive 2009/72/EC:

> [w]ithout a competitive and efficient European electricity ... market, Europe's citizens will pay excessive prices for what is one of their most fundamental daily needs. The electricity ... market is also essential for Europe's competitiveness as energy is an important input for European industry.
>
> Furthermore, a competitive and efficient electricity ... market is a precondition to tackle climate change. Only with a functioning market is it possible to develop an effectively functioning emissions trading mechanism and a renewable energy industry that will meet the ambitious objective, agreed by the European Council of ensuring that the EU's energy mix is sourced 20% from renewable energy sources by 2020.

> Finally, a competitive EU-wide electricity … market is crucial to ensure the security of Europe's energy supply, as only a Europe-wide and competitive market generates the right investment signals and offer fair network access for all potential investors, and provides real and effective incentives to both network operators and generators to invest the billions of euros that will be needed in the EU over the next two decades.[2]

The three pillars of the internal energy market are mutually complemented and correlated. Stable energy supplies are of great significance for the economic development and production capacity of the European economy. Security of them affects competitiveness and energy prices. This enables investment in: building new infrastructure, a grid with interconnectors and generation units (also renewables), as well as improving the situation of energy customers. Development of infrastructure strengthens energy security. Applying new technology results in more efficient energy usage. All these together provide an increased exchange of energy and new market entries. The market is functioning well.

The technical characteristics of electricity, the historical background of the electricity sector, ownership and market factors, production and transfer of electricity in the EU etc., all contributed to the European model of market liberalisation of the energy market, which was based on harmonisation pursued by the Member States and regulatory authorities, and steered by the European Commission and other Union authorities.

The model does not imply retreat from public influence in favour of a pure market, as one might think by focusing only on a shallow sense of liberalisation (linked with libertarianism rather than liberalism). On the contrary, the electricity sector's model is based on public law instruments used by the EU to achieve specific goals, collected in the framework of the internal energy market. The analysed legislative packages containing specific commitments on implementation imposed on Member States clearly show that the EU, on the road towards an internal energy market, has selected and still selects the direction of regulation exercised by public authorities. Thus, liberalisation does not exclude active public participation in reaching the assumed model of the electricity sector within the EU. Unbundling, the concept of TPA, or the idea of independent regulators are the main public legal institutions used in European law to establish market conditions for the energy sector.

Nevertheless, on the grounds of European law, regulation in the electricity sector finds its own dimension, shaped by the provisions of energy packages. It is illustrated by the wording of Recital 12 of Directive 2009/72/EC's preamble, where one may find that:

> [a]ny system for unbundling should be effective in removing any conflict of interests between producers, suppliers and transmission system operators, in order to create incentives for the necessary investments and guarantee the access of new market entrants under a transparent and efficient regulatory

regime and should not create an overly onerous regulatory regime for national regulatory authorities.

Therefore, the presence of the public factor in the energy sector must not be excessive. It cannot lead to elimination of its market character. This proves the described formula of regulation, as an option which fulfils the field between the sphere of the market (market based) and public (state-based approach). Regulation keeps the legal form of the state's impact on the electricity market balanced. The EU's internal energy market links public influence with the market-based attitude, where public law regulation plays the role of a binder. Liberalisation is provided by and through a public regulatory approach.

Another feature of public law regulation in the EU is of a teleological nature. As explained, public law regulation in both its senses, the narrow and broad, is used to establish an internal electricity market. This notion, as well as the concept of market liberalisation derived from energy packages, is founded on three main pillars: competition, security, and environment. Public law regulation is driven by competition, security, and environment. Thereby, it has to enhance and promote competition, strengthen energy security, and protect environment. This relationship imposes these (promotion of competition, strengthening energy security, protecting environment) on regulation. That is why the three components, being determinants of the EU's liberalisation policy within the electricity sector, require being presented by their reference to public law regulation. The following sections link these approaches by a common denominator, i.e. which looks on them from the regulatory perspective.

However, the scope of this book is limited to two of the three mentioned components: competition and environment (linked in the EU with climate issues). Energy security, is a very broad and deep notion, with its external and domestic dimensions (see Nowak 2009, pp. 54–55, 94–102). Perception of it varies among countries, and energy risks are different if assessed in the short or long term (Grevi 2006, p. 1). Besides electricity, it is also necessary to differentiate remarks between oil and gas markets. Giovanni Grevi (2006, p. 1) rightly concludes that "there is … no one-size-fits-all solution: different responses are needed to address different problems". Apart from the provision of Liberalisation Packages, which deal with energy security, this issue is shaped by separate European legislation (e.g. Council Directive 2009/119/EC, Directive 2005/89/EC, as well as Regulation (EU) No 994/2010), as well as policy strategic documents (e.g. European Commission 2000, 2006, or 2011). These circumstances make energy security an area that requires in-depth analysis, which could turn into a separate dissertation or book. Thus, within the scope of this work, only the two mentioned elements of European regulatory policy are examined in a more detailed way.

## Regulation for competition and consumers

Energy Packages are the tools used by the European Union to establish the internal energy market. They were designed to ensure competition and enhance the position of new entrants or energy consumers. To implement competition conditions, concrete regulatory duties as well as powers were established. These were granted to regulatory authorities, both at the national and European level. As early as in 1986 the Council noted the need for "greater integration, free from barriers to trade, of the internal energy market with a view to improving security of supply, reducing costs and improving economic competitiveness".

### *Pro-competition and pro-consumer approach in electricity directives*

Competition is an element of every Energy Package. In the First Electricity Directive the completion of a competitive electricity market was considered an important step towards completion of the internal energy market (i.e. market in electricity must be competitive) (Recital 2 of Directive 96/92/EC's preamble). The Second Directive linked competition with "progressive market opening" (see Recital 21 of Directive 2003/54/EC's preamble). The Third Electricity Directive addressed the electricity internal market and competition issues. It covered a real choice for all consumers, new business opportunities or competitive prices and higher standards of service (Recital 1 of Directive 2009/72/EC's preamble).

In this view, since the First Package, the aim for actors operating in the EU should have been to achieve a competitive market in electricity (see Recital 9 of Directive 96/92/EC's preamble). Article 3 (1) of Directive 96/92/EC enhanced competition, as well as imposing a prohibition of discrimination in market behaviour as regards rights or obligations. This had to be ensured by Member States "on the basis of their institutional organization". It meant using the provision of public law regulation, by introducing legislation to set the correct market attitude. Within the rules of public law regulation, there were rules for access established under Article 17 (negotiated access) or 18 (single buyer procedure) of the First Electricity Directive. Besides, achieving a competitive market in electricity could be implemented by providing an institutional regulatory framework deriving from public law – establishing a regulator responsible for regulatory duties in the energy sector.

From the institutional, public law view, the Second Liberalisation Package provided competition in a more explicit way, setting firm provisions for regulatory action conducted by a regulatory authority. Under Article 23 of Directive 2003/54/EC, pro-competition powers within the duties of ensuring "non-discrimination, effective competition, and the efficient functioning of the market" had to be granted to regulatory authorities as their basic responsibilities. In this field, regulators had to strengthen public law regulatory institutions like unbundling or TPA. The Second Package obliged Member States to enable the regulatory authority to conduct monitoring of the effective unbundling of accounts, as well as the terms, conditions, and tariffs for connecting new producers of electricity (Article 23 (1) (e)–(f) of Directive 2003/54/EC). Apart from these, the regulators had to monitor the level of transparency – and competition (Article 23 (1) (h)). This was correlated with an obligatory report on competition within the electricity sector in each Member State covering "market dominance, predatory and anti-competitive behaviour", which was to be sent by the relevant national authorities to the Commission (Article 23 (8)).

Furthermore, the *pro-competition* approach was intensively developed under provisions of the Third Energy Package. Securing competition fell into the broadened scope of Member States' (as well as national regulators') duties. For example, in executing their duties, they should strengthen access at the cross-border level for new market players, both suppliers and generators. Moreover, they should support diversity of these new entities, representing different energy sources (see Recital 8 of Directive 2009/72/EC's preamble). This is in line with stricter provisions for separation of networks from activities of generation and supply (effective unbundling), aimed at eliminating the risk of discrimination in the electricity market. In this context, in Directive 2009/72/EC, the pro-competition value of ownership unbundling is underlined.[3] Currently, the Third Electricity Directive also provides other legal institutions for public law regulation. For instance, these are compliance programmes set out under its Article 6, with their anti-discriminatory and anti-competitive obligations.

The *pro-consumer* attitude covers ensuring high standards of universal and public service, protection of vulnerable customers, or powers contributing to the full effectiveness of consumer protection measures (Recital 37). As already mentioned, consumers are granted special status within the provisions of the Third Energy Package ("should be at the heart of this Directive"). The EU intends to enhance the consumers' position, and it is the right direction. This brings the electricity sector closer to the individual, enabling dispersion and improving the market fluctuations. As a result, it leads to strengthening market processes within the structure that has often defended itself against market rules. Thus,

> [p]romoting fair competition and easy access for different suppliers and fostering capacity for new electricity generation should be of the utmost importance for Member States in order to allow consumers to take full advantage of the opportunities of a liberalised internal market in electricity.
>
> (Recital 57)

### *Protection of competition and consumers in public law regulation*

With respect to European and national competition law,[4] the protection of competition and consumers' position is also a goal of national energy regulatory authorities. Thereby, the regulators should be granted the power to decide on appropriate measures to ensure customer benefits through the promotion of effective competition (Article 36). Pursuant to Article 36 of Directive 2009/72/EC, the *pro-competition* and *pro-consumer* approaches occur almost in every general objective of the regulatory authority. Seen in this light, national energy regulators should take all necessary measures to:

> [promote] … a competitive … internal market in electricity within the Community, and effective market opening for all customers and suppliers in

> the Community...; [develop] competitive and properly functioning regional markets...; [eliminate] restrictions on trade in electricity between Member States...; [help] to achieve, in the most cost-effective way, the development of ... non-discriminatory systems that are consumer oriented...; [facilitate] access to the network for new generation capacity, in particular removing barriers that could prevent access for new market entrants...; [ensure] that customers benefit through the efficient functioning of their national market, promoting effective competition and helping to ensure consumer protection; [help] to achieve high standards of universal and public service in electricity supply, contributing to the protection of vulnerable customers and contributing to the compatibility of necessary data exchange processes for customer switching.
>
> (Recital 57)

The general obligations are concretised by specific duties and powers of the regulatory authority. For instance, regulators have to monitor market opening verifying its level and effectiveness, as well as monitoring the competition at wholesale and retail levels. The monitoring covers such factors as electricity exchanges, prices for household customers, switching rates, disconnection rates, charges for (and the execution of) maintenance services, and complaints by household customers, or distortions or restrictions of competition (Article 37 (1) (j)). In addition, regulators have to guarantee that consumers have access to information on energy consumption, as well as to ensure it is in an easily understandable format (Article 37 (1) (p)).

A practical dimension of the national energy regulators' pro-competition and pro-consumers approach, was presented in the annual report elaborated jointly in November 2013 by the ACER and the CEER. It analyses the status of the main legal elements of consumer protection, significant from the point of "a safety net for consumers in the liberalised market", i.e. universal service, supplier switching, protection of vulnerable consumers, information requirements, and alternative dispute resolution mechanisms (ACER/CEER 2013, p. 236).

Within this scope national regulators appoint a supplier of last resort (e.g. for consumers who cannot find any other supplier on the market, or in a situation of bankruptcy of another supplier),[5] as well as collect information on this issue. In the field of switching suppliers, national regulatory authorities may approve procedures guaranteeing that the process takes less than three weeks.[6] As regards vulnerable consumers, some Member States apply social tariffs.[7] Also there may be a policy of no-disconnection during winter months is applied for vulnerable consumers of electricity.[8]

An important element of the pro-consumer approach reflected in public law regulation is information ensured to consumers. Under provisions of the Third Energy Packages, Member States are obliged to establish a single point of contact for energy consumers which has to provide consumers with all necessary information. This concerns their rights, current legislation, and the means of dispute settlement available (Article 3 (12) of Directive 2009/72/EC). These provisions are correlated with measures on consumers protection included in Annex I of Directive 2009/72/EC. It is stated that consumers should, *inter alia*, "receive transparent information on applicable prices and tariffs and on standard terms and conditions, in respect of access to and use of electricity services". Also, as stated in Annex I, Member States have to ensure that a electricity service provider specifies, for the consumers' needs, the method of initiating procedures for settlement of disputes, as well as information on their rights, including ways of complaint. Other pro-consumer measures that must be applied by EU's countries relate to guaranteeing consumers' rights concerning payment methods (a wide choice available), changing suppliers (no charges), electricity contracts (to include, *inter alia*, provisions on duration, renewal, and termination of services) (Annex I).

As already mentioned, besides enhancing competition and protecting consumers, public law regulation is aimed at ensuring security of supply as well as environmental protection. Currently, this is clearly proved by the provisions on public service obligations, as provided in the Third Electricity Directive (see Recital 9 of Directive 96/92/EC's preamble). During subsequent steps towards the establishment of the internal energy market, the scope of public service obligations has been extended in the field of environment protection. In this respect, under provisions of the Third Electricity Directive, these obligations may relate to energy efficiency, energy from renewable sources, and climate protection (Article 3 (2) of Directive 2009/72/EC). This highlights the pro-environmental direction of public law regulation increasingly apparent in European legislation.

## Regulation for environment and climate

Apart from the pro-competition nature of public law regulation in the electricity sector (in a broad and narrow sense) the European Union finds another aspect of this approach extremely important – environment and climate change. This attitude may be called *pro-environmental*, i.e. making the regulation exercised by the EU's institutions in the energy sector aimed at providing an activity in which the environment, with its natural resources, should be protected, with respect to sustainable development. Leonardo Massai rightly writes about "the integration of environmental protection", as a consequence of amendments of the TEC, in particular the reference to the integration principle under Article 6 of the Treaty, after passing the Treaty of Amsterdam (Massai 2012, p. 72). However, integrating energy and environment has been a major component of European Energy Policy even in the 1990s. Furthermore, the Single European Act provided an arena for closer integration of environmental policy (European Commission 1998, p. 2; see European Commission 1990). The integration assumption is confirmed by numerous actions conducted by the EC on a strategic level. For example, in 1997, the Commission released the Communication "An overall view of energy policy and actions". Noting the great importance of environmental issues which "emerged at the top of the political agenda", in its report, the EC provided that "[e]nergy ... is a key factor in the achievement of sustainable development" and "[o]ne major challenge for energy policy is ... to render energy and environmental objectives more compatible" (European Commission 1997, p. 3). Also the Communication of 1998, "Strengthening environmental integration within Community energy policy", deals with a call for combining energy and environmental objectives.[9] Subsequently, the idea of *sustainable development* complemented this approach (see European Commission 2001a, 2002, or 2013).

The environmental side of the energy policy driving for integration, as assessed in the 1990s, was "to promote energy efficiency/saving, to increase the share of production and use of cleaner energy sources, and to reduce the environmental impact or the production and use of energy sources" (European Commission 1998, p. 7; see European Commission 1995).

### *Public law regulation for reduction of emissions and climate action*

The European Community, as well as the European Union, have not limited their impact on the energy sector only to these environmental issues. The European agenda finds a much more specific dimension. Besides the environment, the EU distinguishes a separate, very important policy objective: *Climate change* and ways in which the European Union can tackle it with the use of public law regulation, which in this case takes the shape of *pro-climate regulation*. The general legal expression of this approach is the Climate and Energy Package, especially with its "3 × 20% goals". Although this attitude is much more complex, and one may find many other examples supporting this concept.

The need for legislation on climate issues was for the first time officially recognised by the EC in the late 1980s. In response to international activity and developments around climate change (see Kulovesi 2012, pp. 118–119), the Commission proposed a means to launch the European approach to tackle the greenhouse effect (European Commission 1988b). Earlier in the 1980s, the EU tackled emissions from industrial installation. This was done with the use of Council Directive 84/360/EEC of 28 June 1984 on the combating of air pollution from industrial plants. The Directive was the first European legal framework for air pollutant emissions from industrial plants. It established important environmental principles for construction installations. In 1988, this framework was completed by passing a Directive on controlling of emissions from large combustion plants that set new obligations for electricity: standards for emission of $SO_2$ and $NO_X$, as well as emission ceilings for $SO_2$ and $NO_X$ – reduction targets, based on the year 1980, of total national emissions of these two gases from existing plants.

In this context, the Communication on Greenhouse Effect introduced the greenhouse issue and possible action for the European agenda (Massai 2012, p. 49). Deriving from the dichotomy of preventive and/or adaptive actions policies to deal with the greenhouse issues included: research, preventive action, planned adaptation, and cooperation with developing countries (European Commission 1988b, pp. 42–50). This correlates with the political actions at the level of the Council. The Dublin meeting in June 1990, where the European Council urged the adaptation of targets and strategies for limiting the emissions of greenhouse gases (GHG), together with the Environment Council of October 1990, where it was agreed to take actions to stabilise European $CO_2$ emissions at the 1990 level by 2000, may be considered as the first steps towards a European climate policy (Massai 2012, p. 50).

The political background built the basis for legislation, as was clearly expressed by the Environment Council of December 1991 when the Commission was requested to formulate concrete European climate measures. The EC proposed the first package of legislative proposals responding to climate change in the same year. However, the package, intended for adoption prior to the Earth Summit of the United Nations Conference, failed to reach an agreement in the field of energy taxation and its harmonisation. As a result, this initiative was dropped (Massai 2012, p. 50).

Nevertheless, in 1993, the first European legislation on climate change was passed.[10] This was concluded with the use of Council Decision 93/398/EEC. Pursuant to its provisions (Article 2), Member States were obliged to publish and implement national programmes for limiting their anthropogenic emissions. Member States had to include in their national programme details of national policies and measures, which contribute to the limitation of $CO_2$ emissions, as well as measures being taken or envisaged for the implementation of the Community's legislation and policies (see Article 2 (2)). Apart from these data, the national programmes covered information on anthropogenic $CO_2$ emissions by sources, country's 1990 base year for them, or trajectories for national $CO_2$ emissions 1994–2000.

Further, in 1993, the EU and its Member States were already required to initiate legislation for the monitoring of GHG emissions in line with the international climate regime. This was driven by the United Nations Framework Convention on Climate Change (UNFCCC)[11] and the Kyoto Protocol.[12] Both international agreements contributed to the boosting of the EU climate regime and clean energy, as a consequence of what was required by international and EC law (Massai 2012, p. 50).

In addition, new legislation on pollution was passed. In 1996, Council Directive 96/61/EC concerning integrated pollution prevention and control (IPPC) was adopted. As written in its preamble "the implementation of an integrated approach to reduce pollution requires action at Community level in order to modify and supplement existing Community legislation concerning the prevention and control of pollution from industrial plants". Seen in this light, the Directive set a general framework for integrated pollution prevention and control, as well as laying down the measures necessary to implement it. The authorities in Member States had to ensure that the right preventive measures aimed against pollution were provided. For instance, this was done by application of the best available techniques.[13] Emission limit values, parameters, or equivalent technical measures had to be based on them, "without prescribing the use of one specific technique or technology and taking into consideration the technical characteristics of the installation concerned, its geographical location and local environmental conditions". How to determine the technical characteristics of the installation, its geographical location, and the local environmental conditions, was the responsibility of the Member States.

According to its Article 1 the purpose of the Directive was "to achieve integrated prevention and control of pollution arising from the activities listed in Annex I". Within this assumption, the IPPC Directive included establishment of a joint system of environmental licences. Among different activities in different industries,[14] in Annex I there is also energy sector. This includes the following activities: combustion installations with a rated thermal input exceeding 50MW, mineral oil and gas refineries, coke ovens, and coal gasification and liquefaction plants.

At the beginning of the twenty-first century the European agenda on climate change took on a new dimension. In 2001, since the public announcement by the US to reject the Kyoto Protocol,[15] the EU has tried to assume a leading role in the field of climate policy at the international level (Massai 2012, p. 54). This was confirmed in the EU's very strong position at Conferences of the Parties negotiations aimed at ensuring the environmental integrity of the Kyoto Protocol and ambitious GHG emission reduction targets, as well as by the scope of legislation at the Community level aimed at combating global warming (Massai 2012, p. 54). Seen in that light, in 2002, the Council, on behalf of the European Community, approved the Kyoto Protocol (Council Decision 2002/358/EC).

After approving the Kyoto Protocol, EU policy-making on climate change accelerated significantly (see Oberthür & Pallemaerts 2010, p. 42). In 2004, the European climate agenda received a firm legal backbone. This was done by adapting the EU Emission Trading System (EU ETS) by passing Directive 2003/87/EC.[16] On this basis, from the beginning of 2005, as a rule, Member States have to ensure that no installation undertook any activity listed in the Directive's Annex I unless its operator was granted an emission permit issued by a competent authority.[17] Moreover, the EU ETS Directive launched the first, "pilot phase" of emission trade in the EU (2005–2007). It covered only $CO_2$ emissions from energy producers and energy-intensive industry, although almost all allowances were given free of charge (European Commission 2015).[18] The total number of free allowances distributed to companies exceeded the emissions, resulting in the over-allocation of emission allowances in most EU Member States (Macken 2011, p. 3).

Between 2007 and 2009, the European Union's action in the field of climate agenda accelerated. In March 2007, the European Council addressed the leading role of the EU in international climate protection and called on developed countries to commit collectively to reducing their emissions of GHG (Council of the European Union 2007). In this context, the European Council endorsed:

> an EU objective of a 30% reduction in greenhouse gas emissions by 2020 compared to 1990 as its contribution to a global and comprehensive agreement for the period beyond 2012, provided that other developed countries commit themselves to comparable emission reductions and economically more advanced developing countries to contributing adequately according to their responsibilities and respective capabilities.
>
> (Council of the European Union 2007, p. 12)

Further, the Council decided that, until approving a global post-2012 agreement, the European Union would act individually in the area of climate, as it wants to transform itself "into a highly energy-efficient and low greenhouse-gas-emitting economy". Therefore the Council set an individual, European commitment to achieve at least a 20 per cent reduction of GHG emissions by 2020 compared to 1990 (Council of the European Union 2007, p. 12). Besides this goal, the Council emphasised the need to increase energy efficiency in the EU, setting the energy efficiency of saving 20 per cent of the EU's energy consumption compared to projections for 2020. Finally, the March Council endorsed a binding target of a 20 per cent share of renewable energies in overall EU energy consumption should be reached by 2020 (Council of the European Union 2007, pp. 20–21).

With this in light, the Commission, in January 2008, proposed a set of legislation which took the form of the already-mentioned Climate and Energy Package with new rules on the EU ETS. In December 2008, the European Council reached a political agreement on the Package, which in 2009 became binding legislation consisting of Emission Performance Regulation (EC) No 443/2009, Renewable Energy Directive 2009/28/EC, revised EU-ETS Directive 2009/29/EC, Fuel Quality Directive 2009/30/EC, CCS Directive 2009/31/EC, and Effort Sharing Decision No 406/2009/EC.

### *Influencing the scope of liberalisation by using the Climate and Energy Package*

Rules established on the basis of the aforementioned legislation, with the great impact of the Climate and Energy Package, in a very significant way affect the scope of public law regulation of the electricity sector. The analysed provisions of the Liberalisation Packages, especially the newest Electricity Directive 2009/72/EC, prove it. Secured supplies in electricity are the prerequisite of a sustainable climate change policy (see Recital 5 of Directive 2009/72/EC's preamble). This is correlated with the idea of a well-functioning internal market that enhances two components of climate policy: renewable energy sources and energy efficiency.[19]

However, this correlation was noticed even in the First Liberalisation Package era. In 2001, the Commission assessed that

> [t]he creation of an internal market for electricity … has been shown, in many respects, to have had positive environmental impacts due to the

> improvements in generating plants, increased operational efficiency and a switch to cleaner fuels in power production. On the other hand falling energy prices might not be conducive to the development of energy efficiency and renewables.
>
> (European Commission 2001a, p. 21)[20]

The overall intention of the European legislation expressed in the provisions of the preamble is clarifying the specific provisions of Directive 2009/72/EC requiring implementation. For example, as stated in Article 3 (2), Member States with regard to electricity undertakings, may execute a concrete regulatory tool, i.e. impose service obligations. Among their conditions was environmental protection. This broad category is specified in three components of the Climate and Energy Package: energy efficiency, renewable energy sources, and climate protection. Furthermore, introducing long-term planning instruments can strengthen energy efficiency or renewable energy. Finally, where it is appropriate, Member States shall implement measures aimed at achieving the objectives of environmental protection. These cover energy efficiency/demand-side management measures and means to combat climate change.[21] Also earlier legislation provided a basis for similar obligation. For example, Directive 96/92/EC allowed the introduction of public service obligations related to environmental protection, or, in Article 8 (3) and Article 11 (3), gave the possibility to favour generating from renewable energy sources or waste.

Regarding the promotion of energy efficiency, where so provided,[22] the regulatory authority must "strongly recommend" optimisation of electricity usage to the electricity undertakings. This regulatory duty covers energy management services, innovative pricing formulas, intelligent metering systems, or smart grids (Article 3 (11) of Directive 2009/72/EC). In addition, energy efficiency is also used as a tool for addressing energy poverty. Here Member States are obliged to take measures to ensure the necessary electricity supply to vulnerable customers (Article 3 (7)).

Moreover, on the basis of Article 3 (9) of Directive 2009/72/EC, Member State have to ensure that the suppliers of electricity, in their operation, provide information linked with the EU's climate aims. This concerns, *inter alia*, information on environmental impact in terms of $CO_2$ emissions (Article 3 (9) (b)). The duty entails the obligation of the regulatory authority to guarantee that this information is provided.

Aims of the European Climate and Energy Package in the field of the public law regulation may be found also in the provisions of Directive 2009/72/EC on authorisation procedure for new capacity (Article 7). In establishing criteria for granting of authorisations for generators, Member States shall consider: "the protection of the environment, energy efficiency", as well as "the contribution of the generating capacity to meeting the overall Community target of … energy from renewable sources in the Community's gross final consumption of energy in 2020", "and the contribution of generating capacity to reducing emissions" (Article 7 (2) (c), (f), (j), and (k)).

Finally, under Article 36, among the general objectives of regulators, is the obligation to help,

> to achieve … the development of … systems that are … in line with general energy policy objectives, energy efficiency as well as the integration of large and small-scale production of electricity from renewable energy sources and distributed generation in both transmission and distribution networks.
>
> (Article 36 (d)–(e))

Moreover, regulators have to remove barriers preventing the network access of renewable energy sources.

These circumstances show the *pro-environmental* (or the *pro-climate*) orientation of the EU. It has its deep impact on the aims of the energy regulators, which have to operate in space built on this policy. Their goals, linked with the general objectives of public law regulation, are driven by the mentioned policy agenda. Accordingly, this shapes their competence and powers.

Lastly, presented in this chapter, findings clearly demonstrate the impact of European Energy Packages on the scope of public law regulation. One of the more significant findings to emerge from this study is that, apart from liberalisation linked with providing market opening and conditions for competition within the electricity market, the legislative packages on liberalisation and climate set regulation conducted by the national regulatory authorities in the direction of ensuring security of supplies and protecting environment and climate. All these three spheres are correlated with each other. Each of them needs the other.

First, it is competition that steers all Energy Packages. The internal energy market must be competitive. Thereby the European Union, with the use of Liberalisation Packages, introduced legal institutions of public law regulation that had to enhance competition and protect the weakest element of it – consumers. Because of competition, the rules for access to the grid, provisions on non-discrimination, capacity for new electricity generation, and cross-border trade were established. Opening the market for the possibility of switching supplier, unbundling, a pro-consumer attitude in terms of universal and public service, as well as protection of vulnerable customers, highlights the *pro-competition and pro-consumer approach* of public law regulation in the EU.

Besides competition and consumers the goal of public law regulation is to protect the environment. In the European Union this attitude combines environment and climate. Regarding the legal sphere, apart from the provisions of the Liberalisation Packages, this goal finds its special treatment, i.e. it is regulated under the Climate and Energy Package as well as the EU's previous legal acts that dealt with reduction of emissions and sustainable development. On this ground, the goals for reduction of GHG emissions, increasing energy efficiency, and promoting renewable energy sources ("3 × 20% goals"), obligations for electricity regarding $SO_2$ and $NO_X$, duties in terms of information on environmental impact concerning $CO_2$ emissions, or criteria for granting authorisations for the generators considering the protection of the environment or energy efficiency, were established. Further, the legal sphere of an environmental character, does not omit regulators' tasks (e.g. regulators have to remove barriers in the field of access to the grid with respect to renewables). This circumstance distinctly emphasises the *pro-environmental* direction of European public law regulation.

Apart from competition and environment, the purpose of regulation is to ensure energy security. As briefly described, the EU finds it important to build a secure internal energy market. Undoubtedly, European legislation and policy documents confirm this. This correlates with the other components of the common energy market.[23] Thereby, pursuant to Article 4 of Directive 2009/72/EC, Member States have ensure monitoring of the security of supply. In accordance with its Article 7, in passing criteria for granting authorisations for the construction of generating capacity, they have to consider, *inter alia*, the safety and security of the electricity system. Energy security also covers the tasks of Transmission System Operators (contributing to security of supply) (see Article 12 of Directive 2009/72/EC), as well as the general objectives, duties, and powers of the regulatory authorities (see Article 36 and 37). All these provided factors demonstrate that public law regulation in the European Union has a teleological character. In this sense, public regulation has to fulfil the goal of a publicly valid character. In the EU, it is a measure which enables achieving an objective or rather a set of objectives gathered together in the notion of the internal energy market. As provided, this concept is anchored in competition, security, and environment. Public law regulation has to strengthen, promote, protect, and enforce each of them. It is used to implement a system of interrelated objectives for the European policy agenda inscribed in provisions of the legislative packages on energy. The European Energy Packages made it possible to realise the European policy agenda with the use of regulatory tools.

The examined circumstances confirm the thesis of the need for regulation. The model of 28 independent Member States organised in the Union, with separate energy systems and their different structures (in the field of energy mix, as well as market concentration, or strength of the sector), requires coordination and harmonisation if the internal energy market is to become a reality. Centralised control over the electricity sector contradicts the rules of the market. Thereby, the role of national regulators is so important, as a balanced approach lying between state-based and market-based models. In this regard, the regulatory model based on the role of national regulators reconciles European and national interests. The role of national regulators is complemented by the activity of ACER. Together, they establish a comprehensive model linking the top-down and the bottom-up approach.

All things considered, it seems that the road to an effective, competitive, secure, and sustainable European common energy market is to be shorter. The question is whether it can be even shorter still? Relying on the previous assumptions on public law regulations, including at the European level, the accelerator may be used further, together with strengthening public law regulation. I address this matter in the very last element of this work's structure, which is its summary. Although, before doing this I draw conclusions of my research conducted in the book.

## Notes

1 In the Explanatory Memorandum to the proposal for Directive 2003/54/EC, as the basic objectives pursued by the internal market, there were qualified: lower prices, increased competitiveness, high standards of public service, security of supply, and environmental protection. Thus, these core categories of the internal market were maintained. See European Commission 2001a.

2

> It must be acknowledged that a more integrated energy market is a significant additional factor as regards the security of supply for all Member States. Greater interconnection of equipment would make it possible to increase both the solidarity between Member States and the flexibility of the industry. It would therefore increase the emergency resources available in the event of a crisis and create the possibility of additional trading.
>
> (European Commission 1988, p. 6)

3 As written in Recital 11,

> [o]nly the removal of the incentive for vertically integrated undertakings to discriminate against competitors as regards network access and investment can ensure effective unbundling. Ownership unbundling, which implies the appointment of the network owner as the system operator and its independence from any supply and production interests, is clearly an effective and stable way to solve the inherent conflict of interests.

4 The Directive provides herein the basis for close cooperation of national competition, financial, and energy regulators with the Commission, and themselves, on investigations relating to competition law. See Articles 36 or 37 (4) (b).

5 Like in Austria, or Hungary (ACER/CEER 2013, p. 237).

6 For example, in Romania (ACER/CEER 2013, p. 238).

7 *Inter alia*, Belgium, France, Greece, Romania, or Spain (ACER/CEER 2013, p. 241).

8 As in the Netherlands (ACER/CEER 2013, p. 241).

9 A strengthening of the Commission's actions at the European level was assessed as a measure for reaching this objective. As justified in the Communication,

> [w]hile Member States have the major responsibility for integrating the environment within their energy policy, they have a clear interest in closer co-operation in this field. The Commission is prepared to facilitate this co-operation and to help Member States in achieving this goal in the most cost-effective way, while taking fully into account the other Community objectives such as the internal market and sustainable growth.
>
> (European Commission 1997, p. 7)

10 Massai (2012, p. 50) finds here a framework of what in the future is called the European climate policy.

11 Adopted 9 May 1992, entered into force 21 March 1994.

12 The Protocol to the United Nations Framework Convention on Climate Change, adopted on 1 December 1997, entered into force on 16 February 2005 in accordance with Article 23, that is the ninetieth day after the date on which not less than 55 Parties to the UNFCCC, incorporating Parties included in Annex I which accounted

in total for at least 55 per cent of the total carbon dioxide emissions for 1990 of the Parties included in Annex I, have deposited their instruments of ratification, acceptance, approval, or accession. Currently, there are 192 Parties (191 states and one regional economic integration organisation) to the Kyoto Protocol (*UNFCCC Status of ratification of the Kyoto Protocol*, n.d.). As provided in Annex A the Protocol covers: carbon dioxide ($CO_2$), methane ($CH_4$), nitrous oxide ($N_2O$), hydrofluorocarbons (HFCs), perfluorocarbons (PFCs), and sulphur hexafluoride ($SF_6$).

13 Pursuant to Article 2 (11) IPPC,

> "best available techniques" shall mean the most effective and advanced stage in the development of activities and their methods of operation which indicate the practical suitability of particular techniques for providing in principle the basis for emission limit values designed to prevent and, where that is not practicable, generally to reduce emissions and the impact on the environment as a whole:
>
> - techniques shall include both the technology used and the way in which the installation is designed, built, maintained, operated and decommissioned,
> - available techniques shall mean those developed on a scale which allows implementation in the relevant industrial sector, under economically and technically viable conditions, taking into consideration the costs and advantages, whether or not the techniques are used or produced inside the Member State in question, as long as they are reasonably accessible to the operator,
> - best shall mean most effective in achieving a high general level of protection of the environment as a whole.

14 For example, installations for the processing of ferrous metals, installations for the production of asbestos and the manufacture of asbestos-based products, installations for the manufacture of glass including glass fibre with a melting capacity exceeding 20 tonnes per day, chemical installations for the production of basic inorganic chemicals, chemical installations for the production of explosives, etc.

15 In July 1999, the US Senate passed a resolution rejecting the Kyoto Protocol, and in 2001 the Protocol was rejected by the US administration. See Ervin & Smith 2008, pp. 87–88.

16 In 2004 the EU ETS Directive was complemented with Directive 2004/101/EC linking the ETS to the Kyoto Protocol project mechanisms, namely the CDM (Clean Development Mechanism) and JI (Joint Implementation) (Oberthür & Pallemaerts 2010, p. 42).

17 For energy activities these are combustion installations with a rated thermal input exceeding 20 MW (except hazardous or municipal waste installations), as well as mineral oil refineries, and coke ovens (all emitting carbon dioxide).

18 As the Commission explains: "Phase one succeeded in establishing a price for carbon, free trade in emission allowances across the EU and the necessary infrastructure for monitoring, reporting and verifying actual emissions from the businesses covered" (European Commission 2015). See Betz & Sato 2006.

19 See Recital 6. For instance, thereby, in development of their network Member States should introduce the smart grids, and choose solution which enable generation and energy efficiency; see Recital 27.

20 In 2001, completely new legislation on renewable energy sources was passed, based on the Commission's proposal from 2000, i.e. Proposal for Directive 2000, 279 final. It was Directive 2001/77/EC.

21 Article 3 (10) of Directive 2009/72/EC. "Such measures may include, in particular, the provision of adequate economic incentives, using, where appropriate, all existing national and Community tools, for the maintenance and construction of the necessary network infrastructure, including interconnection capacity."

22 Otherwise Member States were responsible for it.
23 "A secure supply of electricity is of vital importance for the development of European society, the implementation of a sustainable climate change policy, and the fostering of competitiveness within the internal market". Recital 5 of Directive 2009/72/EC's preamble.

## References

ACER/CEER 2013, *Annual report on the results of monitoring the internal electricity and natural gas markets in 2012*. Available from: www.acer.europa.eu/Official_documents/Acts_of_the_Agency/Publication/ACER%20Market%20Monitoring%20Report%20 2013.pdf [12 July 2015].

Betz, R. & Sato, M. 2006, "Emissions trading: lessons learnt from the 1st phase of the EU ETS and prospects for the 2nd phase", *Climate Policy*, 6, pp. 351–359. Available from: www.eprg.group.cam.ac.uk/wp-content/uploads/2008/11/betz.pdf [16 July 2015].

Council Decision 93/389/EEC of 24 June 1993 for a monitoring mechanism of community $CO_2$ and other greenhouse gas emissions, OJ L 167, 9 July 1993.

Council Decision 2002/358/EC of 25 April 2002 concerning the approval, on behalf of the European Community, of the Kyoto Protocol to the United Nations Framework Convention on Climate Change and the joint fulfilment of commitments thereunder, OJ L 130, 15 May 2002.

Council Directive 84/360/EEC of 28 June 1984 on the combating of air pollution from industrial plants, OJ L 188, 16 July 1984.

Council Directive 88/609/EEC of 24 November 1988 on the limitation of emissions of certain pollutants into the air from large combustion plants, OJ L 336, 7 December 1988.

Council Directive 96/61/EC of 24 September 1996 concerning integrated pollution prevention and control, OJ L 257, 10 October 1996.

Council Directive 2009/119/EC of 14 September 2009 imposing an obligation on Member States to maintain minimum stocks of crude oil and/or petroleum products, OJ L 265, 9 October 2009.

Council of the European Union 2007, *Council conclusions of 8–9 March 2007*, Brussels, 2 May 2007, 7224/1/07, REV 1.

Council Resolution of 16 September 1986 concerning new Community energy policy objectives for 1995 and convergence of the policies of the Member States, OJ C 241, 25 September 1986.

Directive 96/92/EC of the European Parliament and of the Council of 19 December 1996 concerning common rules for the internal market in electricity, OJ L 27, 30 January 1997.

Directive 2001/77/EC of the European Parliament and of the Council of 27 September 2001 on the promotion of electricity produced from renewable energy sources in the internal electricity market, OJ L 283, 27 October 2001.

Directive 2003/54/EC of the European Parliament and of the Council of 26 June 2003 concerning common rules for the internal market in electricity and repealing Directive 96/92/EC, OJ L 176, 15 July 2003.

Directive 2003/87/EC of the European Parliament and of the Council of 13 October 2003 establishing a scheme for greenhouse gas emission allowance trading within the Community and amending Council Directive 96/61/EC, OJ L 275, 25 October 2003.

Directive 2004/101/EC of the European Parliament and of the Council of 27 October 2004 amending Directive 2003/87/EC establishing a scheme for greenhouse gas emission allowance trading within the Community, in respect of the Kyoto Protocol's project mechanisms, OJ L 338, 13 November 2004.

Directive 2005/89/EC of the European Parliament and of the Council of 18 January 2006 concerning measures to safeguard security of electricity supply and infrastructure investment, OJ L 33, 4 February 2006.

Directive 2009/72/EC of the European Parliament and of the Council of 13 July 2009 concerning common rules for the internal market in electricity and repealing Directive 2003/54/EC, OJ L 211, 14 August 2009.

Ervin, J. & Smith, Z.A. 2008, *Globalization: a reference handbook*. ABC-CLIO, Santa Barbara, CA.

European Commission 1988a, *Commission working document: the internal energy market*, Brussels, 2 May 1988, COM (88) 238 final.

European Commission 1988b, *Communication to the Council: the greenhouse effect and the community. Commission work programme concerning the evaluation of policy options to deal with the "greenhouse effect"*, Brussels, 16 November 1988, COM (88) 656 final.

European Commission 1990, *Communication from the Commission to the Council on energy and the environment*, Brussels, 8 February 1990, COM (89) 369 final.

European Commission 1995, *White Paper of the European Commission: an energy policy for the European Union*, Brussels, 13 December 1995, COM (95) 682 final.

European Commission 1997, *Communication from the Commission: an overall view of energy policy and actions*, Brussels, 23 April 1997, COM (97) 167 final.

European Commission 1998, *Communication from the Commission: strengthening environmental integration within Community energy policy*, Brussels, 14 October 1998, COM (1998) 571 final.

European Commission 2000, *Commission green paper of 29 November 2000: towards a European strategy for the security of energy supply*, Brussels, 29 November 2000, COM (2000) 769 final.

European Commission 2001a, *Communication from the Commission to the Council and the European Parliament: completing the internal energy market*, Brussels, 13 March 2001, COM (2001) 125 final.

European Commission 2001b, *Communication from the Commission a sustainable Europe for a better world: a European Union strategy for sustainable development*, Brussels, 15 May 2001, COM (2001) 264 final.

European Commission 2002, *Communication from the Commission to the European Parliament, the Council, the Economic and Social Committee and the Committee of the Regions: towards a global partnership for sustainable development*, Brussels, 13 February 2002, COM (2002) 82 final.

European Commission 2006, *Commission green paper of 8 March 2006: a European strategy for sustainable, competitive and secure energy*, Brussels, 8 March 2006, COM (2006) 105 final.

European Commission 2011, *Communication from the Commission to the European Parliament, the Council, the European Economic and Social Committee and the Committee of the Regions on security of energy supply and international cooperation: the EU energy policy: engaging with partners beyond our borders*, Brussels, 7 September 2011, COM (2011) 539 final.

European Commission 2013, *Communication from the Commission to the European Parliament, the Council, the European Economic and Social Committee and the Committee of the Regions beyond 2015: towards a comprehensive and integrated approach to financing poverty eradication and sustainable development*, Brussels, 16 July 2013, COM (2013) 531 final.

European Commission 2015, *EU ETS 2005–2012*. Available from: http://ec.europa.eu/clima/policies/ets/pre2013/ [12 July 2015].

Grevi, G. 2006, "CFSP and energy security", *EU Institute for Security Studies Seminar*, Paris, 23 October 2006. Available from: www.iss.europa.eu/uploads/media/rep06-12.pdf [12 July 2015].

Kulovesi, K. 2012, "Climate change in EU external relations: please follow my example (or I might force you to)", in *The external environmental policy of the European Union: EU and international law perspectives*, ed. E. Morgera, Cambridge University Press, Cambridge, pp. 115–148.

Macken, K. 2011, *The EU emissions trading scheme: a review of the first six years of operation*. Available from: www.epa.ie/pubs/reports/air/etu/ETS%20Review.pdf [15 July 2015].

Massai, L. 2012. *European climate and clean energy law and policy*, Earthscan, London.

Nowak, B. 2009. *Energy policy of the European Union: chosen legal and political aspects and their implications for Poland*, Academic and Professional Press, Warsaw.

Oberthür, S. & Pallemaerts, M. 2010, "The EU's internal and external climate policies: an historical overview", in *The new climate policies of the European Union: internal legislation and climate diplomacy*, eds S. Oberthür & M. Pallemaerts, VUB Press, Brussels, pp. 27–63.

Proposal for a Council Directive concerning common rules for the internal market in electricity, Brussels, 21 February 1992, COM (91) 548 final.

Proposal for a Directive of the European Parliament and of the Council amending Directive 2003/87/EC so as to improve and extend the greenhouse gas emission allowance trading system of the community, Brussels, 23 January 2008, COM (2008) 16 final 2008/0013 (COD).

Proposal for a Directive of the European Parliament and of the Council on the promotion of electricity from renewable energy sources in the internal electricity market, Brussels, 10 May 2000, COM (2000) 279 final.

Protocol to the United Nations Framework Convention on Climate Change, adopted on 1 December 1997.

Regulation (EU) No 994/2010 of the European Parliament and of the Council of 20 October 2010 concerning measures to safeguard security of gas supply and repealing Council Directive 2004/67/EC, OJ L 295, 12 November 2010.

*UNFCCC status of ratification of the Kyoto Protocol*, n.d. Available from: http://unfccc.int/kyoto_protocol/status_of_ratification/items/2613.php [12 July 2015].

# 11 Findings and conclusion

The European Union's legislative packages have had a lasting impact on the European electricity sector and the scope of its public law regulation. Traced provisions of the Liberalisation Packages, the Climate and Energy Package, as well as related strategic EU documents, proposals of legislation, reports, opinions, etc., have provided the foundation for this book. On the one hand, some theses require only recapitulation. On the other hand, some theses need additional comments. The formula of this chapter allows for it.

Electricity is nowadays one of the strategic factors determining countries' level of development. In many ways it is absolutely essential for the normal functioning of modern societies and economies. It determines competitive strength and market advantages. It stabilises socio-economic relations, finding opportunities for industry and households. Further, electricity plays a more and more vital role in the world, being preferable for energy usage. Compared to other kinds of energy, its shares in the global market grow faster. There are many indications that the future will belong to electricity.

Its importance influences the public interest attached to it. Also the past shows that, throughout the twentieth century, states controlled the electricity sectors in most countries, owning electricity companies, as well as establishing rules for operation in the sector. Post-war western Europe was dominated by the view that the state should control the energy sector and other main branches of the industry. In many cases, electricity companies were nationalised or the concentration of market entities occurred. Driven by the strategic character of energy, states executed their powers regarding the sector.

This situation persisted until the 1990s in the western part of Europe. The national energy sectors were run by national and state-owned monopolies. They were granted (*de jure* or de facto) exclusive powers in the area of purchase, import and export, or infrastructure. In addition, this system included operation of vertically integrated entities, remuneration based on historical costs, high degree of planning, objectification of consumers, and, as a result, closure to competition. A theoretical background for this practical solution was the traditional paradigm of central control over a synchronised network. In this regard, the electricity sector was a strategic asset for a national economy. Therefore, that made it necessary to provide them with exclusive rights in the field of electricity production, transmission, and distribution. This state-based approach has its roots in theories originating from *mercantilism* as well as concepts related to *interventionism*. They are grounded on an intensive way of steering the energy sector. This was the rationale of the approach to the sector before the 1980s.

Noticing drawbacks of this sector's structures, the European Commission, driven by the need to establish an internal market with the energy market as a component between the 1980s and 1990s, took steps to overcome these monopolies and their powers. The lack of specific legal grounds dedicated to the energy sector resulted in using competition law. In the 1990s, the market-based activity of the European Commission was strengthened by a binding legal basis: the First Energy Package. Aimed at liberalising the electricity sector, eliminating monopoly rights, and enabling different suppliers to compete for customers, the First Energy Package was just a very early step towards broad market reform that was deepened in 2003 by the Second Energy Package, and, in 2009, by the Third Energy Package. Known also as Liberalisation Packages, they are instruments used by the European Union to introduce reform of the energy sector, including electricity.

Packages, and their crucial elements – the Electricity Directives – are the core of this study. Conducted in the book, analysis on the issue of the European Energy Packages can serve as a base for future studies on the legislative packages. My definition of *legislative package* (*a set of interdependent or related legal acts viewed or organised as a unit*) may be applied to other studies. Also other remarks provided on this issue (e.g. concerning package approach in the different EU sectors) can be an added value for ongoing research.

As packages' names suggest, the essence of the reform is to liberalise the energy market. This links with the notion of *liberalisation*. This study has shown that liberalisation has its limits. It does not consider the total withdrawal of public influence from influence on the economy and its industries, like the electricity sector. Individualism with a free and open market, even in liberalism and a market-based approach, has boundaries (not in a libertarian approach). Public presence in the sector does not vanish only due to liberalisation. Liberalisation conducted in the European energy sector, as proved in the book, finds a broad space for public forces executed at the European or national level.

Liberalisation in the European electricity sector is based on the open market, with free possibility of changing energy supplier, as well as accessing the grid, trade, generation, transmission, and distribution possibilities linked with the public influence that provides the EU's policy goals. The EU finds it necessary to create market conditions in the electricity sector through the use of public impact. However, the space for it is limited by the precondition of *market liberalisation*. Nevertheless, the energy market is not a totally free platform. Experience of energy crises, as in California, resulted in the need to restrain the market approach in favour of a public approach.

The real economy could not be a "pure market" in the absolute sense. State (public) interference is necessary. The mechanisms that drive the market and make it work properly are public tools. These are the definition and enforcement of property rights and civil laws that govern contract enforcement. So both enforcement and civil laws were given by the state – i.e. enacted by parliament. This means that it has a public character, even if it is used by individuals. Thereby, they must be provided by a public authority (Sterner 2003, p. 19). Using an example of the collapse of many formerly planned economies that attempted to set a free-market transition without due attention to establishing the necessary institutions, Thomas Sterner (2003, p. 19) illustrates two factors. First, systems with an excessive degree of state intervention (over-regulation) meet difficulties in achieving efficiency (they are ineffective). Second, systems that are extremely marked-oriented, as well as unregulated, may omit social issues and also fail in terms of efficiency. Robert P. Inman finds that neither the institution of government, nor collectively decided and enforced trading, stand as the unarguably preferred models.

> Each institution has its strength and each its weakness. While markets husband information and are responsive to variations in individual preferences and revealed abilities, they are often unable to ensure cooperation behavior in the many instances where cooperative allocations are unanimously preferred. Governments, on the other hand, can enforce a cooperation allocation, but often at the cost of being less responsive than markets to variations in individual preferences and abilities.
>
> (Inman 1987, p. 753)

Lastly, as Sterner rightly observes:

> Although neither absolute anarchy nor totalitarian planning has many serious proponents, policymaking is carried out against a backdrop of intense academic and ideological conflict over the optimal extent of state intervention in the economy. The proponents of free markets focus on efficiency as the engine of economic welfare, whereas the advocates of state intervention emphasize that the markets are imperfect without adequate policies to regulate them and to maximize welfare.
>
> (2003, p. 20)

This dichotomy is supplemented by public law regulation, which covers the space between two extremes. I find public law regulation as the balanced legal form of a state's impact on the energy market. Driven by the European policy agenda, it takes a central place on the axis of the state's influence on the market (with the two extreme points: the total subordination and the total release). As the public element in the market, the energy sector is promoting and strengthening competition (market-based attitude) or ensuring energy security, and environment protection (public policy interests).

In terms of public law regulation, I distinguish two ways of defining it: the narrow and the broad sense. Regulation *sensu stricte* is the activity of the national regulatory authorities conducted on the basis of public law, where regulation is the regulator. Regulation *sensu largo* is any mechanism of control and influence. In the former, a regulator is established to protect public interest, to provide a substitute for competition, or to steer market actions towards it, as well as to promote and enhance it. Regulation has to be conducted by the state, although in the European Union it gains a broader meaning: it includes action at the national and European level. In both senses I find regulation intentional. Besides market forces, social forces, and technologies, regulation covers law.

The narrow sense of regulation stems from an institution – the regulatory authority. It is a materialisation of public law regulation, which is proved by its tasks. Among its powers are enforcing orders and regulations, monitoring the behaviour of operators, promoting competition, strengthening the position of consumers, setting tariffs, etc. Thereby, as liberalisation does not exclude public participation, in a liberalised energy market the existence of independent regulatory agencies is not only possible but also necessary. It seems that the EU has chosen the "regulatory path" towards its way to the internal energy market. This approach is grounded on establishment of a firm regulatory framework. The independent regulatory institutions in each Member State are the regulatory framework's key element.

Therefore, in Europe, the energy (electricity) regulator performs functions more complex than taking the position of the night-watchman. It does not limit its action to the measures of last resort. One of the more significant findings to emerge from this study is that European regulators are of the *day-watchman* type. This is confirmed by different regulatory tools granted to the regulators as well as responsibilities in the field of policy, which transcend national dimensions, reaching the European level. These cover price regulation, licensing, registration, permission, certification, accreditation, or litigation, standardisation, as well as other instruments, which may be linked with controlling, monitoring mechanisms, or enforcing. The regulator being a day-watchman state combines two approaches of regulation: the private (regulation for competition) and the public (regulation for environment/climate and energy security). This creates the centrist model, in which regulation fills a space between extreme points linking them in one comprehensive option. The *day-watchman* regulator is not an active participant in the market. However, he does not withdraw from it. He is vigilant and actively observing. Wherever necessary, he may alter and enter into action. The regulator establishes the rules of the sector and its participants. He ensures enforcement of them, imposing penalties when necessary. Lastly, he balances the public and private interest.

The regulator's activity is based on law. Thus, it is law that covers regulation. Law ensures the concretisation of specific regulatory measures (e.g. sanctions, guidelines, standards, tariffs). Both of them, regulation *sensu stricte* and *sensu largo*, are conducted on the basis of a set of promulgated rules. What grants them legal character are the legislative packages of the European Union. Packages cover a broad range of public law regulation. In their scope, crucial legal institutions aimed at reaching European market reform's aims were established. Each Package gradually intensified influence on public law regulation, as a competitive market does not exist automatically. This involves "step-by-step" moves towards a liberalised energy market.

Hence, the First Energy Package driven by a public law regulatory regime provided the very first basis for shaping the structure of the internal energy market. The general and rather soft character of the provisions of the package revealed their weaknesses. The provisions of the package were assessed as structural obstacles linked with the strong position of the national energy utilities. Further, the early energy market was over-fragmented, being rather a national juxtaposition, with more or less liberalised markets rather than a common energy market. To achieve a fully open market, stronger regulatory tools were necessary. This new wave of influence on the scope of public law regulation covered introducing new instruments, concerning the degree of market opening (quantitative proposals), and the minimum obligations (qualitative proposals) that included access to the network, consumer protection, the unbundling of the transmission and distribution function in integrated gas and electricity companies, and the already mentioned regulation.

This was done by adopting the Second Electricity Package. It established a much more comprehensive legal dimension of regulation. Particularly, it covered the narrow sense of regulation – the institution of the regulator – where Member States were obliged to establish an energy regulator. Under the provision of the Electricity Directive, regulators also received a minimum range of regulatory responsibilities and powers. Hence, their position was strengthened, and Member States had to ensure this. As the priority for the European Union was reaching a harmonisation with this regard, Directive 2003/54/EC formalised the cooperation of national regulators: the ERGEG was established. With this respect, it was a very first sign of the *Europeanisation* of regulation, enhanced by multilateral cooperation on the line regulators-Commission.

Although, in practice, Directive 2003/54/EC's application revealed imperfections of the legal framework. Shortcomings included delays in transposition, and a different scope of transposition undermined by derogations. Other system failures concerned the influence of national government (e.g. by overruling regulators' decisions, depriving powers to impose sanctions) and limits to national regulatory authorities' powers (i.e. granting them insufficient powers, in contradiction with Directive 2003/54/EC). Moreover, the high degree of market concentration, cross-subsidies, primacy of interests of the integrated companies within the same group, and low market liquidity, hindered the existence of competition in the EU market.

Because of these circumstances, the regulatory framework needed improvement. Therefore, the Third Liberalisation Package was passed. It expanded the scope of public law regulation adding to it the concrete European dimension. This European legislation was driven by the need to reach the full energy market, with strong competition and the necessity of overcoming shortcomings within it. The Package enhanced unbundling (where the ownership was model promoted), models of TSOs, operators' duties, and public service obligations on electricity undertakings, as well as provisions on compliance programmes.

Although, from the very beginning, the EU involved public law regulation in its activity, as competition in the energy sector had not been reached independently. The market challenge in electricity has not been left alone. Its driver has been the EU and its institutions using public law regulation based on the provision of the European Energy Packages. The Member States have to guarantee accurate transposition of the European legislation and realise obligations in the field of public law regulation in the field of energy.

As a result, Member States had, *inter alia*, to establish independent regulatory authorities, and, under the provisions of the Third Energy Package (and earlier the Second), enhance the regulatory authorities' positions. This concerned granting them broad independence from Member States' influence. Although with the establishment of ACER, an increasing dependence on regulators by the European Union and its bodies was evident. Further, the Third Energy Package harmonises the legal status of national regulators. The progressive *Europeanisation* of legal regulation in the energy sector is demonstrated by unification (of intensive harmonisation) of the regulators' position, duties and powers.

The public approach stemming from the Energy Packages has established a new quality of regulatory framework in the energy sector. Aimed at achieving a fully integrated internal energy market and market liberalisation the packages provided a broad space for public law regulation. With the use of public law the European Union enhanced the cooperation of regulators and TSOs. This includes the European, as well as the national level. The scale of this cooperation is growing. The Agency is an example of it. It is not a regulator but it may perform some regulatory duties. It has power to take binding, individual decisions. ACER may grant exemption from important regulatory tools (unbundling and TPA). It is also involved in issues of cross-border infrastructure, and on operational security. National regulatory authorities have to comply with actions in these fields. Further, indirectly acting through the EC, the Agency may initiate a binding Commission decision. In addition, ACER may start the process of establishing binding rules on this cooperation of national regulators, where necessary. Moreover, ACER performs typical regulatory functions in the field of monitoring (although with no right to respond on non-compliance).

The Agency fulfils the regulatory space at the European level. Together with the EC, Member States, and national regulators, it acts for the needs of internal markets for electricity. It assists the national regulatory authorities by its recommendations. ACER aimed at coordination, using its expertise, in a soft way (providing its guidelines, opinions, and recommendations) steers regulatory actions at the European level. Further, it is a visible symbol and a core example of a process, which may be called the *Europeanisation* of public law regulation.

Other factors that prove this tendency are related to cooperation of the national energy regulators. This, addressed generally in the Second Electricity Directive,[1] is determined much more extensively under the provisions of the Third Energy Package. Article 6 (1) of Directive 2009/72/EC establishes the grounds for closer collaboration of regulatory authorities (and Member States as well) at one or more regional levels, aimed at integrating their national markets, as "a first step towards the creation of a fully liberalised internal market". Particularly, they:

> shall promote and facilitate the cooperation of transmission system operators at a regional level, including on cross-border issues, with the aim of creating a competitive internal market in electricity, foster the consistency of their legal, regulatory and technical framework and facilitate integration of the isolated systems forming electricity islands that persist in the Community.
>
> (Article 6 (1) of Directive 2009/72/EC)

Further, national regulatory authorities, in performing their duties, apart from close cooperation with the ACER, should cooperate closely with other Member States' regulators (Article 36 (a) of Directive 2009/72/EC). In particular, this regards cooperation in terms of cross-border issues (Article 37 (c) of Directive 2009/72/EC). With reference to this, regulatory authorities shall, *inter alia*, consult each other and shall provide any information necessary for the fulfilment of their tasks (Article 38 (1) of Directive 2009/72/EC). To develop and foster this cooperation, regulators may establish the cooperative arrangements with each other (Article 38 (3) of Directive 2009/72/EC).

As Anna Walaszek-Pyzioł (2002, p. 169) rightly concludes, a lawyer who analyses legislation, when wants to assess it, has to ask him/herself two questions. The first is: what is the aim of this legislation? The second is: does the content of the adopted legislation support achieving these aims? Seen in the light of above-mentioned factors, as well as correlated with them, remarks on the First, the Second, and especially the Third Energy Package, enhance public law regulation in the electricity sector to liberalise it. Public law regulation has become a tool for broad reform of the energy market in the European Union, since the very beginning of the European road towards the common energy market. Moreover, the Liberalisation Packages (as well as the Climate and Energy Package) have influenced the national possibilities of determining the field of regulators' action. This concerns setting public regulation law in the direction chosen by the European Union.

As addressed in this work, public law regulation, in both its senses, the narrow and broad, is used to establish an internal electricity market. Depending on the context, it may be the aim or the measure for achieving primary European energy objectives (its mirror reflection, dualistic nature). Achieving the internal energy market contributes to the realisation that the objectives of the European energy agenda are linked, based on competition, energy security, and environment. Public law regulation, shaped by provisions of the Energy Packages and the Climate and Energy Package, is a measure that enhances and promotes competition, strengthens energy security, and protects environment. Thereby, regulation becomes a means of achieving the objectives inscribed into the internal energy market. Further, this affects the regulation itself, which clearly can be seen, for instance in the responsibilities of the national regulatory authorities. The objectives inscribed into the internal energy market, make public law regulation oriented for energy security, sustainability, and affordability. Therefore, regulation is pro-security, pro-environmental (or pro-climate, pursuant to provision of the Climate and Energy Package) as well as pro-consumer (herein, as it has to lead to the internal energy market it is also pro-competition). Thus, activity at national level can also be grouped under the three selected categories at the European level.[2]

This range has its impact on the actions of Member States, which adapt their domestic law to European law. The broad reform of the energy market does not infringe the principle of proportionality of EU law.[3] The goal of the internal energy market and benefits of completing it are reasons for pan-European action (action at the European level) – this cannot be done individually by Member States. Thereby this goal is a kind of excuse, a cause. And it has a great importance. Furthermore, the move towards the internal energy market is based on coordination of national action, strengthening national regulators, and introducing tools like unbundling or TPA, which improve the situation of Member States' energy markets making them more competitive, on the one hand. On the other hand, this "Europeanisation" respects the possibility of shaping the national energy situation of Member States. This is confirmed by the legal means used to carry it out. As the EU's directives gives Member States a certain latitude in how they transpose them, Member States can implement EU law in the way they deem most appropriate. Nevertheless, national activity must go in the general direction indicated by the EU and approved by its institutions (where three components occur), which is assured by the European Commission and the possibility of legal action based on non-compliance of national law.

Finally, on the basis of the conducted analysis, the following thesis can be formulated:

1 The state's presence in the electricity sector, which is one of the sensitive sectors of the economy, is inevitable; herein, only the legal form of that presence changes; on the axis of the state's (public) influence on the market public law regulation takes a middle place, as it is a balanced legal form of a state's impact on the energy market, assuming existence of the two extreme points of the state's position on the market: a total subordination and a total release.
2 The concept of public law regulation, in terms of defining it, is not homogeneous; although the introduction of certain classifications can point to some of its essential elements; also its range is not uniform – several different types of legal approaches to regulation can be distinguished.
3 The EU uses a comprehensive solution for shaping the energy sector; it takes a form of legislative packages dedicated to this sector; packages covers a broad range of public law regulation, *inter alia*, through legal institutions such as TPA and unbundling, as well as in terms of the requirement imposed on Member States to establish energy regulators with specific responsibilities and certain powers.

4 Provisions of the EU's legislative packages enhance the position of the national regulatory authorities in the field of their independence from Member States, while they increase dependence of regulators on the European Union and its bodies, mainly the Agency for the Cooperation of Energy Regulators.
5 Although the current legal status of ACER does not meet all functions of a typical energy regulator, it can be assumed that, in the future, the Agency will be able to have a stronger impact on the activity of national regulators.
6 Especially the Third Energy Package harmonises the legal status of national regulators: their position (independence), the scope of operation, duties, and powers; it also demonstrates the progressive *Europeanisation* of legal regulation in the energy sector; its next step might be further institutionalisation of regulation in the energy sector at the European level, including the establishment of a European energy regulatory authority.
7 The European Union legislative packages dedicated to electricity (the Liberalisation Packages as well as the Climate and Energy Package) influenced the national (Member States) field of action by setting public regulation law in the direction chosen by the European Union.
8 The nature of the European approach to electricity is to combine it with climate protection; a legal expression of this approach is the Climate and Energy Package, with its "3 × 20% goals"; the provisions of legislation on climate and energy have their impact on the regulation of the electricity sector, making it more *pro-environmental* (or *pro-climate*); apart from climate and environment, public law regulation is aimed at enhancing the energy security.
9 It seems that the model of the energy market formed by EU legislation is not the final one; this is proved by the activity of the European Commission that continuously proposes new legislation on the energy sector.
10 The electricity sector, with its legal basis, both on the European and national level (the need to implement sufficient legal acts), will be in the further interest of the European Union, not only at the operational (executive) level, but also at the strategic level, including adoption of new legal acts determining the dimension of public law regulation of the Member States.

Having discussed the main findings of this book, let us address briefly certain future prospects for public law legislation in the European Union, mainly the idea of the common *European Energy Regulator*. Naturally, this is also linked with questions posed by Anna Walaszek-Pyzioł. As already proved, successive European legislation harmonised the legal status of national energy regulatory authorities in the right direction. In this context, public law strengthened the regulatory authorities' position, with powers and duties, providing them with independence in relation to Member States and the electricity sector. It cannot be excluded that the current legal framework will evolve into a more institutionalised regulatory scheme. This may include establishing the European energy regulatory authority. Herein, ACER is a concrete foundation on which such a structure can be created. However, in the main part of its duties and powers, nowadays the Agency cannot be regarded as a classic regulator.[4] Nevertheless, as shown, some of its duties may be perceived as regulatory functions, and, even in some situations, the Agency issues binding individual decisions. Thus, ACER may form the basis for future legislation activity, which will modify, and again strengthen, public law regulation at the European level. In this view, public law regulation can cover changes in the legal status of the Agency (see Sokołowski & Stankiewicz 2011, pp. 242–243).

With this background, reference to an evaluation of ACER's activities should be made. In January 2014, the EC elaborated the first evaluation of ACER's activities since the Agency's establishment. The EC considers the ACER "a credible and respected institution playing a prominent role in the EU regulatory arena", noticing its focus on the right priorities (European Commission 2014, p. 9). What must be stressed is the fact that the Commission "invites ACER to be more proactive" (European Commission 2014, p. 5). Especially, this covers "diverging approaches and interpretations between NRAs" (European Commission 2014a, p. 5). Furthermore,

> [a]s the [internal energy market] implementation progresses, this will become a more prominent task for ACER. ACER will be called in the future to mediate and arbitrate between [national regulatory authorities] as regards the interpretation of specific provisions of [n]etwork codes.
>
> (European Commission 2014a, p. 5)

The European Commission's findings show that it seeks a more active role for ACER and practical execution of its responsibilities. These would bring the Agency closer to performing regulation at the European level. Thereby, the EC's assessment implies taking into consideration enhancing the position of ACER with the use of the next energy package. This covers granting it more powers. It may concern altering its non-binding character and releasing the Agency from the European Commission's influence.[5] In these terms, the Agency could directly establish binding rules on cooperation among national regulatory authorities and among regulatory authorities at regional and Community levels, instead of making the appropriate recommendations to the Commission. Together with this move the Board of Regulators' scope of tasks could be extended (Articles 14–15 of Regulation (EC) No 713/2009). As a result, this would establish a network of independent regulatory authorities (national and European coordinator–regulator) operating for the needs of the internal energy market and its policy goals.

Hence, the scenario of stronger European regulation (with its further institutionalisation) is conceivable and cannot be easy ignored. First, it was already considered in late 1990s. Conflicts in decision-making processes, the issue of cross-border tariffs, or the objective of having one single tarification system for the whole EU, led to the Commission's proposals, which included the idea of the establishment of the new regulatory instrument administrated by the Commission, or the *European Regulator* (European Commission 1999, p. 27). Nevertheless, it required the creation of a new, much stronger regulatory regime based on public law. On the other hand, it would provide full European unification of the regulatory approach to the energy sector, as well as of the measures taken by Member States. Naturally, this move would entail an examination regarding its compliance with the principle of proportionality.

As demonstrated, the European Union did not find it necessary to implement this regulatory solution in the 1990s. However, the idea of the European Energy Regulator still appeared and still appears in public debates waged on the EU's forum. This concept emerged during discussion of the Third Energy Package and was supported by the former President of the European Commission, José Manuel Barroso, and the former EU Commissioner for Energy, Andris Piebalgs (*New York Times* 2006). Objections of some Member States (like the UK, France, or Germany) blocked this initiative, assessing it as detrimental to independence within energy policy, anti-sovereign, and premature (*New York Times* 2006). Yet it does not change the fact that the President Barroso has favoured improving wide European energy regulation (Taylor 2006).

Furthermore, the concept of a European Energy Regulator still comes back and appears in the current debate on European energy. In March 2014, Iberdrola's Chairman, Ignacio Galán, presented a solution to the EU's energy problem. According to him, the problem "is an eminently European issue, should come from Europe itself, as in the case of the financial problem". Apart from tariffs matters and the balance between energy security, sustainability, and competitiveness, such a move would involve "[s]trengthening the functioning of the market in Europe and establishing a single European energy regulator to promote a stable, predictable and harmonious framework and vouch for compliance with regulations in all Member States" (Iberdrola 2014).

The European Energy Regulator would be a powerful symbol of the direction that the European Union chose to build the common energy market. This direction is the liberalisation of the energy market with the use of public law regulation and its tools. However, even without one authority responsible for typical regulatory action,[6] the impact of European Energy Packages on the scope of public law regulation of the electricity sector is not to be underestimated. The European Union consistently moves towards the establishment of a new and increasingly stronger legal framework grounded on the basis of public law.

As a final point, one may ask about the future of public law regulation in the European electricity sector and prospects for it. An analysis of the recent strategic documents of the European Union shows that regulation will continue to be used as a measure for achieving the objectives of the internal energy market. After the adoption of the Third Energy Package, the European Commission regularly called for its timely and urgent implementation, reaffirming the direction of public law regulation in European legislation.[7] By 2014, the existing European legislation on energy needed to be transposed within all Member States. In the first place, it includes providing the national energy regulatory authorities with the necessary tools and resources to enable them to carry out effective enforcement of European energy legislation (European Commission 2012, p. 2). Nevertheless, in September 2014, infringement proceedings for partial transposition of the energy market directives (electricity and gas) were pending against two Member States.[8] Additionally, in 2014, "the Commission has started to identify and resolve problems concerning incorrect transposition or bad application of the Third Energy Package rules by the Member States (so-called 'non-conformity' problems)" (European Commission 2014b).

It is very probable that the European Union will again make use of the packages mechanism in the energy market field. Electricity, due to its growing importance,[9] will be a continuing interest to the European Union. This includes at operational level (implementing and exercising existing provisions), but also at the strategic level. It means that it is likely that new legal acts determining the dimension of public law regulation in the electricity sector will be proposed and soon their legal shape will be revealed.

A sign of this type of trend could be the concept of an Energy Union,

> where Member States see that they depend on each other to deliver secure energy to their citizens, based on true solidarity and trust ... where energy flows freely across borders, based on competition and the best possible use of resources, and with effective regulation of energy markets at EU level where necessary.
>
> (European Commission 2015, p. 2)

Among five mutually reinforcing and closely interrelated dimensions "designed to bring greater energy security, sustainability and competitiveness", one may find "[a] fully integrated European energy market" (European Commission 2015, p. 4).

Seen in this light, the EC underlines the need for an effective regulatory framework to achieve a state of well-functioning internal energy market needs. In this context, the Commission draws attention to the position of ACER:

> ACER currently acts primarily through recommendations and opinions. It has very limited decision-making rights, e.g. it can only take decisions at the request of the national regulators or if they fail to take a decision within a certain timeframe. EU-wide regulation of the single market should be strengthened, through a significant reinforcement of the powers and independence of ACER to carry out regulatory functions at the European level in order to enable it to effectively oversee the development of the internal energy market and the related market rules as well as to deal with all cross-border issues necessary to create a seamless internal market.
>
> (European Commission 2015, p. 9)

Certainly, part of the future legislation will be further strengthening of the position of the regulatory authorities. As already mentioned, *inter alia*, a proposal to establish a new entity, i.e. the European Energy Regulator, may be considered. Instead of this scenario, the Fourth Energy Package may cover enhancing the position of ACER as highlighted by the Commission, particularly granting it more duties and powers to undertake binding decisions. Regardless of which option would be chosen, public regulation would be strengthened as a result.

Other concepts that may result in passing new legislation can be observed in documents adopted by the European Commission. In terms of further action within this scope, one may also expect activity by the Commission in relation to regulated electricity and gas prices. The EC urges that it ceases to be "perceived by investors as an indicator of political interference which stifles investment" (European Commission 2012, pp. 10–11). With this in mind, at the beginning of 2015, the Commission underlined, "[i]n a number of Member States, regulated tariffs still limit the development of effective competition, which discourages investments and the emergence of new market players" (European Commission 2015, p. 11).

Regardless of these conjectures, as well as the facts that a number of Member States have already allowed energy prices to be free of public impact, and the Commission has agreed with some Member States on a timely phase-out of regulated prices, most of the EU's countries still use regulated price formation (European Commission 2012, p. 10). This accords with the pro-competitive approach manifested in the European regulation, and is not against public regulation in both its dimensions, in a broad and narrow sense. This possible move regarding tariffs would require enhancing regulation further in the field of monitoring market conditions and intervening where necessary.

The next legislation may also include tighter rules on unbundling, with the ownership option, not politically feasible under discussion on the Third Energy Package (Brunekreeft 2011, p. 134). Thus, this completes other areas of European interests in the energy sector, which might be covered by a future legislation package on energy.

Nevertheless, no matter in which direction these considerations would go and how strong further liberalisation measures would be, it is certain that the European Union would not resign from the public law regulatory model of the energy sector. Rather, the EU would continue the move towards an energy market based on competition, energy security, and environmental protection established by public law regulation. The legislation packages on energy – enhancing public regulation in terms of the broad and the narrow sense in subsequent phases of the electricity sector's reform – are clear proof of the fact that the regulatory model would be used in the future. To conclude these considerations, let me quote President Barroso who aptly expounded the relationship of the regulators and the energy sector. As he publicly declared "[i]f you want an internal market to work in Europe in energy then you need more muscle in terms of the regulators" (Taylor 2006).

## Notes

1 As stated in Article 23 (12) of Directive 2003/54/EC "[n]ational regulatory authorities shall contribute to the development of the internal market and of a level playing field by cooperating with each other and with the Commission in a transparent manner".
2 For example, see remarks on legal methods of realisation of energy policy in Poland in the field of environment, competition, and energy security. See Elżanowski 2008, pp. 102–213.
3 As Alexander Türk notices, the principle of proportionality, which is an integral part of the general principles of EU law, "is a valuable tool to protect Member States and individuals against excessive Community acts" (Türk 2009, pp. 135–136). It requires that the measure is suitable or appropriate to achieve the aim in issue. It includes assessment whether the measure is necessary, i.e. whether less restrictive means could have been used to achieve the aim. It also covers analysis if the means employed go beyond the aim to be achieved (Türk 2009, p. 136). See also Craig 2012, pp. 590–640; Kaczorowska 2013, pp. 119–120.
4 Some authors evaluate it as "a step in the right direction", but with a "too vague role". See Mankoff 2009, p. 28.
5 Burkard Eberlein (2012, p. 159) even calls it "a creature of the Commission" that initiated its establishment and supports its operation.
6 According to ACER's vision of a future energy regulatory framework, "[t]he Agency's role in the future will evolve in response to further market integration and as a result of the further development of European energy policies". Seen in this light,

> [t]he Agency should continue to fulfil two key roles: first, to oversee effectively the European regulatory framework, and ensure that the activities of EU bodies (ENTSOs and other newly established bodies) comply with their legal obligations to avoid any 'regulatory gap' (which is discussed below); and, secondly, to support the cooperation of [national regulatory authorities] and to facilitate the coordination of their actions at European level to enable them to respond to the pace of market integration to 2025.
>
> (ACER 2014, p. 25)

7 The European Commission highlighted delays and shortcomings in the implementation of the Third Energy Package. For example, as reported in a non-paper from 2011,

> [e]nergy regulators at national level do not always dispose of the necessary powers and resources to enforce the applicable rules, nor do they have the statutory independence required to enforce correct application of EU legislation in all Member States. Despite many cases of non-compliance with the rules on access to the gas and electricity networks, national regulators often do not have sufficient powers to impose penalties.
>
> (European Commission 2011)

8 Romania and Ireland. See European Commission 2014b, p. 4.
9 The importance of electricity will grow. World electricity demand in the New Policies Scenario is projected to increase from 17 200 TWh in 2009 to over 31 700 TWh in 2035, an annual growth rate of 2.4 per cent, driven by economic and population growth. Over 5900 GW of new capacity will be added worldwide to meet demand growth and replace retired power plants. The scale of these investments is nearly $10 trillion (in year-2010 dollars) (IEA 2011, p. 175).

## References

ACER 2014, *Energy regulation: a bridge to 2025 conclusions paper*. Available from: www.acer.europa.eu/Official_documents/Acts_of_the_Agency/SD052005/Supporting%20document%20to%20ACER%20Recommendation%2005-2014%20-%20%20Energy%20Regulation%20A%20Bridge%20to%202025%20Conclusions%20Paper.pdf [14 July 2015].

Brunekreeft, G. 2011, "Vertical relations and energy networks: selected issues", in *Competition, contracts and electricity markets: a new perspective*, eds J.-M. Glachant, D. Finon, & A. de Hauteclocque, Edward Elgar, Cheltenham, pp. 134–156.

Craig, P. 2012, *EU administrative law*, 2nd edn, Oxford University Press, Oxford.

Directive 2003/54/EC of the European Parliament and of the Council of 26 June 2003 concerning common rules for the internal market in electricity and repealing Directive 96/92/EC, OJ L 176, 15 July 2003.

Directive 2009/72/EC of the European Parliament and of the Council of 13 July 2009 concerning common rules for the internal market in electricity and repealing Directive 2003/54/EC, OJ L 211, 14 August 2009.

Eberlein, B. 2012, "Inching towards a common energy policy: entrepreneurship, incrementalism, and windows of opportunity", in *Constructing a policy-making state? Policy dynamics in the EU*, ed. J. Richardson, Oxford University Press, Oxford, pp. 147–169.

Elżanowski, F. 2008, *Polityka energetyczna: prawne instrumenty realizacji* [Energy policy: legal instruments of realisation], LexisNexis, Warsaw.

European Commission 1999, *Second report to the Council and the European Parliament on harmonisation requirements: Directive 96/92/EC concerning common rules for the internal market in electricity*, Brussels, 16 April 1999, COM (1999) 164 final.

European Commission 2011, *Commission non-paper of 24 February 2011: the internal energy market – time to switch into higher gear*. Available from: http://ec.europa.eu/energy/gas_electricity/legislation/doc/20110224_non_paper_internal_nergy_market.pdf [15 July 2015].

European Commission 2012, *Communication from the Commission to the European Parliament, the Council, the European Economic and Social Committee and the Committee of the Regions: making the Internal Energy Market work*, Brussels, 15 November 2012, COM (2012) 663 final.

European Commission 2014a, *Commission evaluation of 22.1.2014 of the activities of the Agency for the Cooperation of Energy Regulations (ACER) under Article 34 of Regulation (EC) 713/2009*, Brussels, 22 January 2014, C (2014) 242 final.

European Commission 2014b, *Commission staff working document: enforcement of the Third Internal Energy Market Package accompanying the document communication from the Commission to the European Parliament, the Council, the European Economic and Social Committee and the Committee of the Regions "progress towards completing the internal energy market"*, Brussels, 13 October 2014, SWD (2014) 315 final.

European Commission 2015, *Communication from the Commission to the European Parliament, the Council, the European Economic and Social Committee, the Committee of the Regions and the European Investment Bank a framework strategy for a resilient Energy Union with a forward-looking climate change policy*, Brussels, 25 February 2015, COM (2015) 80 final.

Iberdrola 2014, Mr. *Galán calls for competitive energy system in Europe to drive industrial revival*. Available from www.iberdrola.es/press-room/press-releases/national-international/2014/detail/press-release/140303_NP_01_GlobalForumSpain.html [14 July 2015].

IEA 2011, *World energy outlook 2011*, International Energy Agency, Paris. Available from: www.iea.org/publications/freepublications/publication/WEO2011_WEB.pdf [12 July 2015].

Inman, R.P. 1987 "The 'new' political economy", in vol. 2 of *Handbook of public economics*, eds A.J. Auerbach and M. Feldstein, North-Holland, Amsterdam, pp. 647–777.

Kaczorowska, A. 2013, *European Union law*, 3rd edn, Routledge, Abingdon.

Mankoff, J. 2009, "Eurasian energy security", *Council Special Report*, no. 43, pp. 1–50.

*New York Times* 2006, *EU ministers reject energy regulator*. Available from: www.nytimes.com/2006/03/14/business/worldbusiness/14iht-energy.html?_r=0 [14 July 2015].

Regulation (EC) No 713/2009 of the European Parliament and of the Council of 13 July 2009 establishing an Agency for the Cooperation of Energy Regulators, OJ L 211, 14 August 2009.

Sokołowski, M.M. & Stankiewicz, R. 2011, "Ku instytucjonalizacji europejskiej regulacji sektorowej: wnioski płynące z analizy ram ustrojowych Agencji do Spraw Współpracy Organów Regulacji Energetyki" [Towards the institutionalisation of European sectoral regulation: the conclusions of the analysis of the institutional framework of the Agency for the Cooperation of Energy Regulators], in vol. 3 of *Problemy prawa polskiego i obcego w ujęciu historycznym, praktycznym i teoretycznym* [Problems of Polish and foreign law in historical, practical, and theoretical contexts], eds B.T. Bieńkowska & D. Szafrański, C.H. Beck, Warsaw, pp. 223–243.

Sterner, T. 2003, *Policy instruments for environmental and natural resource management*, World Bank, Washington, DC.

Taylor, S. 2006, "Barroso in bid to open up energy sector", *European Voice*, 13 September. Available from: www.politico.eu/article/barroso-in-bid-to-open-up-energy-sector/ [14 July 2015].

Türk, A.H. 2009, *Judicial review in EU law*, Edward Elgar, Cheltenham.

Walaszek-Pyzioł, A. 2002, *Energia i prawo* [Energy and law], LexisNexis, Warsaw.

# Index

For Product Safety Concerns and Information please contact our EU
representative GPSR@taylorandfrancis.com
Taylor & Francis Verlag GmbH, Kaufingerstraße 24, 80331 München, Germany

www.ingramcontent.com/pod-product-compliance
Ingram Content Group UK Ltd.
Pitfield, Milton Keynes, MK11 3LW, UK
UKHW022133190926
475702UK00013B/1787
* 9 7 8 0 8 1 5 3 5 8 3 1 2 *